BRITAIN'S
FORGOTTEN BATTLE

BRITAIN'S FORGOTTEN BATTLE

THE REICHSWALD FOREST CAMPAIGN, 1945

ADRIAN & DAWN L. BRIDGE

AMBERLEY

First published 2025

Amberley Publishing
The Hill, Stroud
Gloucestershire, GL5 4EP

www.amberley-books.com

ISBN 978 1 3981 1491 3 (hardback)
ISBN 978 1 3981 1492 0 (ebook)

British Library Cataloguing in Publication Data.
A catalogue record for this book is available from the British Library.

1 2 3 4 5 6 7 8 9 10

Typesetting by SJmagic DESIGN SERVICES, India.
Printed in the UK.

Dedicated to the memory of former Cameronian Rifleman Adrian B. Bridge (1926–2015) and all his British and Canadian comrades in the First Canadian Army, who fought through the bloody, muddy battlefields of the Reichswald, and onwards towards the Rhine, between 8 February and 11 March 1945.

CONTENTS

PREFACE

'It is better to die in freedom than to live with a German gun to your head.'

This was how one civilian from Nijmegen, in the Netherlands, explained the attitude of civilians living on the front line from September 1944 to February 1945. For five months the city was the most forward Allied position on the Western Front, and in this period far more civilians died than in the previous five years of German occupation. Operation Market Garden had brought freedom to the people of Nijmegen and the surrounding villages, but not safety. Operation Veritable, which is the subject of this book, would finally bring security and the prospect of peace. The almost nightly showers of German grenades ended, the army moved on and, for the first time in months, the people of Nijmegen could emerge from their bomb shelters without fear and start to rebuild their lives.

On the German side of the border, the stakes were even higher: Operation Veritable (a major part of which was the Battle of the Reichswald) brought liberation after twelve years of Nazi dictatorship, but it also ushered in destruction, military occupation and great uncertainty. Settlements that stood in the path of the offensive, such as Kleve and Wesel, were reduced to rubble, with less than 10 per cent of all houses still standing (let alone habitable) at the end of the war. Within these ruins, the first years of the post-war period would be marked by hunger, epidemics and a focus on day-to-day survival. In these conditions, infants and the elderly died in large numbers. Yet the Allied military campaign that brought so much destruction also brought what the National Socialists had never been able to deliver: a peaceful future for Germany.

In the post-war period, Operation Market Garden is commemorated in large ceremonies, attended by hundreds of veterans and thousands of locals. These commemorations grew in popularity after the release of the blockbuster movie *A Bridge Too Far* in 1977. Today the commemorative events last more than a week and span dozens of locations. Yet, Operation Veritable was largely forgotten. Decades later, few locals had heard the name of the operation and for many veterans the Battle of the Reichswald was a terror they would rather not recall.

On both sides of the border, some locals did try to change things. In 1975, historians H. Bosch and W. Haas produced the German documentary *Krieg am Niederrhein*. It consists of huge quantities of original footage by Allied war correspondents and paints a palpable picture of this battle. Up until the present day, the Freedom Museum in Groesbeek highlights Operation Veritable by screening this documentary every February and March. In 2002, the Freedom Museum, then called the National Liberation Museum, became the first to add a modest display about the battle to its permanent exhibition. Annual commemorations of Operation Veritable have been held by the Groesbeek Airborne Friends at the Canadian War Cemetery near Groesbeek since 2004.

Recognition for what historian W. D. Whitaker described as 'the battle to end the war' was slow to come. In 2012, the director of the Freedom Museum even wrote a letter to Steven Spielberg, hoping to convince him to produce a movie that would put the forgotten battle on the map. This attempt was unsuccessful but perhaps one day some talented producer will pick up this book and see an opportunity to be the first to bring this story to the big screen. In 2019, the museum decided to take matters into its own hands: the new permanent exhibition dedicated an entire hall to the battle, with historic items on display and a 19-foot-high screen displaying footage to underline the importance of the story being told. For visitors to this museum today, there can be no doubt that this is a battle of at least equal importance to Operation Market Garden. Gradually, this awareness is sinking into the general consciousness of the population.

Operation Veritable was the start of the Rhineland Offensive. The largest offensive ever to be launched from Dutch soil, the Rhineland Offensive turned out to be the biggest Allied attack in western Europe during the Second World War. The subsequent crossing of the Rhine was the beginning of the end of Hitler's Germany, bringing the liberation of the north of the Netherlands and starting the final push to Berlin. The Allied Forces moved straight through Germany to meet the Russians and defeat the German army on 8 May 1945. As such, the Battle of the Reichswald played a crucial role in the last year of the war, making it a matter of global importance. Therefore, it deserves a prominent place in our collective memory, now and for generations to come. Take this book and know that you are holding an account not of a single battle, but of a turning point in history.

Wiel Lenders (Director) and Rense Havinga (Curator) of the
Freedom Museum in Groesbeek, the Netherlands

FOREWORD

Canadians share hundreds of years of history and common heritage with our British Allies, partners and friends. There are more family linkages between us than we can even begin to count. We have the same monarch, similar governmental, legal and commercial systems, substantial two-way trade and investment, lively cultural and academic ties, extensive scientific exchanges, and a deep reservoir of respect and trust rooted in a set of values that we have promoted and defended together, and for which we have always been prepared to make sacrifices. Our deeply connected military traditions are of particular note, giving powerful, poignant meaning to the words 'shoulder to shoulder'. At important times and places throughout history, Canadian and British soldiers, sailors, air crews, engineers, intelligence agents, special ops personnel and many others have faced the scourge of war, on the front lines, together. Historically and now, they have made and make a coherent team, and they have always had each other's backs.

The greatest combined military campaign in world history was, of course, the D-Day landings in 1944 in which Britons and Canadians fought tightly and successfully together, alongside all our other Allies. But thereafter, there was almost another year of hard slogging – multiple smaller, but crucial battles, before VE Day in May 1945.

This book highlights the critical importance of one of them – the tough, soggy campaign through the Reichswald Forest on the eastern edge of the Netherlands, between the Rhine and the Maas rivers, conducted jointly by British and Canadian forces from 8 February 1945 onwards. Codenamed Operation Veritable, this campaign involved the First Canadian Army under the command of Lieutenant-General Harry Crerar and the British XXX Corps led by Lieutenant-General Brian Horrocks.

Through nasty physical conditions and bad weather, Anglo-Canadian skill, strength and valour prevailed, hastening the Allied crossing of the Rhine, and thus accelerating victory over the Nazis in Europe.

The authors, Adrian and Dawn Leyland Bridge, tell a compelling story about the strategic nature of this campaign, the collaboration that secured its success, and the courage and determination of individual Canadians and Britons who led the fight. Thousands died, now memorialised in cemeteries proudly attended by succeeding generations whose very freedom was made possible by these brave departed souls.

I am grateful to the Bridges for shining a light on what happened in the Reichswald Forest in February 1945. The world needs to be reminded.

Freedom is never free. But Canada and the United Kingdom must never flinch from our combined dedication to protect democracy, human rights, the rule of law, the rules-based international order, and our free, respectful, inclusive way of life.

Lest we forget.

H. E. Hon. Ralph Goodale, PC
High Commissioner for Canada in the United Kingdom
of Great Britain and Northern Ireland
Canada House, Trafalgar Square, London

ACKNOWLEDGEMENTS

The authors are indebted to a number of archivists, academics and organisations in the UK, Europe and Canada for their invaluable help and assistance in producing this book. The Freedom Museum in Groesbeek, the Netherlands, formerly known as the Vrijheidsmuseum, does perhaps more than any other organisation to keep alive the memory and significance of the offensive known as Operation Veritable, launched just to the west of the Reichswald Forest, in February 1945. The museum's director, Wiels Lender, and curator, Rense Hovinga, couldn't have been more supportive of our endeavours, and the German and Dutch historians we encountered via the Freedom Museum (including Paul Klinkenberg and Wolfgang Wegener) provided insights into the events surrounding Operation Veritable which were truly invaluable. In particular, we thank the Freedom Museum director and curator for their thought-provoking preface to this book.

In the UK, Mike Taylor at the Low Parks Museum in Hamilton, Scotland, couldn't have been speedier or more helpful in supplying us with the full, original war diaries, including all annexes, for the 9th Battalion of the Cameronians

(Scottish Rifles) for February and March 1945. At this point, we would also like to express our thanks to the archivists and other staff at various locations throughout the UK and Canada who maintain, and in some cases publish, the war diaries without which this book could not have been written. The archivists at King's College Archive Centre, Cambridge, and Radley College, Oxford, were also enormously helpful in providing the authors with access to information relating to the histories of Ronald Balfour and Anthony Paget prior to their participation in Operation Veritable. The authors also acknowledge the help and advice given by individual members of the online ww2.wartalk.com network. The detailed insights provided by some contributors, over many years, have been impressive to say the least, and have led us on, with great accuracy, to pursue individual and regimental records in the National Archives at Kew. Finally, in the UK, we need to thank the National Army Museum in Chelsea for sourcing a number of quite powerful photographic images for use in the book.

The authors' friends and colleagues in Canada were helpful from the very onset of this project. In particular, Shannyn Johnson, at the Canadian War Museum in Ottawa, answered all our queries and questions with unfailing courtesy and professionalism. Our considerable thanks also need to be expressed to the Honourable Ralph Goodale PC, Canada's High Commissioner to the UK, who took time out from a very busy schedule to write a foreword to this book.

Finally, last but not least, we need to express our gratitude to Adrian's father, Adrian Broomhall Bridge (1926–2015), who was a teenage rifleman in the Cameronians, and fought through the Reichswald campaign, crossed the Rhine, and then assaulted die-hard German positions on the River Elbe in the last days of the Second World War. His recollections of the fighting, given in old age, provided the original inspiration for writing this book. His was, indeed, a very fine generation.

INTRODUCTION

At five o'clock in the morning on 8 February 1945, 1,053 British and Canadian heavy and medium guns began a huge bombardment of German defensive positions in and around the Reichswald Forest region,[1] at the extreme northern edge of the Siegfried Line, which lay just inside Germany's border with the neighbouring Netherlands. The barrage lasted for over five hours, and was the largest Commonwealth artillery bombardment since El-Alamein in October 1942. The roaring cacophony created by the firing of so many artillery pieces at the same time had to be heard to be believed. The sound deafened Allied soldiers in rear areas for hours, and the ground itself seemed to reverberate with the constant noise of guns being fired and shells exploding.

Once the shelling had stopped, 50,000 British and Canadian soldiers, supported by tanks and other armoured vehicles, moved forward from their various start lines and launched the great military offensive known as Operation Veritable. Initial attacks were launched just to the north of the Reichswald Forest, another attack pushed just to the south, and one British division – the 53rd Welsh Division – smashed straight through the dense centre of the forest area, which was 6 miles long and 3 miles wide. The subsequent fighting during Operation Veritable, and in the later breakout phase – dubbed Operation Blockbuster – was some of the hardest and most savage of the entire war in Europe. A mere three months before the Second World War in Europe ended, the Reichswald campaign was fashioned as part of a massive northern pincer movement, under First Canadian Army leadership, which would turn the northern flank of the German defensive Siegfried Line, link up with the American 9th Army pushing up from the south, and thereby trap or destroy substantial German forces on the west bank of the Rhine.

A week before British and Canadian forces launched the northern arm of this pincer movement, there was a substantial thaw in the German winter weather. The few roads in the Reichswald area, previously frozen solid and easily traversed by tanks and other armoured vehicles, rapidly became quagmires. Whole tanks, as well as men, could and did disappear into the muddy abyss, and entire stretches of the campaign battlefields were transformed into rain-drenched hellholes reminiscent of the worst aspects of the fighting around Passchaendale, on the Western Front, in 1917. Lieutenant-General Brian Horrocks, the head of Britain's XXX Corps, was the actual battlefield commander at the Reichswald, charged with accomplishing the broader strategic objectives set for him by General Harry Crerar, who commanded the First Canadian Army, and by Bernard Montgomery, who led the Allied 21st Army Group, which encompassed British, Canadian and some American armies.[2]

Horrocks went on record on many occasions to say that the Reichswald campaign was the hardest he ever fought. The weather and subsequent flooding, aided and abetted by the Germans intentionally opening many of the dykes in the Rhine area, was not the only difficulty faced by the British and Canadians as they attacked on 8 February, and continued to attack, day and night, for the next month. The Germans, outnumbered and outgunned, fought with considerable tenacity and resourcefulness. This fact was quickly recognised by Allied generals. Montgomery, for example, said that in order to prevent the Anglo-Canadians from breaking through the Reichswald area 'the enemy parachute troops fought with a fanaticism unexcelled at any time in the war'. He subsequently added that 'the volume of fire from enemy weapons was the heaviest which had so far been met by British troops in the campaign'.[3] Montgomery's comments were, however, only partially true. Some of the Germans involved were undoubtedly propelled into resistance by the fanaticism imbued by years of National Socialist indoctrination. Many other Germans, though, were simply motivated by the fact that the British and Canadians were now invading German soil. The desire to defend one's 'hearth and home' was a powerful motivating factor in Nazi Germany as well as in the opposing Allied nations.

As will be seen, the military challenges presented to the British and Canadians during the Reichswald Forest campaign were immense and varied. To the north, the Canadians were engaged in largely amphibious warfare, attacking and neutralising German outposts marooned on isolated strips of land which had survived the flooding of the Rhine. In the Reichswald Forest itself, the Allied attackers faced the difficult task of coping with what the *Yorkshire Post*'s war correspondent described, on 14 February 1945, as 'this strange, wild forest fighting'.[4] Even putting aside the flooding, the densely packed trees in the forest made it difficult to deploy tanks to good effect. Between the long rows of beech and oak trees, there were clear, narrow open rides which gave German defenders ideal opportunities to set ambush positions and await advancing Allied infantry, who could be mown down by short bursts of accurate Spandau machine gun fire.

Away from the forest itself, the British and Canadians had to fight their way through the streets of nearby strategically important Rhineland towns such as Kleve, Goch and Weeze.[5]

These towns had already been badly damaged by Allied bombing prior to the commencement of Operation Veritable, and prising German soldiers out of their defensive positions in ruined streets and houses proved to be extremely slow and dangerous work. Lieutenant-General Horrocks had contemplated speeding through the Reichswald, seizing the key nearby towns and closing on the Rhine (perhaps even seizing a bridge across it along the way) within a matter of a few days. The reality proved to be very different. Deliberate flooding, and the winter thaw, put paid to all thoughts of swift military progress. As Eisenhower pointed out after the end of the war, the Reichswald campaign encapsulated 'some of the fiercest fighting of the whole war' and involved 'a bitter slogging match in which the enemy had to be forced back yard by yard'.[6]

In the end, of course, the Germans were forced back 'yard by yard' to the east bank of the northern stretches of the Rhine, though achieving this took more than a month rather than a few days. Even so, the achievements of the British and Canadian armies in the Reichswald campaign of February–March 1945 were considerable. The veterans of both armies, together with the newly conscripted, fresh from school and basic training, combined to surmount all the difficulties presented to them, and were ultimately triumphant. At the cost of considerable blood and treasure, the German army which opposed the British and Canadians in the Reichswald sector was eventually pushed back and defeated.

The heavy fighting in the Reichswald battles is certainly better remembered on the continent of Europe, and in Canada, than it is in the UK. For instance, the campaign remains a permanent focus for study and exhibitions at Groesbeek's Freedom Museum in the Netherlands. Dutch and German historians study the wartime archaeology of the Reichswald, and in the period just prior to the 2020–2022 Covid pandemic, the Dutch Veritable Society commemorated the events of February–March 1945 with military re-enactments, and an historically accurate mock-up of a British military headquarters in Gennep was recreated. Even in Germany, the efforts of Major Ronald Balfour, of the King's Royal Rifle Corps, to save local artefacts from destruction during the Reichswald fighting were remembered with considerable affection by many locals for decades after the end of the war in Europe.[7]

Canadian consciousness of its pivotal role in the Reichswald campaign has been demonstrated on numerous occasions, well into the twenty-first century. During November 2016, for example, Canadian historians and broadcasters Wayne Abbott and David O'Keefe presented a well-researched documentary (as part of Canadian television's *War Junk* series) on a military billy can discovered in the depths of the Reichswald Forest which had once belonged to Major Frederick Bermingham, who'd fought during Operation Veritable as an officer in the 2nd Canadian Anti-Tank Regiment.[8] Bermingham had dropped his can – used as a receptacle for eating food and drinking – during the height of the Reichswald fighting. The major survived the campaign, and seventy-one years later, O'Keefe, Abbott and Canadian TV brought Bermingham's two surviving twin daughters all the way from Alberta to view the Reichswald battlefields and to be reunited with the long-lost memento (which had his name still etched into the side). Canadian broadcasters and historians have also successfully focused attention on that country's involvement in the savage tank battles in the Hochwald Gap during the latter stages of the Veritable campaign.[9]

In contrast to the situation in Canada and the Netherlands, British reactions to the Reichswald campaign have always been rather muted. During the period of the fighting itself, in 1945, the Reichswald campaign was front-page news in many British newspapers. For over a month, between February and March 1945, reports appeared regularly about the fighting in the Reichswald Forest, Kleve, Goch, Weeze, Xanten and other nearby locations. In the post-war period, however, British memories of the Reichswald Forest campaign seemed to fade fast. On 7 July 1957, Sir Brian Horrocks appeared on the BBC, delivering the last of his television series entitled *Men in Battle*. During the programme, he described the Reichswald fighting as 'the battle no one has heard of, although it was one of the most decisive of the war'. Horrocks was probably right in making this observation, and during the following seventy-five years, between 1945 and 2020, only one detailed text about the Reichswald campaign was ever produced, written by Peter Elstob, in 1970.[10] The seminal Thames TV series *World at War*, produced during the early 1970s, contained only a brief reference to the destruction and capture of Kleve, which was a key moment in the Reichswald campaign, before the focus moved on to the crossing of the Rhine in late March 1945. Even into the 2020s, British television documentaries still paid little attention to the events of Operation Veritable. The documentary series *World War II: Battles for Europe*, for example, originally produced – with some European investment – in July 2019, and aired in Britain on numerous occasions during the early 2020s, contained a welcome emphasis on Canadian efforts on the Scheldt during late 1944 but said little of note about the savage fighting in and around the Reichswald, and the adjacent Rhineland plains, during February and March 1945.

Horrocks' comments in 1957 about the Reichswald campaign remain as true now as they were all those years ago. In the run-up to the eightieth anniversary of the launch of the Reichswald campaign, in 2025, some timely studies of the topic have appeared, and not before time. If the 14th Army of General Slim, which fought so hard and for so long in the Far East, was Britain's 'forgotten army' of the Second World War, there is a good case for labelling the Reichswald Forest campaign as Britain's 'forgotten battle' of the war. Sandwiched as it was between better-known military events such as Operation Market Garden in September 1944, the Battle of the Bulge in December 1944, and the Rhine crossings of late March 1945, Operation Veritable and the Reichswald Forest campaign of February–March 1945 has certainly been a neglected field of study.

On the surface, the reasons for this apparent neglect seem rather unclear. On 8 February 1945, close to 40,000 British service personnel assaulted German defensive positions in and around the Reichswald Forest, supported by roughly 12,000 Canadian troops, who swept into flooded German-held territory on the banks of the Rhine. During the following month, the Canadian military contribution to the campaign increased exponentially, and both British and Canadian troops fought in horrendous conditions, day and night, through forests, mud, water and freezing temperatures, against an implacable and determined enemy. By the end of the campaign, tens of thousands of British, Canadian, German and American soldiers had been killed or wounded, but – as will be seen in the coming pages – the significance of the battles in the Reichswald, Kleve, Goch, Weeze, the Hochwald and elsewhere was immense.

The fact that the Reichswald campaign, and Operation Veritable as a whole, encompassed battles that 'no one [in Britain] has heard of', as Horrocks said in 1957, may have something to do with the fact that the British fought as part of the First Canadian Army during the brutal battles of February and March 1945. Commonwealth military formations had fought as part of larger British armies for a considerable period of time – during Montgomery's North African campaign, for instance, the 8th Army contained substantial contingents of men from New Zealand, Australia and South Africa. At the start of the Reichswald offensive, however, exactly the opposite was true. British divisions, in a late flowering of the ethos of Commonwealth and Empire, formed a huge part of Canada's First Canadian Army, and they went into battle commanded by a Canadian general. As time progressed, Commonwealth links loosened and British wartime memories receded, and this did perhaps lead to the Reichswald campaign and Operation Veritable becoming one of the forgotten aspects of Britain's military efforts in the Second World War. The fighting was looked upon as being a purely Canadian affair, when in reality the situation was very different. The Reichswald campaign, and Veritable in its entirety, was very much a joint Anglo-Canadian military endeavour, conducted in the very last months of the war in Europe, which was ultimately triumphant, and certainly helped hasten the end of German resistance in the West. The authors hope that the following pages will shed some much-needed light on the multi-faceted yet neglected story of Britain and Canada's Herculean military efforts to dislodge German forces from the Reichswald Forest and the adjacent Rhineland plains during early 1945.

I

THE ROAD TO THE REICHSWALD

> I must say that it [Operation Market Garden] is designed not only to carry out most effectively my basic conceptions with respect to this campaign but it is in exact accordance with all the understandings that we now have.
>
> Supreme Allied Commander Dwight D. Eisenhower[1]

In order to fully understand why between 170,000 and 200,000 British and Canadian service personnel were massed along the Dutch–German border, just to the west of the Reichswald Forest, on 7 February 1945, it is necessary to say more about the military events which took place in north-western Europe during the preceding five months.

By autumn 1944, German forces had been driven out of France and Belgium, and it appeared that the once invincible German Wehrmacht was teetering on the brink of total collapse in the west. Both the Supreme Allied Commander, Dwight Eisenhower, and his deputy, Bernard Montgomery, seemed to believe that the German army in the west was on its last legs. On 5 September 1944, for example, Eisenhower wrote, 'The defeat of the German armies is now complete and the only thing needed to realise the whole conception is speed.'[2] Given Eisenhower's comments, it was no surprise that he proved to be an enthusiastic supporter of Montgomery's radical plan to launch a rapid, narrow military thrust north-east into the Netherlands. Codenamed Operation Comet, this thrust was designed to isolate the German 15th Army from the rest of the retreating German forces and press it back towards the sea and the Scheldt estuary. In addition, it was hoped that success might see Comet forces turn the northern flank of the Siegfried Line, the German defensive line that stretched from the Netherlands down to the border with Switzerland. Once this was done, a military advance to the south-east could well cut German access to the vital industrial resources of the Ruhr, and might even bring the war in the west to a rapid conclusion.

On 6 September 1944, elements of the British Second Army broke out of Antwerp and attacked in a north-easterly direction as part of the Comet plan. German resistance proved to be much stronger than anticipated, however, and it soon became apparent to Montgomery that ground forces alone were insufficient for a rapid advance north-east into the Netherlands. The outcome might be very different, though, if airborne and ground troops could be used together, to pave the way for a swift advance through the Netherlands. This was the genesis of Montgomery's daring plan for Operation Market Garden, which involved British, American and Polish airborne forces seizing key bridges across canals and rivers in the north-eastern Netherlands. Britain's XXX Corps, led by Brian Horrocks, would then advance across these captured crossing points with as much speed as possible. The last and ultimate prize was to be the capture of the bridge over the Neder Rijn at Arnhem. Once XXX Corps had crossed the bridge at Arnhem and advanced to the Zuider Zee, it could then wheel to the south-east, outflank the Siegfried Line, and begin to achieve Montgomery and Eisenhower's strategic objective of depriving the Nazi regime of the Ruhr's industrial resources. If all went well at Arnhem, and the Neder Rijn was crossed, it was intended to launch a major attack into the Reichswald Forest region in late September 1944.

Of course, all didn't go well at Arnhem, which did indeed prove to be 'a bridge too far'.[3] Of 10,000 members of Britain's 1st Airborne Division dropped over the Wolfheze and Oosterbeek landing zones on 17 September 1944, 8,000 were killed, wounded or captured. General Roy Urquhart's 1st Airborne Division was effectively destroyed as a viable fighting force. Roughly 600 paratroopers under John Frost's command held on at Arnhem for more than four days against wave after wave of German attacks, but eventually even they had to give up, and German forces reoccupied the bridge and the devastated town of Arnhem after what the official German military report of the battle described as bloody hand-to-hand fighting, in which Frost's lightly armed battalion had killed or wounded over 3,300 enemy combatants.

In the end, Operation Market Garden – which both Eisenhower and Montgomery were equally enthusiastic about – failed because it was overly ambitious, and because it underestimated the extent to which the German military machine in the west had recovered from its disasters in France and Belgium during summer and early autumn 1944. To an extent, the German armies in the west had recovered their poise, and it was a recovery which would cause the Western Allies many problems in subsequent battles along the Scheldt estuary, in the Huertgen Forest, at the Reichswald and elsewhere. Lax intelligence, perhaps caused by a degree of complacency, also meant that the unfortunate British paratroopers of the 1st Airborne, and the Polish paratroopers of the 1st Independent Parachute Brigade, were unknowingly dropped close to where two divisions of the II SS Panzer Corps were refitting, a few miles to the east of Arnhem.

The failure to secure a bridgehead over the Neder Rijn at Arnhem was an undoubted reverse for the Allies. Nevertheless, in other rather neglected aspects, Operation Market Garden had been a success. The German defensive strategy in the southern Netherlands, based largely on its canals and rivers, had been virtually destroyed. More importantly, Nijmegen – and the bridge over the River Waal at Nijmegen – had been secured during the operation. The bridge had been captured largely as a result of a spectacular daylight assault launched by members of Brigadier-General Gavin's 82nd U.S. Airborne Division in open-topped boats. Horrocks' XXX Corps arrived to bolster the American hold on Nijmegen, and further American reinforcements were rushed in to consolidate and expand the bridgehead, which proved to be of crucial importance to the Allies in the period between September 1944 and the beginning of February 1945. The resulting salient was a narrow one, but it was expanded eastwards almost to the German frontier and was regarded as the gateway to the Reich by both Hitler and a number of his leading generals. Moreover, it was from within the Nijmegen salient that the men and materiel were amassed to eventually launch the Reichswald Forest campaign on 8 February 1945.

The setback at Arnhem was, initially at least, only supposed to delay plans for an Allied attack through the Reichswald for a very short period. A new provisional date of 10 October 1944 was set for a concerted 21st Army Group attack through the Reichswald Forest, and then on to the Rhineland plains. In the event, even this new start date had to be cancelled. By early October 1944, Allied supply lines were becoming seriously overextended. It was no longer possible to supply all the Allied armies advancing on Germany with enough fuel, rations and other war materiel to sustain the overall forward momentum. A new and nearer deepwater port was needed to replace the temporary artificial harbours set up at Normandy after D-Day. The Allies had captured the Belgian port of Antwerp on 6 September, and if supplies could be unloaded there and then distributed to the various armies advancing on Germany, logistical problems would be reduced dramatically. Unfortunately, Antwerp lay 60 miles inland from the sea, along the Scheldt estuary, and the Allies had neglected to clear German forces from this area. Effectively, the Allies had secured a working port, but one which was blockaded by the Germans positioned in strength at various points along the Scheldt. The Germans had to be ejected from the Scheldt before Antwerp could be used as a main Allied supply port, and this became the overwhelming priority for Eisenhower, Montgomery and the planners at SHAEF (Supreme Headquarters Allied Expeditionary Force), hence the delay of the commencement of the Reichswald offensive from 10 October to 10 November 1944. However, even this later date had to be cancelled when the Germans began attacking the eastern and northern flanks of the Nijmegen salient. Sensibly, perhaps, Montgomery felt that it was unwise to launch an offensive around the northern edge of the Siegfried Line before enemy threats to the flanks had been neutralised.

As the exceptionally cold winter of 1944 began to envelop all sides on the Western Front, little of significance (at least on the German side) seemed to be happening. But Montgomery had pledged that, whatever the weather conditions, German forces would be pressured and pushed back wherever they were found. A new start date of 1 January 1945 was issued for the commencement of the Reichswald offensive, and, anticipating a quiet Christmas, Montgomery requested that Eisenhower allow him leave to return to England in order to visit his son. Leave was granted, and Montgomery also found time to attend a 51st Highland Division investiture on 14 December 1944. During the investiture, Montgomery stated that the German armies in the west were largely finished; this speech was certainly tempting fate, because on the following day Hitler launched his desperate last-ditch offensive against weak American forces positioned in the Ardennes. During the resulting Battle of the Bulge, the overwhelming Allied military priority shifted to halting and then defeating the German offensive, so the proposed Reichswald attacks were postponed yet again.

By this time, an offensive in the Reichswald area had been envisaged and then delayed on no fewer than four occasions. However, Montgomery and Eisenhower remained remarkably consistent in their pursuit of overall strategic military objectives.

Crossing the Rhine and capturing the key industrial areas of the Ruhr had been a fundamental goal since at least September 1944, and an offensive across the Reichswald and its adjacent Rhineland flood plains was a key requirement if these overall goals were to be achieved. Thus, plans for a huge offensive around the northern flank of the German Siegfried Line were again activated. After a generals' conference at Maastricht in December 1944, the offensive through the Reichswald Forest and on into the Rhineland had been given the codename Operation Valediction. This name was later dropped in favour of the codename Operation Veritable, and a new and final start date of 8 February 1945 was agreed. Even before the Battle of the Bulge was completely at an end, Montgomery's eyes had turned to the Reichswald. He wanted Brian Horrocks, head of XXX Corps, to lead the charge through the forest, under the command of General Harry Crerar's First Canadian Army.

'How many divisions do you want'? Montgomery apparently asked Horrocks on the telephone.

'Seven,' replied Horrocks.

He got what he wanted, and the great, much-delayed Reichswald Forest campaign finally began on the morning of 8 February 1945.[4]

2

STRATEGY AND PLANNING FOR THE CAMPAIGN

> Battles cannot be run like board meetings and though a wise commander will always listen carefully to the advice of his experts ultimately the plan is his and his alone.
>
> Lt-Gen. Brian Horrocks, commander of XXX Corps

The above comments, espoused by a reflective Horrocks as he wrote his introduction to Elstob's 1970 account of the Battle of the Reichswald, undoubtedly contained a great deal of truth. As the on-the-spot battlefield commander, Horrocks was the ultimate arbiter of the destinies of all those who crossed their various start lines at the commencement of the great Operation Veritable Anglo-Canadian offensive. It was Horrocks who also had ultimate responsibility for the Reichswald battle plan which unfolded on 8 February 1945, one devised in circumstances where Horrocks felt he had 'no room for manoeuvre and no scope for cleverness'.[1] The low-lying lands on his left flank had been flooded by the Germans, and the flood waters were also rising on his right flank. In addition, the road network in the forest was desperately poor. There were no paved roads running from east to west and only two which ran from north to south, these converging at Hekkens, midway along the southern border of the forest. Given the constraints of weather and topography, Horrocks and his XXX Corps and 21st Army Group planners believed that they had little option but to launch Operation Veritable as, in essence, a straightforward frontal infantry assault, aided by air and armoured support wherever possible, and preceded by a massive artillery barrage against prepared German defensive positions.

Although Horrocks had the delegated authority to launch the Reichswald offensive in any way that he saw fit, his plans for the battle were certainly not produced in a void; he had to secure the approval of his immediate military superiors, and his tactics had to fit in with the overall strategic aims and objectives pursued by those higher up the military chain of command. It was, for instance, entirely logical and predictable that Horrocks should lead the initial west-to-east charge into the Reichswald area, with five British divisions supplemented by two Canadian divisions, because the ultimate aim of the campaign was to link up with General Simpson's U.S. 9th Army, also under Montgomery's command, which was to cross the Maas, push northwards and encircle the German armies in the Reichswald and Rhineland areas within a giant pincer movement. The codename given to the U.S.-led southern arm of this grand, classical campaign of encirclement was Operation Grenade. Once the northern arm of this pincer movement – the combatants involved in Operation Veritable – had joined with the Americans after the successful execution of Operation Grenade, both sets of armies were to move up to the Rhine, where Montgomery wanted the British in the centre, the Americans on the right and the Canadians on the left. Hence, it made sense in general terms if the offensive through the Reichswald was, to begin with at least, one which involved more British than Canadian front-line troops. The tenacious Canadians, however, were keen to play a greater role in the operation from the very start. Horrocks and his XXX Corps were attached to the First Canadian Army during the Reichswald campaign, and Horrocks was keen to emphasise the fact that he thought of himself as fighting a Canadian battle. Lieutenant-General G. G. Simmonds, commander of the II Canadian Corps, complained to Crerar that it would be unfortunate if battle commenced without some Canadian involvement. Probably as a result of this observation, the II and III Canadian divisions were added to the forces used by Horrocks in his initial attacks, and Canadian forces as a whole went on to play a very distinguished role in the overall Reichswald campaign.

General Crerar established the overall strategic direction of the Reichswald campaign, and the context within which Horrocks had to work, at a very early stage. On 25 January 1945, Crerar issued instructions to his Corps commanders confirming that the Reichswald offensive would be carried out as stated in his earlier directive of 14 December 1944. The attack was to be launched on 8 February 1945, and in his much-quoted instructions, the overall campaign was to be divided into three main phases. Phase 1 had Horrocks and XXX Corps right at the epicentre of the fighting, in which the Reichswald Forest was to be cleared of German troops, and advances were to be made to the towns of Gennep, Asperden and Kleve. Once the Gennep–Asperden–Kleve line had been reached and secured, Phase 2 of the campaign could be launched, breaching the enemy's second defensive system to the east and south-east of the Reichswald Forest and capturing the towns of Weeze, Udem, Kalkar and Emmerich. The lines of communication between these strategically located towns had to be secured before the third and final phase of the campaign, which involved breaching the German Hochwald 'Layback' defence lines and advancing to secure the towns of Geldern and Xanten. This last phase proved to be desperately hard.

Crerar's complex three-phase campaign strategy required a vast amount of planning, and in several key areas the logistical demands generated by a 200,000-strong army, about to go on the offensive, were simply staggering. The old Napoleonic adage about an army marching on its stomach was as true in the Reichswald as it was in every other theatre of war. British and Canadian quartermasters achieved the impressive feat of lodging 2.3 million rations in forward dumps for feeding soldiers involved in the fighting. These forward-dump food stocks could then be utilised by individual units at appropriate times as they moved around during the campaign.

The artillery shells used in the massive bombardment of German positions before Allied infantry and armour moved forward also had to be transported to numerous Allied gun sites. This in itself was a massive exercise: on 7 February alone, the 399th Company of the Royal Army Service Corps (RASC) used twenty 3-ton trucks to transport 2,400 rounds of 17-pounder high explosive artillery shells to forward ammunition dumps. Journalist Thomas Longville Bowen, editor of the *Merthyr Express*, found himself attached to the 53rd Welsh Division as it moved into the Reichswald Forest on 8 February. He reported in the *Merthyr Express* of 17 March 1945 that over 750,000 shells were fired into German positions during the first few hours of the offensive alone.[2] Longville Bowen stayed with the Welsh Division throughout the forest phase of the fighting, and later reported on the division's street-fighting activities in Goch and elsewhere. In modern parlance, he was really an 'embedded' journalist – a senior Welsh newspaperman reporting on Welsh troops fighting in a major European campaign. British and Canadian shelling wasn't confined to just the preliminary bombardment which preceded the move forward of Allied infantry and armour. The sheer weight of munitions brought forward to Allied gun positions can be adjudged by the fact that during five separate bombardments on 8 February, an average of at least 9 tons of shells burst on each of 268 pre-selected German defensive positions. Thirteen German forward positions were also saturated with rockets fired by the 1st Canadian Rocket Battery.

In addition to the vast quantities of munitions, food and troops brought into forward assembly areas, blood plasma and anaesthetics were needed, and 8,000 miles of four different kinds of cabling were made ready for use. Allied amphibious vehicles were to play a crucial role in the offensive from the very start, and 10,000 smoke generators were used to disguise the movements of these vehicles, and to shield the advance of infantry and armour over open country. The internal components of artillery pieces, tanks and other vehicles were also protected from rust via the liberal use of fog oil. More than a million gallons of fog oil were made available during the course of the campaign, but this still didn't prevent mechanical breakdowns being a major cause of concern during the incessant rain in the Reichswald and the Rhineland during February and March 1945.

Fuel was the vital ingredient which kept mechanised armies going during the Second World War, and the lack of it was a major reason why the Panzer armies which crashed through the Ardennes in December 1944 finally ground to a halt. No such fuel shortages were likely to impede the progress of the British and Canadians in the Reichswald Forest campaign. The problem of overstretched supply lines, which had caused the British and American armies to pause and stutter during their advance across France and Belgium in late 1944, was ended when Antwerp became a fully functioning port. Fuel could then be unloaded and transported quite rapidly, and on 7 February 1945, the Deputy Director of Supply and Transport at First Canadian Army Headquarters reported that there was enough fuel immediately on hand to drive XXX Corps forward for 150 miles. On top of this, fuel reserves could be accessed which sustained XXX Corps for another 150 miles. The Canadian II Corps were designated to take over many of XXX Corps' offensive duties during the second phase of Crerar's campaign plan, and there was another stockpile of fuel available which would probably keep the Canadian outfit going for another 200 miles.[3]

Securing sufficient food, fuel and ammunition, along with the myriad other resources needed by an army about to go on the offensive, was just one of the many challenges faced by British and Canadian army planners. Equally as important was the task of ensuring that men and materiel could be moved from one location to another with the maximum possible speed and efficiency. For this to happen, road and rail networks needed to be up to scratch and, in the context of the south-east Netherlands (where the military buildup took place), this also meant that enough bridges had to be in place to ensure that First Canadian Army assets and resources could cross the country's many rivers, dykes and canals. The massive scale of the construction work undertaken in preparation for the Reichswald campaign was recognised even at the time of the fighting. *The Scotsman* newspaper of 10 February 1945, for example, reported that the campaign presented 'an engineering problem as well as a tactical one. Never had pioneers and engineers played so vital a role in actual battle.'

The undoubted truth of *The Scotsman's* comments was confirmed by the fact that in the run-up to D-Day on 8 February, fifty companies of engineers, twenty-nine companies of Pioneers, and three road construction companies worked around the clock to repair and improve 400 miles of roads, and to construct a hundred miles of new roads. Nearly a hundred new bridges, including rail bridges over the Maas, were also constructed with considerable speed. Hundreds of trains were commandeered for the offensive, and some 35,000 road vehicles of all shapes and sizes were utilised by the First Canadian Army during the campaign. In the eight days between 1-8 February, the RASC's 399 Company utilised 237 3-ton vehicles in order to complete a wide variety of tasks, including the collection and delivery of 17- and 25-pounder artillery shells, small arms ammunition rounds, coal, tank tracks, blankets, loud hailers, jerry cans, DERV, petrol, oil and lubricant (POL).[4] In addition, between 8 and 25 February, the RASC's 62nd Company made use of seventy-nine 3-ton trucks and six DUKW amphibious vehicles in order to carry out its allotted tasks. The enormous scale of the demand for motor vehicles can also be illustrated by the transport requests put forward by Captain J. Sawbridge, adjutant of the 9th Cameronians (Scottish Rifles) just five days before D-day on 8 February. In his Transport Administration Order, Sawbridge requested for his battalion at least one ambulance, two scout cars, five jeeps, six cars (including one for the chaplain), thirteen 15-cwt trucks and thirty-eight carriers (for troops, mortars and other equipment).[5]

This huge buildup of military vehicles in the Nijmegen salient, to the west of the Reichswald Forest, was regulated by the activities of the Special Traffic Office (STO). The STO was a force of some 1,600 men, and one of its chief responsibilities was to try and ensure that military convoys moved with as much secrecy as possible. Movement was restricted to the nighttime hours, and headlights were not allowed. The troops, armour and supplies of the Welsh Division, for example, moved up to their assembly areas in the woods around Groesbeek in the pitch-black dead of night, in trucks with doused headlights, along roads flooded with 18 inches of mud and water. The fact that the division made it on time to their designated start lines without attracting undue attention was in itself a considerable achievement. In his *Merthyr Express* article of 17 March 1945, Longville Bowen rather colourfully described this nocturnal move-up as being 'comparable with the task of moving the whole population of Cardiff and its effects to Swansea, without the people of Swansea being aware of the move'. Reconnaissance parties were the only military units given permission to move during daylight, and even then they had to remove formation patches from their battledress and travel in Canadian vehicles accompanied by Canadian liaison officers.

Elaborate camouflage techniques were instituted to try and hide as many as possible of the 1,053 guns being assembled to the east and south of Nijmegen. Dummy-gun positions were erected which were later replaced by real artillery pieces, and camouflage experts from 21st Army Group Headquarters sited many ammunition dumps in hedgerows, kitchen garden plots and patches of scrubland. On a wider strategic level, increased military wireless traffic was employed, along with other ruses, to encourage the Germans into the mistaken belief that Montgomery's main offensive would be either further to the south, in the Venlo area, or in the north, directed towards northern Holland. By this time in the war, the Germans claimed to be more aware of the British capacity for devious behaviour. Nevertheless, when the rain-sodden Anglo-Canadian military thunderbolt struck through the Reichswald Forest on 8 February 1945, it did come as a surprise to most – if not all – German military planners.

3

THE AIR CAMPAIGN

> I believe that the first great principle of war is that you must first win your air battle before you fight your land and sea battle. The second great principle is that Army plus Air has to be so knitted that the two together form one entity.
>
> Bernard Montgomery during the 1943 Italian campaign[1]

The Reichswald Forest campaign, and Operation Veritable as a whole, was supported principally by six major Allied air formations: the Eighth and Ninth U.S. Air Force, RAF Bomber Command, and the RAF's No. 2 Group, No. 83 Group and No. 84 Group, which were all part of the RAF's 2nd Tactical Air Force (2TAF), created on 1 June 1943. In broad terms, the objectives of the air campaign were twofold. The heavy and medium bombers of RAF Bomber Command, the 8th U.S. Air Force and No. 2 Group of 2TAF were really focused on pre-planned attacks on strategically located towns, road bridges, rail links and communication hubs. The fighter-bombers of 2TAF's No. 83 Group, meanwhile, were concerned primarily with preventing Luftwaffe interventions and isolating the Reichswald battlefield by instituting a massive programme of interdictions on the enemy's rear areas across the Rhine. This interdiction programme really involved attacking any targets of opportunity which appeared, such as ferries, locomotives, rail carriages and road transports. By smashing these targets, and obliterating bridges and rail tracks, 2TAF sought to cut off the Reichswald battlefield from any hope of military support or supply from the rest of Germany. The fighter-bombers and bombers of the U.S. 9th Air Force, under Major-General Otto Weyland, were also engaged, like the RAF's No. 83 Group, in supporting the Reichswald offensive by laying waste to the enemy's Rhineland communications system. Unlike No. 83 Group, and the U.S. 9th Air Force, the aerial resources of 2TAF's No. 84 Group were focused primarily on the battlefield itself. No. 84 Group fighter-bombers were engaged in providing close support and protection for ground troops, performing reconnaissance and attacking pre-arranged enemy headquarters, communications and forward ammunition dump targets.

Montgomery always professed a strong desire to see armies and air forces working together as one indissoluble entity, and during the Reichswald campaign several concrete steps were taken to bring about the desired level of unity between ground forces and the six principal air formations involved in the fighting. To begin with, a senior RAF Bomber Command representative was attached to No. 84 Group during the planning and execution of Operation Veritable. This representative had sufficient authority to make decisions on behalf of Bomber Command without the necessity of seeking permission from Harris or any of his deputies. One of the key discussions which took place between Bomber Command and Horrocks at the start of the campaign concerned the type of bombs to be used during the initial attacks against German targets. If Kleve and Goch were to be destroyed, Horrocks and the First Canadian Army accepted that cratering of roads and streets was likely to occur. Such cratering could and did occur, slowing down the Allied advance through these towns. In other nearby villages and small towns attacked on the night of 7 February, however, Allied bombers used incendiaries and anti-personnel bombs specifically in order to avoid cratering. Horrocks also accepted the RAF argument that cratering was inevitable if bombs heavy enough to destroy German concrete defensive installations on the strategically located Materborn Ridge, overlooking Kleve, were used. In the open spaces around Nutterden though, it was agreed that bombers would attack German troops with non-cratering airburst bombs – such bombs would kill Germans in rather grisly fashion, but at least the roads would be left intact, and easily traversed by Allied armour and infantry.

The Bomber Command raid on Kleve during the night of 7 February 1945 proved to be the best-remembered and most-written-about aspect of the Reichswald heavy bombing campaign. It featured in an episode of Thames TV's seminal early 1970s *World at War* documentary series, in which an elderly Brian Horrocks recounted his sadness at acquiescing in the destruction of a medieval town once the home of Henry VIII's fourth wife, Anne of Kleves.[2] In reality, when General Crerar asked Horrocks whether he wanted the town 'taking out' or not, Horrocks had little choice but to reply in the affirmative. Kleve was massively important in a strategic sense, and Horrocks had to ensure that the town could not be used with ease as a forward assembly point for German reinforcements, which could then be moved on to various points on the battlefield, as and when necessary. A force of 295 Avro Lancaster bombers and ten Mosquitos carried out the task of trying to obliterate Kleve on the night of 7/8 February. The actual bombing was carried out by 285 Lancasters, which dropped 1,384 tons of explosives on the town but no incendiaries. A further 285 Avro Lancasters, led by ten Mosquito pathfinders, also attacked the nearby towns of Weeze, Udem, Geldern and Kalkar during the same evening. In total, 464 Bomber Command aircraft, including 156 Lancasters, 292 Halifaxes and sixteen Mosquitos, were also directed to attack Goch.[3] The Goch raid came to a premature end after only 155 planes had bombed the town, but considerable damage was still inflicted on this strategically crucial German communications hub.

No. 84 Group of 2TAF was working with XXX Corps for the first time during preparations for the Reichswald offensive. Therefore, a whole set of new procedures were created in order to ensure that targets identified by ground formations were passed rapidly to No. 84 Group fighter-bombers flying overhead. Staffs of ground formations were all briefed in some detail about how to submit targets to No. 84 Group via the First Canadian Air Support Signals Unit. At XXX Corps headquarters, a Forward Control Post was also established which operated a 'cab rank' of fighter-bombers overhead, who could all be despatched to attack agreed targets within a few minutes of orders being received. In addition to this, a Mobile Radar Control Post was created for directing aircraft in bad weather – a crucial service given the almost continuous rain and cold temperatures which existed during the period of the campaign.

The procedures for ensuring Montgomery's desired seamless unity between army and air were a little different with regard to the U.S. 8th and 9th Air Force, but overall, the arrangements made for integrating U.S. forces within the air campaign as a whole seem to have worked quite well. Requests for U.S. 8th Air Force resources were, for example, channelled to SHAEF via Headquarters, RAF 2TAF. One such request led to 8th Air Force heavy bombers attacking road and rail bridges across the Rhine at Wesel, prior to the launch of the 8 February ground offensive. American bombers returned to attack the road bridge at Wesel on 14 February, and, in a clear example of Anglo-American air cooperation, a force of Bomber Command Lancasters returned to bomb Wesel yet again on 16 February. Wesel was an important forward base for German troops moving up to the Reichswald area, and as a result of the synchronised air activity of the British and Americans, movement through the town and across the Rhine became virtually impossible.

Ensuring that army and air worked together as one united entity was probably easiest with the three air formations involved in 2TAF. Harry Broadhurst, Air Officer Commanding (AOC)

No. 83 Group, and Edmund Hudleston, AOC No. 84 Group, had both gained senior commands in the RAF's Desert Air Force (DAF), which supported Montgomery's North African campaign. Basil Embry, No. 2 Group's dynamic AOC, had also been seconded to the DAF, in October 1941, as an adviser. Montgomery went on record on many occasions to express his gratitude to the DAF for its many bombing and strafing exploits during the 8th Army's long march westwards from the gates of Cairo to Tunisia. Broadhurst, in particular, was renowned for insisting that his pilots were trained intensively in the techniques necessary to strafe and bomb enemy vehicles, tanks, transport and communication lines. The tactics he inculcated in his pilots helped form the basis of ground-attack principles used at D-Day, and later on in the Reichswald campaign. Moreover, Broadhurst had a reputation for being totally committed to cooperation with the army. Hudleston, an Australian, commanded a mixed force of Typhoons, Spitfires and American Mustangs, and he was a senior RAF officer of considerable charm, very adept at dealing with inter-service relations. By February 1945, Basil Embry was leading No. 2 Group's DeHavilland Mosquitos, which had a record of panache, precision bombing and aircraft serviceability which was the envy of much of the rest of the Allied air force. Together, the No. 2, No. 83 and No. 84 Groups of 2TAF made up a formidable strike force, and one which achieved much in the skies above the Reichswald Forest, and the Rhineland, during February and March 1945.

On D-Day, 8 February 1945, RAF 2TAF made more than 1,000 sorties. Spitfire and Typhoon fighter-bombers attacked German infantry positions in the Reichswald Forest, and strafed slit trenches with cannon fire. Mitchell B25 and Boston bombers also unloaded high explosives on German troop concentrations situated less than 1,000 yards from British and Canadian front lines. Further afield, fifty German motor transports heading towards the battlefield were destroyed, along with fifty-five locomotives, and 160 rail trucks. Rail tracks were also cut in twenty-seven different locations. West of the Ruhr, at Hamborn, Typhoons set two oil storage tankers ablaze, and a power station at Arnhem was attacked with rockets. RAF 2TAF's efforts were more than matched by a massive contribution from the U.S. 9th Air Force, which flew 953 fighter-bomber, 505 bomber, and 98 reconnaissance sorties on the opening day of the Reichswald offensive alone. The 9th dropped 1,236 tons of munitions over German Rhineland communications during the course of 8 February, losing seven fighter-bombers and one bomber in the process.

Both 2TAF and the U.S. 9th Air Force were particularly keen on attacking German trains, locomotives and rail infrastructure. According to journalists who wrote censored accounts of the fighting for British newspapers of the time, this was because there had been a marked increase in German rail traffic since the end of the Battle of the Bulge in late January 1945. As the bulge in the Allied line had been straightened out by U.S. and British forces, the German army had been forced to retreat, and a vast number of their motorised vehicles had been destroyed as they headed eastwards. Scottish newspapers carried particularly detailed accounts of the Reichswald campaign – undoubtedly because of the heavy representation of Scottish regiments in the fighting – and the *Dundee Courier* of 17 February 1945 claimed that that more than 4,500 German vehicles had been destroyed on just the two days of 22 January and 23 January 1945. As a result, the Germans had little option but to move more supplies to their troops in the Reichswald via rail. Consequently, Allied forces focused much attention on strafing trains and marshalling yards. On 9 February 1945, the *Birmingham Evening Despatch* claimed that 2TAF and the U.S. 9th Air Force had together damaged or destroyed 21,000 railcars, 200 locomotives, and severed rail tracks at 150 separate locations.[4] These figures, like those reported by the *Dundee Courier* for German vehicle losses at the Battle of the Bulge, were undoubtedly exaggerated. Nevertheless, it is true to say that, whatever the real figures were for German rail and motor vehicle losses, the air campaign objective of crippling the entire Rhineland railway system to isolate the Reichswald battlefields was very largely achieved within a comparatively short period of time. Rhineland communications were paralysed across a large stretch of territory between Nijmegen and the River Moselle south of Echternach.

The role of 2TAF on the battlefield, with No. 84 Group in the vanguard, differed according to the priorities of the Allied generals on the ground. At the start of the Reichswald campaign on 8 February, General Horrocks made attacks along the road to Kranenburg, which ran just to the north of the Reichswald Forest, an absolute priority. Horrocks' intention was to advance along the road to Kranenburg and then seize the Materborn Gap, a narrow neck of high ground between the forest and Kleve. Once the gap was secure, Allied troops would pour through into the plains to the east of the Reichswald Forest before sufficient German reinforcements could arrive to stop them. As a result of Horrocks' strategy, air attacks on German positions located in this northern corridor were given maximum priority on 8 February. As the ground battles moved to the east and south of the Reichswald Forest, in the later phases of General Crerar's overall campaign strategy, the focus of Allied air attacks also began to shift. By 16 February, the town of Goch, some 8 miles to the south of the Reichswald Forest, was the scene of heavy fighting. British and Canadian forces advancing on Goch were met with determined German resistance. Reuters correspondents were telling various British and American newspapers that the German resistance in Goch was being stiffened by supplies channelled through the nearby towns of Udem and Weeze. In order to disrupt this supply route, both towns were, in the words of Reuters, 'smothered' by 2TAF medium bombers during 16 February. At the same time as 2TAF bombers were engaged in flattening Udem and Weeze, British and Canadian troops were fighting a heavily contested battle with German forces for control of the Asperden–Hassum highway, which lay to the north-east of

Goch. British and French Spitfires dropped substantial quantities of high explosives and incendiaries on German strongpoints and dugouts along the highway, while other Spitfires attacked ammunition dumps and an enemy church tower observation point in Hassum itself.

By the time Operation Veritable was launched on 8 February 1945, the German Luftwaffe was but a pale shadow of the mighty aviation force which had blazed a trail of terror and destruction across much of the continent of Europe. The demands of total war, on two fronts, had bled it dry of many of its best pilots, and by February 1945 the German air force had lost forever its supremacy in the skies over Europe. Nevertheless, even three months before the end of the war in Europe, the Luftwaffe could still pose a serious threat: a mere six weeks before the commencement of Operation Veritable, on 1 January 1945, the German Luftwaffe had managed to put 1,035 aircraft into the skies, as part of Operation Bodenplatte, which involved a surprise attack on seventeen Allied airfields in France, Belgium and the Netherlands. The object of the operation was to destroy as many Allied aircraft, hangars and airstrips as possible. German medium bombers and night-fighters acted as pathfinders, but the Luftwaffe strike force was mostly made up of single-engine Messerschmitt Me109 and Focke-Wulf Fw 190 fighter planes. Operation Bodenplatte achieved considerable tactical surprise, and a great many 2TAF planes were destroyed on the ground.

As it turned out, Bodenplatte was the very last large-scale offensive operation launched by the Luftwaffe in the war, and it led to the capture or death of many of Germany's most experienced remaining pilots. Even so, Operation Veritable air planners had to guard against the Germans launching a similar, even if smaller, surprise attack over the Reichswald battlefields. No. 84 Group fighter-bombers sought to neutralise this Luftwaffe threat by carrying out pre-emptive strikes on German airfields north of the Ruhr. Fighters from 2TAF assembled in the skies in their various 'cab ranks' ready to shoot down German aircraft well before they entered Reichswald Forest airspace on 8 February. In its coverage of the opening phase of the Reichswald campaign, the *Birmingham Evening Despatch* of 9 February reported that ten German aircraft had been shot down: five Stuka dive-bombers were destroyed by a Royal Canadian Air Force (RCAF) Spitfire squadron south-east of Wesel, three Me 109 fighters were shot down by RAF Hawker Tempest fighter planes as they attempted to take off from various Luftwaffe airbases, and a Junkers Ju 88 fighter-bomber and a Focke-Wulf Fw 190 were brought down south of Bremen. Newspaper reports of aircraft losses were always rather unreliable, but the Luftwaffe's attempts to intervene in the Reichswald campaign were clearly only minor and intermittent. There were simply not enough trained pilots left to mount an effective aerial challenge to the Allies as they moved through the Reichswald Forest, its nearby towns and villages, and on towards the Rhine.

Nevertheless, the Luftwaffe's irregular appearances above the Reichswald battlefields still created a vivid impression, because many of the planes it used to attack Anglo-Canadian positions were Messerschmitt Me 262 jet-propelled fighter-bombers, which were at the cutting edge of world aviation technology. A number of British battalion war diary entries recorded the fact that German jet fighter-bombers were making attacks in the area. These attacks were concentrated on the Kleve area during mid-February 1945. On 14 February, for example, the war diary of 190 Field Regiment, Royal Artillery (RA) recorded the fact that a 'sharp attack' by jet-propelled planes had been made in the vicinity of Kleve. These immensely fast German fighter-bombers had dropped several bombs, but no casualties had been inflicted. The war diary entries for 131 Field Regiment RA suggest that there were probably two Me 262 jet fighter-bomber attacks during the day on 14 February – one in the morning and one in the afternoon – but that neither attack caused much damage. By late February, German jets were attacking First Canadian

Army positions further to the east. Allied fighter and bomber activity had been restricted during much of February by fog, rain and occasional snow. Visibility had improved by 21 February, and RAF Typhoons resumed large-scale strafing activities. At the same time, however, the improved weather allowed Luftwaffe Me 262 jets to resume their bombing sorties. During the late afternoon of 21 February, the 181 Field Regiment RA war diary stated that Me 262 jets had bombed Allied positions at Schloss Kalbeck, and the Argyll & Sutherland Highlanders war diary entry suggests that German jets were also active in the Bucholt area. But the overall impact of these Luftwaffe jet-propelled aircraft, as they streaked across the Rhineland skies at speeds far beyond those achievable by nearby Spitfires and Typhoons, was still negligible. There were just too few of them in service to make much of a difference.

4

THE GERMAN DEFENCE

> Good luck and good hunting. Not for nothing is the lion our divisional symbol. Fanatically loyal to our concept of people and Fuhrer, we shall fight like a sworn band of brothers, and victory will be ours against a world in arms.[1]
>
> Order of the Day, Maj.-Gen. Heinz Fiebig,
> 84th Infantry Division commander

At the onset of the Allied ground campaign on 8 February 1945, the Reichswald sector of the German Westwall, or Siegfried Line, was held by the Wehrmacht's 84th Infantry Division, commanded by Major-General Heinz Fiebig. The division, comprising roughly 10,000 men, has generally received a poor press from British and Canadian historians. In his Official History of the Canadian Army, C. P. Stacey described the 84th as being mostly made up of raw recruits who were poorly equipped. British war correspondents who accompanied the First Canadian Army through the Reichswald campaign also had a tendency to describe the 84th as being soldiers of poor quality.[2] Undoubtedly, by February 1945, the division had been weakened severely by the heavy casualties it had sustained in

Normandy during 1944, and many of its new recruits certainly lacked experience. The ranks of the 84th had been decimated during fighting in the Falaise pocket at Normandy, but enough experienced soldiers had survived to ensure that it remained a viable fighting force. By the time of the Reichswald battles, the 84th Division consisted of the 84th Fusilier Battalion, the 1051st Grenadier Regiment, the 1052nd Grenadier Regiment and an assortment of military units shattered during the Normandy campaign and later brought together as Battle Group Katzmann. In December 1944, the Battle Group Katzmann was reconstituted as the 1053rd Grenadier Regiment.[3] The three Grenadier Regiments were each made up of two battalions, and there were roughly 500 men in each battalion. Every battalion was subdivided into three companies, and there were three platoons in every company. As an addition to these resources, on 6 February, the 2nd Parachute Regiment, composed of 2,000 crack Luftwaffe paratroopers, was placed under 84th Division command. This particular formation had already fought the British and Canadians at Bergen op Zoom, during the Allied operations to clear the Scheldt estuary, and had established a tough and tenacious fighting reputation for itself.

The men of the 2nd Parachute Regiment were positioned in the German line between Katerbosch and a point just to the south of Gennep. The sector of the German line between the Rhine and the village of Wyler, some 3 miles to the west of Kranenburg, was occupied by the 2,000 men of the 84th Fusilier Battalion, with the 1051st and 1052nd Grenadier Regiments positioned to the south of the fusiliers. Two battalions of the former Battle Group Katzmann were also positioned between Grafwegen and Katerbosch. Behind the various grenadier regiments, the fusiliers and the parachute infantry, German reserves in the immediate vicinity of the Reichswald were decidedly thin.[4] Fiebig could call upon the services of the Sicherungs Battalion Munster, which was comprised of older men who were usually employed in guarding static military installations. Additionally, German commanders could, if necessary, make use of the 276th Magen (Stomach) Battalion, composed of recruits with chronic digestive ailments which made them unsuitable for regular army service. Later on, long after the clamour of battle in the Reichswald had subsided, Fiebig told Allied interrogators that he'd made use of the Magen Battalion in preference to the Ohren (Ear) Battalion because the hearing loss prevalent in the latter would have made them unable to hear 'even the opening barrage of an attack'. Also, in early February 1945, First Canadian Army sources identified the presence of what they called the Brockenbusch Battalion, composed of between 500 and 800 Organisation Todt workers who'd been ordered to dig defensive trenches in the vicinity of Millingen, Kekerdom, Niel and Duffelward. These men could, it was thought, be used to bolster the German front lines if necessary, though how effective they would have been is certainly open to question. German infantry in the Reichswald front line was supported by a range of small arms weaponry: the 1051st and 1052nd Grenadier Regiments were supplied with six 81mm mortars and six heavy machine guns (HMGs) per battalion. German armour, however, was in noticeably short supply. The only armour actually present in the Reichswald area on 8 February comprised thirty-six self-propelled guns belonging to the 655th Heavy Anti-Tank Battalion. In total, Fiebig only had about 100 artillery pieces he could lay his hands on at the start of the Anglo-Canadian onslaught against German positions in the Reichswald sector.

In general, XXX Corps and First Canadian Army intelligence concerning German army numbers and dispositions proved to be remarkably accurate – there were no glaring gaps or omissions in Allied intelligence as there had been during the Arnhem Market Garden campaign. General Crerar's planners suspected that the German 7th Parachute Division could be positioned to the east of the Reichswald, whereas at least part of it had in fact been edged northwards by General Alfred

Schlemm, who had been appointed as the overall commander in the area on 28 January 1945. Schlemm had a Luftwaffe background, and was a veteran of many of the bloody battles on the Eastern Front. He was also a skilled tactician, and very adept at organising tactical retreats. He proved to be one of the very few senior German commanders who believed the Allies would launch a major offensive through the Reichswald (which is why he quietly moved part of the 7th Parachute Division to the north). Other reserves, in addition to elements of the 7th Parachute Division, were also within comparatively easy reach of the Reichswald area. General Johannes Blaskowitz's armoured reserve was at Dulken, 12 miles south-east of Venlo. The XLVII Panzer Corps made up this reserve, which comprised the 116th Panzer Division and the 15th Panzer Grenadier Division. Unfortunately for the Germans, however, both divisions were only at half strength, and able to muster a total of just ninety tanks between them. The further away from the key Rhineland sector the German commanders were, the more sceptical they seemed to become about the possibility of a major Anglo-Canadian offensive turning the northern flank of the Westwall. Field Marshal Gerd von Rundstedt was the overall commander of German forces on the Western Front, and on 5 February his chief intelligence officer told key commanders of Army Group H (which defended the western borders of Germany between the North Sea and just north of Dusseldorf) that an Allied offensive across the Maas was more likely than a full-blooded thrust through the Reichswald. General Blaskowitz was the commander of Army Group H and, like Alfred Schlemm, he'd moved into this position only recently, on 28 January. He told Schlemm that there was no real evidence of large-scale Allied activity in the Nijmegen area.

This uncertainty and confusion among members of the German High Command about where and when the great Allied offensive in the west would take place was certainly exacerbated by Hitler's preoccupation with the great military advances being made by Soviet forces in the East. Nevertheless, by 10 February it was clear to German strategists that the Anglo-Canadian offensive through the Reichswald was a massive one, and no feint, so reinforcements were sent into the area. The order to commit the XLVII Panzer Corps to the battle was given on 10 February, and its tanks assembled at Udem on the following evening under their immediate commander, Heinrich von Luttwitz. The corps was given the objective of either securing Kleve or ensuring its recapture, and von Luttwitz was given one regiment of the 346th Infantry Division to support him. The 6th German Parachute Division was also brought in closer on the German right.

Intelligence staff at both the First Canadian Army and the 21st Army Group were certainly aware of the threat posed by German reinforcements. On 4 February 1945, Montgomery's intelligence chiefs estimated that von Rundstedt might be able to assemble up to eleven panzer and panzer grenadier divisions which could, in theory, be deployed against the Anglo-Canadian armies pushing through the Reichswald. In reality, though, the Germans had to guard against the threat posed by both Simpson's 9th U.S. Army and Omar Bradley's group of armies further to the south on Germany's long Western Front. As a result, only a minority of von Rundstedt's possible reserves could be deployed against the First Canadian Army on the northern edge of the Westwall. First Canadian Army planners issued 'modest estimates' of how quickly the Germans would be able to reinforce their positions, which were issued to Allied formations down to battalion level prior to the great move forward on 8 February (D-Day). By the end of D+1 it was estimated that one extra enemy infantry division could enter the battle area. By the end of the fourth day of the offensive, D+4, it was reckoned that one complete panzer grenadier division and one complete panzer division could be fighting the British and Canadians, and one week after the launch of the campaign it was predicted that two extra German infantry divisions could be committed to the struggle.[5] Speed was clearly of the essence if the First Canadian Army was to break through the Reichswald Forest and spill out into the Rhineland plains. However, rapidity of advance was made extremely difficult by rising flood waters, and by the fact that Allied infantry and armour had to overcome three different tiers of prepared German defences.

By the time that substantive German reinforcements were arriving in the Reichswald area, the German Forward Line defences had been largely overrun. Even so, at dawn on 8 February, the Forward Line presented some formidable obstacles to the 50,000 British and Canadian infantry, supported by some 500 tanks, who were about to attack it. The line itself lay roughly 2 miles to the west of the Reichswald Forest and the Siegfried Line, and consisted of a number of strong outposts situated in woods, houses and along roads, which were very largely manned by members of the German 84th Division. British and Canadian patrols gathered a considerable amount of intelligence about the defences which made up the German Forward Line. They identified a considerable number of enemy bunkers, and earth and wooden strongpoints, along with at least one anti-tank ditch, between 10 and 12 feet wide, with a drop to the water of at least 6 feet.[6] In fact, so many bunkers and strongpoints were identified that it was soon realised that the Germans simply didn't have enough men to fill them all – some bunkers and strongpoints were obviously empty, and other alleged strongpoints were clearly dummy positions constructed to deceive the British and Canadians. Patrols encountered few pill boxes west of the Siegfried Line, and they also found little evidence of barbed wire being used as part of the German Forward Line defences. The identification of German minefields in the Forward Line proved to be particularly difficult. British and Canadian patrols couldn't locate specific minefields, though they expected at least one to be in existence. The lack of information about enemy mines did not bode well for the Anglo-Canadian offensive once it had begun, and many Allied formations, including the 9th Cameronians, suffered casualties as they inadvertently advanced into undetected German minefields.[7]

Once British and Canadian infantry and armour had moved successfully through the German Forward Line, they immediately had to tackle the Reichswald sector's Westwall/ Siegfried Line defences. The so-called Siegfried Line had been constructed along Nazi Germany's western boundaries in fits and starts since 1936, and it ran north from the borders of Switzerland to Kleve and the Netherlands frontier. Originally, the defences had been constructed to counter the French Maginot Line, but once German forces had successfully conquered most of western Europe the purpose of the Westwall seemed rather unclear. Further building programmes were resumed with some intensity from 1944 onwards, and by February 1945 the Westwall ran for some 400 miles and contained more than 18,000 bunkers, tunnels and tank traps. The main Westwall defences in the Reichswald sector were located to the north and south of the forest itself. Within the forest, German defences basically consisted of a line of trenches, with few if any concrete pill boxes and strongpoints. The German Defence Line here was to be largely based upon small arms fire rather than tank and artillery support. On 9 February, the war correspondent Christopher Buckley followed British troops into German trenches on the western fringes of the Reichswald Forest. He encountered two lines of shallow trenches constructed by conscripted labour during autumn 1944. Buckley described these trenches as forming a continuous zigzag line, dotted here and there with rudimentary dugouts. These shallow trenches had no adequate embrasures for machine gun positions, according to Buckley, and rather resembled waterlogged early First World War defensive positions.[8]

The German trenches on the western fringes of the Reichswald Forest were backed up with further defensive trench systems situated just to the east of the forest, which followed the line of the towns Kleve, Bedburg and Goch. This second belt of defences was still in the process of being constructed but was intended to consist of a double line of trenches separated by a large tank ditch. Trench lines were defended with quantities of barbed wire, and there was some evidence of mines being laid. Another line of trenches was also under construction, linking the defences at Kleve with those on the River Niers. Like the defences linking Kleve, Bedburg and Goch, the trench system between Kleve and the Niers was also unfinished. In fact, work on the northern part of the system had barely begun. This was in stark contrast to the situation in the southern part of the defences, where the trench system was virtually complete.

The overall objective of the Reichswald campaign was to outflank German armies defending the northernmost part of the Westwall and move the First Canadian Army up to the western banks of the Rhine. Once the Reichswald Forest had been cleared of German troops, and key towns such as Kleve and Goch had been captured, the next objective for the First Canadian Army was to wheel to the south-east, and smash through a third tier of German defences which ran along undulating ground roughly 10 miles to the east of the Reichswald Forest. This third German defensive line – known as the Hochwald Layback – ran southwards from the left bank of the Rhine, opposite Rees, along the western edge of the Hochwald and Balberger Wald, and continued to the town of Geldern. The long, boomerang-shaped ridge with the Hochwald at the northern end and the smaller Balberger Forest to the south was defended with dogged determination by the Germans, and the Allied campaign to breach the Hochwald Layback, spearheaded by the Canadians, led to some of the most savage fighting of the entire Operation Veritable campaign.

Together, the Hochwald Layback, the Westwall defences and the Forward Defence Line, together with rising flood waters and incessant rain, were certainly successful in slowing down the British and Canadian offensive. Allied hopes for a swift success faded as the campaign slogged on for over a month. However, probably the most successful German tactic in slowing down the British and Canadian offensive had little to do with the effectiveness of its armies or defensive lines and everything to do with the successful destruction of the sluice gates at the Schwammenauel dam, on the River Roer, during the night of 9/10 February 1945. The Schwammenauel was the largest of three Roer dams, and it lay just to the east of the Huertgen Forest. The dam was situated roughly 120 miles to the south of the Reichswald Forest, but more importantly it lay just at the point where General Simpson's U.S. 9th Army was about to cross the Roer and then push north-east as part of the southern pincer movement which was intended to trap Schlemm and Fiebig's forces fighting in the Reichswald area. Capturing the Schwammenauel had never been a major Allied priority. During General Courtney Hodges ultimately failed attempts to capture the Huertgen Forest in autumn 1944, in which U.S. forces suffered more than 33,000 casualties and the more or less complete destruction of two divisions, capture of the dams had never even been an objective. RAF Bomber Command later made unsuccessful attempts to breach the Schwammenauel dam, and on 5 February 1945, General Omar Bradley's First U.S. Army also tried, unsuccessfully, over three days, to seize the dam. The task was finally given to the U.S. 9th Infantry Division, supported by the 78th Infantry and other armoured elements, and they were making good progress when the Germans, with Hitler's personal approval, blew up the Schwammenauel's sluice gates. The effects of the carefully planned destruction were immediate – 100 million tons of water flowed into the surrounding countryside, and the water level of the Roer rose by 5 metres. Moreover, the Roer was flowing so rapidly that it couldn't be spanned by pontoon bridges.

Montgomery met with Simpson on 10 February, and Operation Grenade, the southern pincer of the Reichswald campaign, was delayed for at least eleven days. The Anglo-Canadian forces fighting in and around the Reichswald were on their own. During the course of the Reichswald campaign, von Rundstedt built up his forces to include three infantry divisions, four parachute infantry divisions, one panzer grenadier division, and two panzer divisions. By the beginning of March 1945, the German First Parachute Army also possessed 700 mortars and more than 1,000 guns of various calibres, together with various additional self-propelled artillery pieces. The Germans could only reinforce their armies facing the British and Canadians to such a great extent because of the successful destruction of the Schwammenauel dam. For a short time, at least, American ground forces had been prevented from crossing the Roer and could play no part in the unfolding events of Operation Veritable.

5

INTO THE VALLEY OF HELL

> The assault will be launched in great strength and with most powerful fire support. Whatever the difficulties of ground and weather, the forward thrust through the enemy and his defences will be pressed without respite...
>
> General H. D. G. Crerar, 7 February 1945[1]

The huge artillery bombardment which launched the Operation Veritable ground offensive during the early morning of 8 February 1945 involved every conceivable type of gun. Large 122mm field guns opened up at long range on German defensive positions. A second line of 280 4.5-inch and 5.5-inch guns also opened up on the Germans, supported by seventy-two anti-aircraft guns and the massed firepower of 576 25-pounder artillery pieces. British and Canadian divisions waiting to attack from the Nijmegen salient also added to the unimaginable cacophony of deafening noise by launching their own 'pepperpot' attacks on the Germans. These pepperpot attacks involved divisional tanks, anti-tank guns, Bofors guns, mortars, medium machine guns and rocket projectors, which all offloaded a prodigious quantity of munitions upon a variety of enemy positions lying in the path of the intended Allied advance. At 0740 hours the bombardment ceased temporarily, and smoke canisters were fired from British and Canadian positions, as if to disguise the advance of infantry and armour. Surviving German gunners emerged, somewhat dazed, from their positions and fired into the smoke. Unfortunately for these dogged Germans, the cessation of the bombardment was merely a trap. Allied sound and flash rangers identified the origin of their fire, and when the British and Canadian bombardment resumed at 0750, the vast bulk of the German positions were obliterated. At 1000 the Allies again began laying down a smokescreen ahead of their men, and in the closing stages of the bombardment, British and Canadian gunners concentrated on trying to smash German central defensive positions.

Charles Lynch, a Reuters special correspondent attached to the First Canadian Army, watched the scene as thousands of soldiers and vehicles moved eastwards from the Nijmegen salient across a shallow, saucer-shaped valley in the general direction of the Reichswald Forest. With a dramatic but entirely justifiable literary flourish, he told readers of the *Coventry Evening Telegraph* on 9 February 1945, 'I saw the pastoral strip of country over which the new offensive was launched become a valley of hell.' Lynch's probably intentional literary allusions to Tennyson's Charge of the Light Brigade into the Valley of Death weren't entirely inappropriate, because the scene just to the west of the Reichswald Forest was entirely one of death and destruction. When the Allied guns stopped, the shallow valley between the Nijmegen salient and the Reichswald Forest had begun to look like something out of Dante's *Inferno*. Lynch himself counted more than 200 fires. In the far distance, on the horizon, the fires caused by the overnight bombing of Kleve were still imbuing the skies with an ominous orange glow. Nearer at hand, countless German military vehicles along with farms, houses and trees were all ablaze. Shrapnel and shell fragments were later found embedded in vast numbers of Reichswald Forest trees.

Most of the men Lynch saw advancing towards the Reichswald Forest were members of the 53rd Welsh Division, which was given the major responsibility of driving German forces out of the 17,000 acres of forest land. The German Forward Defence Line west of the forest was overrun with little opposition, and the men of the Welsh Division then entered the north-west part of the Reichswald Forest, spearheaded by forces from the division's 71st Brigade. A few Churchill tanks had managed to follow the 71st into the forest, though most of the other brigade vehicles had become immersed in the soft ground and considerable mud of the Valley of Hell. An Allied division at the time of the Reichswald campaign contained approximately 10,000 men, and the brigades which made up an individual division usually possessed roughly three battalions of infantry (about 2,700 men). In addition, a brigade would have between sixty and seventy tanks, a field artillery regiment, a battery of anti-tank guns, a troop of self-propelled light anti-aircraft guns, one machine gun company with a heavy mortar platoon, and a field company of engineers.

In reality, brigades were self-contained miniature armies in their own right, able to supply all their own needs and requirements with the exception of air support, which had to be arranged externally on a case-by-case basis. The self-reliant, all-arms character of brigades during the Reichswald struggles proved to be of crucial importance in light of the restricted nature of the British and Canadian advances – in most cases the Allied forces, hemmed in by flooding, poor roads, minefields and German military activity, could only manage brigade-wide attacks and advances. During their failed attempts to breach the Siegfried Line in the Huertgen Forest during autumn 1944, the Americans had incurred enormous casualties because they tried to advance with insufficient forces in an area where the ground was good and where the Germans had myriad opportunities for establishing effective defensive lines. The problem in the Reichswald campaign was the opposite: Montgomery certainly gave Crerar and Horrocks enough men to break through – roughly 180,000 in total – but the areas in which they could work were severely circumscribed by constant rain, flooding and mud. As a consequence, much of the bloodletting occurred in comparatively narrow fighting corridors in which British divisions were in action 'one brigade up' at a time.

Nowhere were the fighting corridors more narrow than in the Reichswald Forest itself. Once into the north-west part of the forest, the Welsh Division's 71st Brigade, together with the division's other brigades and battalions, faced a difficult task in ridding the area of its German occupants. In fact, Major Lewis Hastings, who worked as one of the BBC's radio commentators, stated that 'the clearing of the Reichswald Forest was the most difficult problem the 21st Army Group has ever faced'.[2] The Welsh Division moved diagonally through the forest, from the north-west to the south-east, using a single waterlogged 3-mile track nicknamed Chewing Gum Alley by the troops. Resupply in the forest was so precarious that at least one battalion of the Welch Regiment lived entirely for five days and nights on chocolate, biscuits and tea brewed in slit trenches, dug among the Reichswald's dense bracken, scrub and mixed oak and beech trees. Initially at least, the main axis of Chewing Gum Alley was too narrow and too wet to support motorised traffic. Wounded had to be carried by stretcher bearers to the edge of the forest, where they were operated upon by the light of nearby burning buildings and constant explosions overhead. The forest floor, meanwhile, was in perpetual shade or darkness, and the way forward at night was lit artificially by ground searchlights nicknamed 'Monty's moonlight'. Monty's Moonlight certainly illuminated the way ahead for advancing soldiers, but it also made them clear targets for German snipers hidden in the undergrowth.

Achieving control of the Reichswald Forest was effectively a matter of seizing the higher ground and dominating the few significant roads which either skirted the east and south of the area or cut directly through the forest, such as the Kleve–Hekkens road. By early afternoon on 8 February, the 1st Battalion of the

Oxfordshire & Buckinghamshire Light Infantry, which operated as part of the 71st Brigade, had seized the Brandenberg heights in the northern part of the forest. Unusually, given the difficulties of the terrain, the 53rd Welsh Division then pushed eastwards in a two-brigade front to seize the forest's other significant areas of higher ground. On 9 February, two infantry arms of the 160th Brigade worked together to successfully capture the Stoppelberg – the 4th Battalion of the Welch Regiment (4th Welch) began the task during the morning by seizing the approaches to the Stoppelberg, an extinct volcano, and then the 2nd Monmouthshire Regiment (2nd Mon) followed up by taking the heights themselves. To the right side of 160 Brigade, elements of 158 Brigade, including soldiers from the 5th Battalion of the Welch Regiment (5th Welch) supported by Royal Armoured Corps (RAC) tanks, secured higher ground to the west and north of the Geldenberg feature.

After these strategic successes on 9 February, the pace of the Welsh Division's sweep eastwards through the forest slackened somewhat. The road surface of Chewing Gum Alley had collapsed by the end of the day. Consequently, on the 10th, Welsh Division soldiers could do little more than patrol and consolidate a line of advance which lay along the Kleve–Hekkens road. While this was happening, Canadian lumberjacks were busy felling trees to create a 'corduroy road' of laterally laid logs on the main axis of advance to allow greater traffic. On 11 February, the division's 158th and 160th brigades resumed their advance eastwards with the intention of reaching the Kleve–Asperden road by the end of the day. During the advance, the 4th Welch captured the village of Dammershof, and the 1st Battalion of the East Lancashire Regiment (1st Lancs), together with a company of men from 5th Welch, pushed German forces out of the village of Am Klosterhof. By nightfall, 1st Lancs had actually made it to the Asperden road, though the 1/5th Welch and the 7th Battalion of the Royal Welsh Fusiliers (7th RWF) had been halted by increasing German resistance. All three groups were ordered to dig in where they were and resume the advance the following day. The 1st Lancs were counter-attacked aggressively on the Asperden road by members of the German 2nd Parachute Regiment but managed to beat off repeated determined assaults. This particular engagement involving the 1st Lancs was just one of a series of savage, close-quarter fights involving the men from east Lancashire. The 1st Lancs commanding officer later described the Reichswald Forest fighting as 'a terribly wearing business for the men, psychologically and mentally. It was nearly all bayonet, sten and grenade fighting. The Bosch reserves fought very well [and were] stubborn, and had to be dug out with the bayonet.'[3]

12 February 1945 proved to be a key date in the Welsh Division's battles for control of the Reichswald Forest. By early afternoon, the 1st company of 5th Welch had successfully cut the Kleve–Asperden road, with the assistance of sixteen tanks from the Royal Tank Regiment (RTR). The men of 2nd Mon and 4th Welch had also managed to clear the north-eastern sector of the forest. Indeed, soldiers of the 4th Welch actually emerged from the twilight world of the forest to straddle the strategic Kleve–Goch road which skirted the eastern boundaries of the Reichswald, and they dug in on open land to the east of the important highway. Here, during the afternoon, the Welsh Division's leading units clashed with two fresh battle groups of the German 15th Panzer Grenadier Division. The 104th and 114th Panzer Grenadier regiments had been rushed into the Kleve area to deal with XXX Corps' expected emergence through the Materborn Gap to the north. Instead, they found themselves facing westwards to confront the forest fighters of the Welsh Division. The censored British wartime press, together with many military strategists in more modern times, have criticised the Germans during the Reichswald campaign for the unthinking use of their reserves. In particular, they have been accused of hurling their men forward, mostly in company strength, to 'plug holes' rather than in pursuit of any sensible overall strategy.[4] Such criticism is probably overstated, but in the case of the 15th Panzer

Grenadier Division, two regiments composed of numerous companies, and supported by artillery, mortars and self-propelled guns, were thrown against the 6th RWF and 5th Welch in a frontal assault. At a range of 300 yards, they were cut to pieces by soldiers of the Welsh Division. Further to the south, the 1st Lancs beat off two similar attacks with the aid of artillery support.

By the end of a hard day's fighting, the men of the Welsh Division were masters of most of the Reichswald Forest. Mopping-up operations were still needed, and an anti-tank ditch and some concrete emplacements remained to be cleared in the extreme south-east corner of the forest. The 53rd attacked again on 13 February, with the 158th Brigade sweeping as far south-east as the Niers, which was a right tributary of the Maas. This last south-easterly thrust was a key prerequisite for a First Canadian Army advance on the vital town of Goch, and it came at the cost of another seventy Welsh Division soldiers being killed or wounded. On the night of 16/17 February, the 53rd Welsh Division fully emerged from the forest and made itself ready to participate in the subsequent phases of Crerar's overall Reichswald campaign. Specifically, the division was charged with the task of clearing the area between the Reichswald Forest and the smaller Kleve Forest to the east.

The overall cost of the fighting in the Reichswald Forest had been extraordinarily high. The 34th Armoured Brigade, which followed the infantry through the forest, had been severely mauled. On 12 February, for instance, Major Ronald Grantham of the Royal Tank Regiment (RTR) led a squadron of Churchill tanks into battle in support of one of the many infantry assaults made on that day. Within a short period of time, eleven out of the fifteen Churchills involved were either put out of action by German fire or bogged down in mud and slime. Grantham's own tank seems to have been immobilised, but from his disabled vehicle, and then on foot, he proceeded to break up four German counter-attacks. For these actions, Grantham was awarded a Bar to the Military Cross he'd won five years earlier during the retreat to Dunkirk.[5] The 9th Battalion of the RTR lost thirty-eight out of its fifty-two tanks, and the Royal Armoured Corps lost half of its entire strength. The butcher's bill for the infantry was little short of appalling: during the course of the war in Europe, from the D-Day landings in June 1944 to the end of the war on 8 May 1945, the Welsh Division endured some 10,000 casualties. A quarter of these casualties occurred during the fighting in and around the Reichswald Forest. In little more than a few weeks, 2,500 men were either killed or wounded while assaulting the Brandenberg heights, traversing the narrow, open rides that ran between the densely packed trees or fighting through the nearby Rhineland towns and villages. Despite the difficult terrain, the constant rain and the close-quarters nature of much of the fighting in the Reichswald, the Welsh Division kept on moving forward, and it cleared the forest in what remains a little-known but nonetheless epic feat of arms.

6

'TINY' BARBER AND THE ROAD TO SKYE

> The Corps Commander [Horrocks] addressed all officers of the Division in the ENSA Hall, Tilburg. He gave a detailed description of the bigger picture and of Operation Veritable. He emphasised that the whole success rested mainly on 15th (S) Division.
>
> 6th Battalion, King's Own Scottish Borderers
> war diary, 4 February 1945

At the onset of the Reichswald campaign, Major-General Colin Muir Barber, in command of the 15th Scottish Division, certainly cut an impressive figure. The forty-seven-year-old was 6 feet 9 inches tall in his stockinged feet and kilt, making him the tallest officer in the entire British army. Given the ironic nickname of 'Tiny' by his superiors and subordinates, Muir was a vastly experienced soldier and commander. Although he was born in Birkenhead on the Wirral, he had been a soldier in Scottish regiments for nearly thirty years, and he commanded the 15th Scottish during its post-D-Day battles across north-western Europe.

Tiny Barber's 15th Scottish Division played a crucial role during the opening phase of Operation Veritable, when its forces headed eastwards from Groesbeek, and then advanced along the main Nijmegen–Kleve road, which skirted the northern perimeter of the Reichswald Forest. For four days between 8 February and 12 February 1945, the endeavours of the 15th Scottish were at the very epicentre of Horrocks' and Crerar's plans for a rapid and successful outcome to the opening phase of Operation Veritable. Tiny Barber's men were expected to push along the advantageous northern Nijmegen–Kleve axis of advance, seize the Materborn heights overlooking the strategic town of Kleve, occupy Kleve itself, and then allow other brigades and divisions to debouch into the German Rhineland plains, and possibly capture at least one bridge over the Rhine at Wesel. The importance of Kleve was recognised by both the Anglo-Canadians and the Germans. The town was a port which received and dispatched goods via the Spoy Canal, and it had received the economic rights and privileges of a city in charters granted way back in 1242. At the onset of war in 1939, it had a population of 21,784, most of whom were subsequently made homeless by RAF bombing during the night of 7/8 February 1945.[1] If the Germans could successfully ensconce themselves in the rubble of Kleve before the British arrived in the town, it was highly likely that they could prevent a rapid Anglo-Canadian advance to the Rhine.

Barber's men were given a massive amount of support as they drove eastwards along the Nijmegen–Kleve road, including 176 Churchill tanks from the 6th Guards Tank Brigade (some with flamethrowers), two regiments from the 79th Armoured Division, the 2nd Household Cavalry Regiment, and a wide variety of mobile artillery pieces. The 15th Scottish advanced along two roads, codenamed Skye and Ayr. Skye was the main road between Nijmegen and Kleve while Ayr was a narrower, unsurfaced track just to its right. The division intended to move on the basis of 'two brigades up', moving side by side at the same time. However, the front was so restricted, and hemmed in by rising water levels, that only companies and battalions from each brigade could be pushed forward at the same time. The Skye route was allocated to 272 Brigade, while the smaller Ayr route initially became the preserve of 46 Brigade. The problems along the Skye route were immediately apparent, because the Germans had breached the dykes along this crucial axis even before the 15th Scottish set off on its eastwards drive to the Materborn heights and Kleve. Between 1 p.m. and midnight on 8 February, water levels just north of the Skye route rose by 18 inches, and by 10 February some 5 miles of the road lay under 2 feet of water. In this increasingly aquatic fighting environment, the 15th Scottish placed great reliance on using Kangaroo vehicles, which were tanks with their turrets removed to carry infantry. The 6th Battalion of the King's Own Scottish Borderers (6th KOSB) were, for instance, carried into battle on Kangaroos operated by the 1st Canadian Armoured Personnel Carrier Regiment.

Roads were soon blocked by rising water levels, and because of the immense amount of traffic moving eastwards towards Materborn. When movement on Skye broke down completely early on 8 February, movement along 46 Brigade's Ayr route became virtually impossible because the narrow track had to cope with the men and machines of both 227 and 46 Brigade at the same time. Bulldozers had to be used to move bogged-down vehicles, and traffic bottlenecks became even worse when Horrocks ordered the 43rd Wessex Division forward from reserve in the mistaken belief that the Materborn Gap had been secured by the 15th Scottish. The Wessex men were supposed to race along in the wake of the 15th Scottish, move through the secured Materborn feature and then spread through the plains beyond Kleve. As it turned out, this key divisional movement simply added to the gridlock along the Skye and Ayr routes, producing one of the largest traffic jams in recorded military history.

Traffic chaos was evident across the whole of the Anglo-Canadian front during the Reichswald campaign, and not just in the sector occupied by the 15th Scottish. Montgomery himself was caught in one such traffic jam on 11 February, during a battlefield visit to troops and generals. At an undisclosed

Reichswald location, the frustrated Field Marshal was recorded as having leapt from his stranded car and yelled, 'Let's get this thing moving.'[2] Mud, floods and traffic congestion certainly scuppered Tiny Barber's original plan to advance the 15th Scottish by leapfrogging its various brigades and battalions in successive fashion along the Skye and Ayr road routes. Such an approach often helped share out the fighting between the various units, and it kept soldiers and armoured groups fresh and rested. Unfortunately, in the circumstances of the Reichswald campaign, it simply wasn't possible to alternate units with ease. Thus, some battalions and brigades fought for sustained periods simply because their replacements were too far down the line of traffic to be leapfrogged into action.

All 15th Scottish brigades and battalions suffered from unremitting rain, floods and occasional snow during the course of the campaign. However, battle experiences could be very different. The 2nd Battalion of the Gordon Highlanders (2nd Gordons), for example, spent the first day of the offensive simply resting and waiting in the wooded area just to the north of Groesbeek. In direct contrast to this, the 2nd Battalion of the Argyll & Sutherland Highlanders (2nd Argylls) were pitched into a maelstrom of activity from the very start. Even before the battalion reached its start line in the valley to the east of Groesbeek, on the morning of 8 February, it had problems traversing British-laid minefields in the area. Once into the German Forward Defence Line, supporting Scots Guards tanks and Crocodiles were delayed by boggy ground, and B Company of the 2nd Argylls walked straight into an undetected anti-personnel minefield. One soldier was killed and six were wounded before a gap in the minefield could be found. One other unnamed private soldier was recorded as missing at subsequent battalion roll calls, but on 9 February he was discovered still lying in the minefield with his foot blown off. Having languished all night in freezing temperatures, drenched in rain, blood and mud, surgeons still felt he stood a good chance of survival.

Scots Guards tanks eventually made it through the German Forward Defence Line, but other armoured units advancing in support of the 2nd Argylls faced severe difficulties. As the 2nd Argylls' war diary entry for 8 February records, 'Flails [tanks], Crocodiles and AVREs on which so many hopes had been built, were delayed first crossing a stream and then [by] a series of boggy patches, and they were never able to catch up with the battle.'[3] Many Argylls had to launch their initial assaults on the German defensive positions on foot, through vast quantities of mud and water, unsupported by armoured units. The battalion's A Company managed to get through the minefield but then ran straight into a heavy German defensive line which put up strong resistance. The company's commanding officer (CO), Major Bruce, was wounded during attempts to overcome this German defence. Lieutenant Hutton was killed and there were several other casualties. Colour Sergeant-Major (CSM) Green rallied the men for a successful attack on the enemy line, for which he received a Distinguished Conduct Medal (DCM); the DCM ribbon was pinned to Green's chest by Montgomery some two weeks later.

Once the various elements of the 15th Scottish had arrived at the northern corridor, in the vicinity of the Skye and Ayr routes to Kleve, the scale of the challenge that awaited them soon became apparent. If the division was to advance upon and then capture Kleve, it had to break through a succession of German Westwall trench systems which stretched all the way back to defensive sites on the high ground around Materborn. A series of prepared fire positions running from woodland at Frasselt to the main Nijmegen–Kleve road also needed to be overcome. Matters were further complicated by a huge anti-tank ditch east of Frasselt, which extended northwards from the Kranenburg area and eventually ended at the Alter Rhein. Moreover, there were several settlements along the axis of advance that would have to be cleared. In some places German resistance was minimal, but throughout the 15th's advance there were times when the fighting was intense and sustained.

On the extreme west of the corridor which led to Kleve, B Company of the 2nd Argylls spearheaded the attack on German positions at the small settlement of Elsenhof. The attack took place on 8 February, only shortly after the Argylls had emerged from their struggles through the German minefield and Forward Defence Line, but it proved to be entirely successful. B Company occupied Elsenhof and took eighty German prisoners at the cost of just one casualty. While the Argylls were dealing with Elsenhof, the 9th Cameronians (Scottish Rifles) attacked the nearby village of Frasselt. Like the 2nd Argylls, the 9th Cameronians (9th Cam) had endured a tough opening to the Reichswald campaign. As they moved east of Groesbeek on 8 February, they moved into an undetected enemy minefield, and were later hit by 'friendly' artillery fire.[4] Nevertheless, by late afternoon on the 8th, C Company of the Cameronians had managed to advance on Frasselt, carried by Churchill flame-throwing Crocodile tanks and supported by artillery fire. Within ninety minutes the village was captured, and by the end of the day 115 POWs were in Cameronian hands, mostly from the 1051st Grenadier Regiment and the 58th Fusilier Battalion of the 84th Division. Resistance had been minimal.

The main strategic significance of Frasselt lay in the fact that the village was situated just to the west of a substantial Westwall anti-tank ditch. During the night of 8 February, 9th Cam patrolled up to the ditch, gathering intelligence about possible crossing points and the number of enemy troops defending the position. In fact, 9th Cam established that there were relatively few German troops in the vicinity, and when the 44th Brigade's Special Breaching Force arrived at the ditch during the early morning of 9 February, they had few problems in bridging the ditch at three separate points. The 6th KOSB then crossed in Kangaroos and quickly exploited their rapid passage by attacking the German-held village of Schottheide, which lay just 300 yards to the east. After a brief but intense firefight, the Germans surrendered. At the cost of ten killed and wounded, 6th KOSB took nine officers as POWs, together with 204 other ranks (ORs).

Seizing the town of Kranenburg, which straddled the main Skye route to Kleve, presented the 15th Scottish with a serious military challenge. Kranenburg, like Kleve, was a town steeped in history. Immediately to its west a large anti-tank ditch had been constructed which, by the morning of 8 February, was entirely filled with water. Unfortunately for the town's German defenders, a bridge across the ditch had been left intact, and this bridge was later used by both infantry and one lone tank as an entry point into Kranenburg. The task of capturing the town was principally the responsibility of the 10th Battalion of the Highland Light Infantry (10th HLI), who were supported by the 2nd Argylls. Once the overall offensive began on 8 February, 10th HLI advanced through the German Forward Defence Line using the gaps created in enemy minefields by the 2nd Argylls and then went straight on to attack Kranenburg. Three companies of light infantrymen were used in the attempt to overcome the German defenders of Kranenburg, along with the 2nd Argylls. C Company of the HLI moved across the anti-tank ditch and set about clearing the western part of the town. They were supported in these endeavours by just one tank as all the others, together with most of the battalion's motorised carriers, had been bogged down in soft ground en route. Even the battalion's wireless communication sets needed to be brought forward on foot.

As the infantry advanced into Kranenburg they were shelled and mortared from high ground in the Reichswald area – probably from the Galgansteen ridge, which projected outwards from the north-west part of the forest region. From about 4 p.m. onwards, 10th HLI's C Company were increasingly successful in clearing the western part of Kranenburg, but A and B Companies, along with the Argylls, were held up by determined German resistance dug in around the railway station. Increasing amounts of small arms fire were coming from the station, and the Germans were also firing a Nebelwerfer, a multiple-rocket launcher, at the advancing Scottish infantry. By about 6 p.m. on 8 February, despite the fearsome Nebelwerfer, German resistance at the railway station had been neutralised, and by the end of the night the Argylls and the HLI were largely in control of the town. During the course of the fighting, 10th HLI had taken 200 prisoners. The Argylls stayed on in Kranenburg during 9 February and took 250 Germans as POWs. In the very early morning of 9 February, the 2nd Gordons arrived in the town, having endured a long journey from Groesbeek which had been delayed by enemy mines, abandoned British military vehicles and felled trees placed across roads by retreating German soldiers. The 2nd Gordons' official war diary entry for 9 February 1945 described the continuing German resistance in Kranenburg as 'very slight'.

The 2nd Gordons had been spared the necessity of fighting at Kranenburg, but they endured their own baptism of fire later in the day at the small village of Nutterden. At first light on 9 February, the 2nd Gordons, supported by one company from the 8th Battalion of the Royal Scots Fusiliers (RSF), advanced to attack German positions at Nutterden, which lay roughly 3 miles east of Kranenburg. By 10 a.m. the village was largely in British hands, though the 2nd Gordons spent the rest of the day in house-clearing and other mopping-up operations. During the fighting, the Gordons took 135 German prisoners, and another twenty soldiers from the German 84th Division surrendered to the RSF. Throughout the day the Gordons had been plagued by intermittent shelling from an unidentified German artillery position, and at 8 p.m. the battalion command post received a direct hit. Eleven Highlanders were killed instantly, and five more were wounded.

While the Gordons were engaged at Nutterden on 9 February, the 2nd KOSB immediately moved on from their capture of Schottheide to assist the 6th RSF in the seizure of the Wolfsberg and Hingstberg knolls, which stood between Nutterden and the Reichswald Forest. In an ideal world, a different unit would have been leapfrogged into action to take the place of the KOSB, but given the traffic chaos on the Skye and Ayr road routes, no replacements were immediately available. Thus, the Borderers piled into their Kangaroos and, supported by the tanks of the Grenadier Guards, attacked the Wolfsberg and Hingstberg knolls as ordered. The Wolfsberg was secured with ease, though 6th RSF experienced considerable harassing fire as it attempted to seize the Hingstberg. During the operation to seize the two knolls, at least ten German officers and 230 other ranks were taken as prisoners. Although the British position on the knolls seemed secure enough during daylight hours, the situation at night was somewhat different. During the night of 9/10 February, two KOSB positions were attacked by probing German patrols. C Company of the Borderers successfully fought off one German attack, but a twelve-strong German patrol succeeded in temporarily overrunning a 2nd KOSB position and destroying three guns before disappearing into the darkness. The patrol did, however, leave behind one soldier in a B Company slit trench, who was taken as a POW by KOSB soldiers while still trying to operate his intact German wireless set. There were no further German probing attacks up either the Hingstberg or Wolfsberg knolls on the following day, though KOSB positions were shelled on a few occasions, and on 11 February the battalion left the high ground to move closer to Kleve.

By 11 February, the battalions and brigades of the 15th Scottish Division were closing in on Kleve. In addition to the capture of the Wolfsberg and Hingstberg knolls, much of the other higher ground along the approaches leading to the town had already been seized. On 9 February, the 8th Royal Scots captured the strategically located Esperance Hill with considerable ease, taking seventy German prisoners in the process. On 10 February, the 2nd Argylls moved on to the crucial Materborn heights and occupied deserted German gun positions equipped with elaborate dugouts containing electric lighting, wooden flooring, stores and bunkbeds. To the north-west of Kleve, the 6th RSF were given the task of clearing woods and overrunning strategically located German positions at the Kleverberg promontory. On 10 February, the battalion set up its HQ in Kleverberg's beerhouse and organised a combined attack by infantry and armour on German outposts which involved the use of flamethrowing tanks. The attack achieved its objectives, though at the cost of a number of killed and wounded, and only seven POWs were taken. On the following day, the Germans counter-attacked in company strength to try and dislodge 6th RSF from their positions. The attack was unsuccessful, and one German officer and thirty-five other ranks were taken as prisoners. The RSF battalion was then redeployed to woods overlooking Kleve, where D Company was attacked on its left flank in determined fashion by German forces, and the RSF's A Company suffered seven casualties as the result of an unfortunate 'friendly' fire incident.

The operation to break through the Materborn Gap, seize Kleve and then debouch into the Rhineland plains had fallen behind schedule almost immediately. Time had been lost because of floods, mud and traffic jams along the Skye and Ayr routes, compounded by Horrocks' decision to bring forward the 43rd Wessex Division and deploy them along Skye and then through the Materborn Gap. Once through the gap, it was the intention of Major-General Thomas, who commanded the 43rd Division, to bypass Kleve and push his men onwards to the vital town of Goch. The decision to deploy the Wessex Division was certainly premature, with fighting continuing to rage in the area. On 10 February, the entire 227 Brigade of the 15th Scottish was ordered to step aside on the Skye route to allow brigades from 43rd Division to pass through. Still, the 43rd Division's 129 Brigade couldn't make much progress along the Nijmegen–Kleve axis of advance.

To avoid the massive traffic queues, Thomas took the decision to shift 129 Brigade onto a secondary road which headed from the Nutterden area down through the south-east section of the Reichswald Forest, and then emerged just to the south-west of Kleve. By taking this circuitous and rather obscure route, Thomas's brigade, led by the 4th Wiltshire Regiment and with supporting armour from the Nottinghamshire Yeomanry, could bypass Kleve and move on towards Goch. The brigade finally emerged on one of the main roads leading to Kleve. Whether or not they really intended to take this road, or whether they'd missed their turning in the dark, has exercised the minds of military historians for some time. The question, however, is largely irrelevant. For whatever reason, the brigade had ended up on the south-western outskirts of Kleve, and German reinforcements from the 16th Parachute Regiment, who'd been drafted in from Arnhem to deal with the 15th Scottish Division troops pushing in from high ground on the west and north, now had to deal with a threat to their rear. German troops defending Kleve had been caught in a perhaps unintentional pincer movement by the 15th Scottish to the north and west and the 43rd Division to the south-west, and this had largely sealed the fate of the town. The German paratrooper reinforcements turned to face the newcomers from the Wessex Division, and for the next fifty hours or so, between 10 and 12 February, 129 Brigade was involved in some of the most ferocious fighting of the entire Reichswald campaign. The West Country infantrymen of the Wiltshire Regiment and the Somerset Light Infantry, supported by Nottinghamshire Yeomanry tanks, just about managed to hold on, but there was no question of them being able to advance any further. Something of a stalemate then ensued between 129 Brigade and the German forces that surrounded them on the south-western outskirts of Kleve.

Further to the north, however, the Wessex Division's 214 Brigade had also given up trying to move along the largely impassable Nijmegen–Kleve road, and swung south along a minor road which led them to the village of Materborn, where they engaged in some brutal fighting with German forces during the night of 10/11 February. The German defenders of Kleve and its approaches were now assailed on all sides. Infantry and armour from the 15th Scottish resumed their advance on Kleve during the early hours of 11 February. The 2nd Gordons had been involved in clearing the small Tiergarten Forest, just to the north of Kleve, which had once been at the heart of the town's spa tourist trade.

By 1400 hours on 11 February, however, the battalion had actually moved into the northern parts of Kleve, and established its headquarters in a deserted shoe factory. Company-strength Gordon patrols were then sent out towards the Spoy Canal area, with the objective of securing bridgeheads over the canal, which could then be used by the 10th HLI to clear the rest of north-east Kleve. During the Gordons' endeavours to ensure that the HLI could successfully 'leapfrog' ahead of it and secure the rest of north-east Kleve, the battalion encountered only light opposition, taking forty-six POWs.

Further to the west, the 2nd KOSBs emerged from fighting on the promontory at Bresserberg and advanced into Kleve during the early hours of 11 February. The KOSB advance wasn't without incident; at 0645 hours the Borderers' reconnaissance party was ambushed by a German patrol and had to retreat, and it wasn't until 1000 hours that the battalion as a whole moved off to Kleve, with considerable tank support. The KOSB finally arrived in south-east Kleve at around midday, at which point it was able to relieve the battle-weary survivors of the 43rd Division's Wiltshire Regiment. Patrols from other battalions present in the town, such as the 6th RSF, also came back with similar reports. By daylight on 12 February, German forces in and around Kleve were no more. On the fifth day of the Reichswald Forest campaign, after four days and nights of heavy and continuous fighting, the crucial town of Kleve (or at least what remained of it) was in the hands of Harry Crerar's First Canadian Army.

7

WATER RATS, WEASELS AND BUFFALOS

> Down into this lit-up area came great wallowing monsters – amphibious Buffalos, breathing fire as the helmsman steered them past the almost submerged roofs of cottages and over perilous obstacles provided by the jagged walls of half-demolished houses beneath the surface.
>
> *The Sphere*, 3 March 1945

At a press conference with war correspondents held on the eve of the First Canadian Army's Reichswald ground offensive, General Crerar emphasised the fact that just one-quarter of the Allied soldiers involved would actually be Canadian. With considerable generosity of spirit, he therefore urged the assembled journalists to ensure that in all their written dispatches they gave 'proper recognition to English, Scottish and Welsh formations'. Despite this imbalance in numbers between Canadian and non-Canadians at the start of the Reichswald fighting, however, Canadian divisions were given some significant tasks to perform right from the start, and the scale of Canada's involvement in the subsequent phases of the Operation Veritable offensive grew exponentially.

Prior to the launch of the campaign, the whole Allied front in the Reichswald sector was held by troops from Major-General Albert Matthews' Canadian 2nd Division. Other infantry and armour which advanced towards German positions on the morning of 8 February had to pass through the Canadian 2nd Division in order to reach their start lines. As a result of the 2nd Division being dispersed along the Allied line, the tasks allotted to it at the start of the campaign were limited but still exceedingly difficult to accomplish. Just one brigade – the 5th Infantry Brigade – was given the responsibility of achieving Canadian 2nd Division military objectives on the opening day of the offensive. Specifically, the division's infantry was tasked with seizing a crucial triangle of land which dominated the Nijmegen–Kleve road. Enemy troops had to be ejected from this area in order to protect the left flank of the 15th Scottish Division as it advanced towards Kleve and the Materborn Gap. The 2nd Division's French-Canadian Le Regiment de Maisonneuve was used to attack and occupy the village of Den Heuvel, where at least forty-six Germans were killed trying to defend the village, and after the fighting had ceased the French-Canadian regiment moved on to occupy the village of Hochstrasse. Le Regiment de Maisonneuve suffered relatively light casualties during its battle for the two villages – two killed and twenty wounded. While the French-Canadians were fighting for Den Heuvel, the Calgary Highlanders were ordered to assault the village of Wyler, which was located near the strategically vital Nijmegen–Kleve road. Wyler, and its adjacent hill, proved to be very difficult to capture. The area was littered with minefields, including the particularly deadly *schumines*, which were small, box-like anti-personnel mines with few metal parts. These were difficult to locate with mine detecting equipment, and were the cause of a number of Calgary Highlander casualties.[1] Fighting for Wyler and its nearby hill lasted all day, and it was only through a flank attack, aided by artillery and air strikes, that the Highlanders finally captured both the hill and the village at around 1830 hours on the evening of 8 February. The Highlanders lost fifteen killed during the battle for Wyler, including one company commander and at least one platoon leader, and a further fifty-five Highlanders were wounded. After this the deadly minefields in and around the village had to be cleared, and it wasn't until around 2100 on the 8th that military traffic again began to move on the nearby road. Their objectives achieved, units of the 2nd Division were not committed to the overall Reichswald offensive again for another six days.

Major-General Daniel Spry's 3rd Canadian Division began its involvement in the Reichswald ground campaign during the early evening of 8 February 1945. Whereas the other British and Canadian divisions moved forward at 1030 hours, Spry's division, by prior agreement, started its campaign at around 1830 hours in the evening. The 3rd Division was given the job of protecting the left flank of the First Canadian Army's offensive by clearing German forces from the flooded areas between the Waal and the Nijmegen–Kleve road. In order to cross this man-made waterworld, Canadian troops needed to use amphibious vehicles rather than tanks, and in the context of western Europe in early 1945, there were few military formations with more experience of amphibious warfare than the 3rd Canadian Infantry Division. Indeed, Montgomery himself had given the 3rd Division the nickname of 'the Water Rats' following their exploits fighting in the muddy, wet and marshy margins of north-west Europe following the D-Day landings. During the long and exhausting battles to clear the Scheldt estuary of German troops, in late 1944, 3rd Canadian Division forces utilised specialised amphibious vehicles on many occasions, and they did so again during the early days of the Reichswald campaign.

In order to attack German positions on the Anglo-Canadian left flank, Canadian 3rd Division troops climbed aboard Weasels, Terrapins and Buffalo amphibious vehicles operated by the British 79th Armoured Division, the only all-armoured division in the entire British army. The 79th was uniquely placed to assist the Canadians because none of its armour was of a standard design. Instead, the division offered specialist amphibious equipment and vehicles that would allow infantry to simply float over the anti-tank ditches, barbed wire and minefields delaying the Allied advance on other sectors of the Reichswald front. The 79th Armoured Division was commanded by Major-General Percy Hobart, a pioneer of technical innovation in warfare whose adapted amphibious vehicles – often described as 'Hobart's funnies' – played a major role in ensuring that the British and Canadians secured their beaches during the D-Day landings with only limited casualties.[2] On 8 February 1945, in order to facilitate the north-easterly advance of the Canadian 3rd Infantry Division across the flooded polders south of the Rhine, 79th Armoured supplied Spry's troops with 114 Buffalos, along with M29 Weasels and Terrapins. The American-made Buffalos were more accurately referred to as Landing Vehicles Tracked (LVTs), and the LVT-2 Buffalos deployed in the Reichswald campaign possessed both machine guns and armour, having originally been developed during the mid-1930s for use in swampy areas such as the Florida Everglades. Handy as armoured personnel carriers, they were able to carry up to twenty-four infantry at a time – more than sufficient for the needs of Spry and his men.

The M29 Weasel tracked vehicle, on the other hand, was much smaller than the Buffalo, and only able to carry a few troops at a time. Built by American car manufacturer Studebaker, it was intended specifically for use in muddy and wet conditions, and was therefore of great use in the Reichswald campaign. Unlike the Weasel and the Buffalo, the Terrapin amphibious vehicles used by the Canadian 3rd Division at the Reichswald were of British design, and built by the commercial vehicle arm of Morris Motors Ltd of Birmingham. Terrapins had already been used with some success during the battles for control of the Scheldt, and were operated by specialist 79th Armoured Division Royal Engineer assault teams, who coaxed the maximum performance possible from machines which had a number of key design flaws, including relatively poor driver visibility.

The LVT-2 Buffalos, M29 Weasels and Terrapins involved in the 3rd Canadian Division's amphibious assault fanned out in a north-easterly direction towards the German positions on the flooded lands south of the Rhine. On occasion, units of the advancing amphibious force were themselves cut off and marooned by the flood waters, which mostly ranged between 3 feet and 8 feet in depth. The German defenders were equally hampered by the floods, which prevented resupply and hindered communications. The 8th Canadian Infantry Brigade spearheaded the advance on the left side of the 3rd Division's front, while the 7th Infantry Brigade led the amphibious charge forward on the right side. The village of Zyfflich fell to the 7th during the first evening of the offensive, captured following a swift attack by the Regina Rifle Regiment supported by heavy smoke cover and, where possible, the tanks of the 13/18th Royal Hussars. As in other sectors of the Reichswald theatre of operations, 'Monty's moonlight' lit up the battlefield, and within two hours fighting had ceased and more than a hundred German troops had surrendered.

At the extreme right of the 7th Brigade's advance, the Canadian Scottish Regiment attacked the village of Niel in Buffalo amphibious craft with almost Nelsonian flourish, guided only by their shipboard compass bearings. They inadvertently encountered a German defensive screen of fortified houses, set up just south of Niel, which had to be overcome before the village itself could be captured. Fighting lasted all night, and Niel finally fell into Canadian hands very early on the morning of 9 February. Two companies of Canada's North Shore Regiment were carried into battle at Zandpol on Hobart's 79th Armoured Division Buffalos; they had cleared the area of enemy troops by about 2100 hours on 8 February, ready for a push into the vicinity of Millingen. Not all British and Canadian troops, however, had the luxury of being transported into battle on Buffalo vehicles. On some occasions Allied troops were forced to advance, retreat and patrol on foot despite terrible conditions. The French-Canadian Regiment de la Chaudier, for example, marched through the night of 8/9 February on foot in waist-deep freezing water in order to attack Leuth. Not surprisingly, the advance took considerable time, but the wet and tired troops still managed to capture the village in an early-morning assault on 9 February.

During the sweep north and east, the 3rd Canadian Division faced some of its most serious fighting at Duffelward, where German troops held out in pill boxes and fortified houses, and at Rindern, where German paratroopers repeatedly counter-attacked Canadian positions. On 10 February, Stormont, Dundas & Glengarry Highlanders, together with the Highland Light Infantry of Canada, climbed into their 79th Armoured Division Buffalos and advanced to the Spoy Canal, north of Kleve. By 12 February, the 7th Canadian Brigade was actually in Kleve, and able to relieve the British KOSBs and other regiments who'd been fighting their way towards Kleve since 8 February. Once in Kleve, the first phase of the Canadian military involvement in the Reichswald campaign was over. Canadian divisions now prepared for a much wider role in assaulting German positions to the east and south of Kleve, and desperate battles still had to be fought against well-defended enemy positions in Moyland Wood, the Hochwald Layback and elsewhere.

8

TO BRUUK AND BEYOND WITH THE 51ST HIGHLAND DIVISION

> This was no glamour story. There were no pipers, no kilts to hang out on the Siegfried Line. It was a real honest-to-God infantry battle, with no punches barred.
>
> Unnamed Highland officer, *London Daily News*, 26 February 1945

The 51st Highland Division attacked on the southern, right-hand flank of the overall Anglo-Canadian Reichswald offensive. The main strategic goal of the division's advance was undoubtedly to open up the main road around the southern edge of the Reichswald, which connected the towns of Mook, Gennep, Hekkens and Goch. Furthermore, the crucial crossroads at Hekkens also possessed a road which branched north-east through the forest to Kleve, making it all the more valuable. With the main Nijmegen–Kleve road bogged down by poor weather and heavy traffic, Horrocks had informed the 51st Division commander, Major-General Thomas Rennie, that the immediate opening of the southern route to Kleve – by capturing Hekkens – was a military objective that should be achieved at the earliest possible moment. Only after it was done could resupply and maintenance of the Allied divisions in the northern sector be assured.

The artillery barrage chosen by Rennie to launch his push into the Reichswald on 8 February was somewhat different from the bombardments which presaged the eastward advance of the other four divisions involved in the opening day of the Reichswald campaign. There was no general creeping barrage on the 51st Highland Division's part of the front; Rennie felt that he was aware of all the enemy locations facing his troops, so concentrated fire support was brought to bear on these strongpoints. A more general bombardment would, in Rennie's opinion, have left at least some German positions untouched. With their sector of the front particularly narrow, the division advanced from its start line on the late morning of 8 February with just one brigade in the vanguard – the 154th Brigade, reinforced with an extra battalion from the 5/7th Gordons. The 153rd and the 152nd Brigades then followed in column formation. One squadron of tanks accompanied each brigade, and these tanks had a variety of different functions: there were Flail and Crab tanks, for instance, which had rollers and weighted chains attached in order to clear mines, and there were also tanks carrying fascine bundles to cross ditches and other battlefield obstructions.[1]

The 154th Brigade moved forward towards the Reichswald Forest with the 1st and 7th Battalions of the Black Watch in the lead. In fact, the 7th Black Watch formed the right flank of the entire Anglo-Canadian army as it crossed its start lines at the beginning of the campaign. Both battalions advanced along three narrow lanes to capture the towns of Breedeweg and Bruuk. They were then ordered to cross a substantial anti-tank ditch which lay between the two settlements and the edge of the forest. All three road axes had to be cleared of mines by Flails and Crab tanks, but Breedeweg was still captured without too much difficulty. The same could not be said of Bruuk, however, nor of the anti-tank ditch, which had once been a key drainage channel known as De Leigraff. D Company of the 7th Black Watch was ambushed in the Bruuk area by German soldiers positioned in the ruins of a farm building. The company commander, Major Lowe, was killed along with two of his lieutenants, and four other Black Watch soldiers were wounded. Lowe's loss, together with that of the other two officers, caused some temporary delays and difficulties, and it was only with the assistance of tanks from B Squadron, 107 Royal Armoured Corps (RAC) that the remainder of the company was able to push through to the edge of the forest.

In the meantime, the scene at the anti-tank ditch was one of considerable confusion and mayhem. The verges of the ditch were festooned with enemy mines, and in the areas not covered by mines the ground was sufficiently boggy and waterlogged to prevent most kinds of vehicle movement. Even AVRE (Assault Vehicle Royal Engineers) bridge-laying tanks were being ditched in the boggy ground before they'd even arrived at the anti-tank bridging points. Nevertheless, despite the incredible difficulties presented by the waterlogged terrain, and the discovery of large numbers of enemy mines, four bridges over the anti-tank ditch were still constructed, and given the incongruously poetic codenames of Wordsworth, Tennyson, Shelley (1) and Shelley (2). Conditions were particularly difficult at Shelley (1) and Shelley (2), which had been allotted to the 7th Black Watch as crossing points. Specialist tanks from 222 Assault Squadron, Royal Engineers had piled rubble, carts and burned-out German trucks into the ditch, preparatory to ramps being laid across the top. Sherman crab tanks from the 1st Lothian and Border Yeomanry flailed the ground for 500 yards up to the ditch itself, detonating thirty mines. Nearby, two Churchill tanks were bogged down irretrievably in the mud by the ditch, and another Churchill tank had hit a mine. Sergeant Cox of the 1st Lothians manoeuvred his Sherman crab tank around the two sinking Churchills; he went on to clear six mines before his tank was hit by German bazooka fire and set ablaze. Cox baled out but was machine-gunned as he did so; he was killed instantly, and two other crew members were badly wounded.[2]

By late afternoon on 8 February, all German resistance at Breedeweg and in the quagmires of Bruuk had come to an end. The 7th Black Watch had done its job for the day, and the battalion dug in some 200 yards short of the forest, having suffered thirty-four casualties (ten killed, twenty-three wounded and one missing) during its first day of operations. The successful seizure of Breedeweg and Bruuk allowed the Highland Division to move on to the second phase of its operations: the occupation of the higher ground in and around the south-western corner of the Reichswald Forest. Specifically, the division was charged with capturing a long ridge of higher ground just inside the forest called the Freudenberg. Pyramid Hill, which formed the extreme southerly point of the ridgeline running across the western edge of the Reichswald, also needed to be cleared of German troops, and once this was done Rennie intended to wheel his men to the west and occupy the higher ground of St Jansberg and Kiekberg.

As the Welsh Division had learned further north, fighting in the forest could be a savage and somewhat surreal experience. Visibility was limited by densely packed trees and undergrowth, and snipers and ambushes were endemic. Soldiers fought in constant rain, mud and freezing temperatures, sometimes breathing their last in the vivid monochrome glare of 'Monty's Moonlight', searchlight beams bounced off the low-lying forest clouds. In these circumstances, it wasn't surprising that some soldiers became lost. On one occasion during the Highland Division's initial fighting in the forest, a lost party of soldiers commanded by the Glaswegian Corporal William Charlesworth stumbled across their divisional general, Thomas Rennie. A fighting man who had been wounded in the Normandy campaign, it was no surprise to find Rennie at the head of his men. When he encountered Charlesworth and his men in the forest, a somewhat stilted conversation ensued between the corporal and the general. 'Having a good battle?' enquired the placid, pipe-smoking Rennie, in the rather clipped tones of the 1930s and 1940s. 'Enjoying every minute of it, sir – I don't think,' came the somewhat feisty reply of Charlesworth. Rennie then explained to the corporal how he and his men could rejoin their battalion.[3]

Some of the Highland Division's youngest soldiers, fresh from basic training in the UK, proved to be particularly adept at the brutal business of forest fighting, at least according to some laudatory articles which appeared in the censored British wartime press. The *London Daily News* of 26 February 1945, for instance, commented on the role of teenage recruits in an hour-long Highland Division battle against German defensive positions three-quarters of a mile inside the Reichswald Forest. A Company, largely made up of teenagers, was reported as charging German lines with Sten guns, Bren guns, rifles and grenades, killing fifty enemy soldiers and taking 164 POWs. These raw recruits were given the nickname 'the Dead End Kids' by Highland Division veterans like Colour Sergeant Major James Leys, from Orkney, who witnessed their actions. The teenagers may well have formed platoons within the 5/7th Gordons. Corporal Frank Felton, from Cannock in Staffordshire, was a senior NCO in one of these platoons, and before he was killed in action on 12 February he certainly seems to have let it be known that the soldiers he served with, and commanded, were indeed some of the fabled 'Dead End Kids'. These young soldiers were named after a tough and uncompromising group of New York youths who had appeared in numerous gangster movies during the late 1930s. These films were obviously popular with Allied soldiers, as well as the British press, and the reports on the Highland 'Dead End Kids' certainly put a positive spin on the often grim fighting which took place in the Reichswald Forest.

Precisely when and where the Dead End Kids fought their first engagement is unclear, but the Highland Division's first fighting inside the forest took place on the northern and southern knolls of the Freudenberg. The 1st Battalion of the Black Watch attacked the northern edge of the long ridge, while the 5/7th Gordons focused on the south after leapfrogging the 7th Black Watch. The 1st Black Watch had successfully seized the northern stretch of the ridge by nightfall on 8 February, capturing over 100 POWs at the cost of four killed and seventeen wounded, but the 5/7th Gordons' fight for control of the southern stretch was far more intense. A Company of the Gordons moved up the slopes of the southern knoll during the early evening but was halted by determined German resistance. The Gordons resorted to an outflanking manoeuvre along a path called the Heiland Track in order to surround the Germans, and the position was finally secured at the cost of thirty Gordons killed, wounded or missing.

Pyramid Hill was situated at the extreme southern end of the long ridgeline which ran across the western edge of the Reichswald Forest, and it was the object of concerted attacks by the 5th Black Watch from about 1300 hours onwards on 8 February. Fighting for control of Pyramid Hill lasted all night, and once the Pyramid positions were secured, the 1st Gordons moved ahead of the 5th Black Watch and then attacked German units on the high ground of St Jansberg and Kiekberg. By late afternoon on 9 February, the 1st Gordons had taken both St Jansberg and Kiekberg, and forced more than 350 German paratroopers – mostly from the 1/2nd Parachute Regiment – to surrender. While the 1st Gordons were fighting for St Jansberg and Kiekberg, the 5th Black Watch moved down the slopes of Pyramid Hill and attacked German positions around Kanonskamp. By 1500 hours on 9 February, Kanonskamp was in the hands of the Black Watch, at the cost of two killed and thirteen wounded. Significantly, the capture of Kanonskamp meant the Highland Division sat astride a highly strategic road between Mook and Gennep.

South of the Reichswald, the Highland Division's main priority was to secure the main road network which linked the towns of Gennep and Mook in the south-west with Goch in the south-east. This was the intended main axis of advance for the division as it plunged deeper into the Rhineland, and towards the Rhine.

Rennie's division launched a two-pronged assault, with 152 and 154 Brigades focused initially on capturing the village of Hekkens and its crucial crossroads while 153 Brigade advanced south-east towards the small town of Gennep, just inside the Dutch border. During the morning of 11 February, 152 Brigade emerged cautiously from the Reichswald Forest canopy and began to march on Hekkens but was halted in its tracks by determined resistance from German paratroopers based in Westwall pill-box defences dotted around the village. Roughly twenty-four hours before 152 Brigade's advance, C Squadron of the 2nd Derbyshire Yeomanry, which was attached to 153 Brigade, had launched reconnaissance probes east of the small settlement of Ottersum. The Derbyshire troop of armoured cars advanced through Aaldonk and Zelderheide with no problem at all but was hit by concentrated bursts of German anti-tank fire at the Hekkens crossroads. Three armoured cars were destroyed, their occupants either killed or wounded, and the troop leader, Lieutenant D. G. Partridge, was captured by the Germans (though he later managed to escape). Clearly, German commanders were aware of the strategic importance of Hekkens and would put up a strong fight for control of both the village and its crossroads. More resources were needed if Rennie was to speedily secure Hekkens and its road junctions for the Allies, and during the afternoon of 11 February he launched a rapid, full-brigade attack which was supported by XXX Corps' entire artillery firepower.

The Highland Division's assault on Hekkens was launched by 154 Brigade at 1530 hours, when three battalions of infantry moved forward from a forest track situated roughly 2,000 yards to the north-east of the village. The 1st Black Watch then advanced down the left-hand side of the main road to Hekkens, with the 7th Black Watch on the right-hand side and the 7th Argyll and Sutherland Highlanders providing flank protection for the advancing force. The massive creeping barrage provided by XXX Corps proved to be very effective indeed, with high explosives dropped at timed intervals just ahead of the advancing troops. There seem to have been no incidences of shells dropping short among the advancing soldiers, and as soon as the defending German forces emerged from shelter the Black Watch were among them. The two Black Watch battalions were in Hekkens – and across German defensive positions – within 90 minutes of the start of the attack, and by 1900 hours they were in full control of the village with more than 200 German paratroopers taken prisoner.

The military operation which led to the capture of Gennep proved to be far more complex than the Hekkens attack, lasting for three days between 10 and 13 February. Gennep was enveloped by the River Meuse to the west and the Niers – one of the Meuse's tributaries – to the east, making it a vital strategic target for the Anglo-Canadian forces pushing south from the Reichswald Forest. Removal of all German forces from the land between the Rhine and the Meuse was the broad strategic goal of the entire Reichswald campaign, so the strong German forces in and around Gennep had to be neutralised. Moreover, with an eye on the future, the east bank of the Meuse had to be cleared of Germans so that bridges could be built across the river. Along these bridges would come the supplies and materiel necessary for the continuance of the Rhineland campaign and the future assault across the Rhine.

The 5/7th Gordons was given the task of attacking Gennep. On the morning of 10 February, the battalion began to advance along the main road to the town, and as a twin objective it also sought to capture the bridge over the Niers at Gennep. By the afternoon, the 5/7th Gordons had made good progress and captured the village of Ottersum, which lay close to Gennep. However, the battalion failed to capture the bridge over the Niers, which was blown up by German forces at about 1500 hours. The Germans defended this line with some determination, and two Gordons were killed and nine wounded during skirmishing in the area.

With the bridge across the Niers destroyed, the 5th Black Watch now took the lead, crossing the river in assault boats about a mile downstream from Gennep during the night of 10/11 February. The 5th Black Watch then entered the town from the north-west, in a rather audacious night-time manoeuvre which certainly took the German defenders of Gennep by surprise.[4] First they cleared the area around the town's church and hospital, and then they moved straight down the main high street, called the Zandstraat, advancing as far as the crossroads situated in the southern part of the town. As the battalion edged forwards, they were shelled and sniped at constantly, and resistance was particularly fierce in the Picardie Street area of the town. Here, C Company of the 5th Black Watch were halted by German forces, and later counter-attacked during the night by a fifty-strong company of German infantry. They just about managed to hold their ground, but only at the cost of another twenty casualties.

On the afternoon of 11 February, the 1st Gordons managed to cross the Niers at roughly the same point taken by the Black Watch, and they set about clearing German troops out of the southern part of Gennep. By this time, fighting in the town was severe, and two troops of Buffalos from the 79th Assault Squadron were used to ferry ammunition and artillery across the Niers to the hard-pressed soldiers fighting in the town centre. Both the 1st Gordons and the 5th Black Watch were involved in some savage close-quarter fighting with German troops during house clearance activities in Gennep. The common approach was for one soldier to break down the front door with his rifle butt while another threw a hand grenade into the interior, with both soldiers moving in once the smoke had cleared. Gennep held many dark cellars occupied by German troops, and the men of the Black Watch and Gordons preferred to clear them by dropping bricks down the cellar steps; in most cases the occupiers darted out and surrendered, thinking the brick was a grenade, and a number of veterans went on record to say that they preferred this 'less messy' approach.

House clearance down the Zandstraat was particularly fraught with danger. A Company of the 5th Black Watch cleared houses on the right side of the street, while C Company concentrated on the left side. Thomas Renouf, a veteran of A Company, recounted in his book *Black Watch* how he leaped through a smashed shop frontage on the Zandstraat and found three German soldiers, whom he took prisoner. One of the Germans had a bad leg wound and was carried out into the street on a wooden plank by his two comrades. Here, amid a multitude of house-to-house skirmishes and street battles, the unfortunate German's leg fell off, and Renouf had to leave the prisoners – with the injured man screaming in agony – as he rejoined his men struggling down the Zandstraat.

By the end of 13 February, significant military operations in Gennep had largely come to an end, and the town was securely in the hands of the First Canadian Army. Even so, Gennep was a dangerous place to be based. The town was shelled on a regular basis by the Germans, and many 51st Highland Division command-and-control functions had to be hidden away in basements and cellars. The division had played a significant role in accomplishing two of General Crerar's key objectives for Phase 1 of the Reichswald campaign – it had helped clear southern parts of the Reichswald Forest, and it had also advanced southwards and captured the strongly defended citadel of Gennep. All that remained was for the Highland Division to move eastwards and capture the tiny village of Asperden, which lay some 2 miles to the north-west of the town of Goch. The seizure of Asperden had been a central feature of Crerar's campaign strategy from the very start, largely because the village lay at the centre of an important road junction which could be used by the First Canadian Army as it moved through Goch and the rest of the Rhineland towards the banks of the Rhine.

The Highland Division's 152nd Brigade was given the task of seizing Asperden, which had already been bombed and shelled heavily by Allied forces. The capture was planned to take place as part of a two-phase advance which went under the codenames of 'Apple' and 'Banana'. Apple involved the securing of a stretch of woodland, a road junction, and fortified medieval monastic remains in the Graefenthal area. These objectives were attacked by the 2nd Seaforth Highlanders on the night of 16 February, and just after 2200 hours the 2nd Seaforths gained control of all three locations. The 5th Seaforths then leapfrogged the 2nd and advanced on Asperden, aided by a heavy artillery barrage and yet another application of 'Monty's moonlight'. The scene that greeted the advancing troops was one of considerable devastation, with the 5th Seaforths' battalion history recording that 'half the village seemed to be in flames, and the church [St Vincentius's] blazed like a torch in the middle of it'.[5] Fortunately for the Seaforths, casualties were light, with only one killed and three wounded during the assault. There was some enemy machine gun fire from the area of the village's railway level crossing, but the rest of the German force in Asperden had pulled back to occupy defensive positions in and around Goch.

The first phase of the Anglo-Canadian Reichswald Forest campaign was now over. Crerar's plan to advance eastwards through the forest and establish a line running from Kleve in the north to Asperden and Gennep in the south had been achieved in just over eight days. However, much hard fighting remained. The Germans were piling their reserves into the area, and the Americans were still unable to launch their side of the pincer movement. For the time being, the First Canadian Army would have to fight on alone.

9

THE BATTLES FOR MOYLAND WOOD AND THE GOCH-KALKAR ROAD

> The Regina Rifles and the Canadian Scottish Regiment drew the task of clearing half of Moyland Wood, a mixed forest cloaking a low, hilly escarpment.[1] The Reginas' forming-up place was marked by the yet unburied bodies of Scottish soldiers who had fought their way through the western end of the woods, adding to the sombre mood of men hesitant to enter a dark forest right out of *Grimms' Fairy Tales*.
>
> Army Part 43, *Legion: Canada's Military History Magazine*, 1 November 2002

In order to pursue the second phase of the Operation Veritable masterplan, which involved an advance east and south-east of the Reichswald Forest as far as the towns of Emmerich, Weeze, Udem and Kalkar, General Crerar reconfigured the armies and command structures at his disposal. The first phase of the Reichswald campaign had been fundamentally a British affair, spearheaded by Horrocks' XXX Corps, with Canadian forces providing flank protection and other mostly defensive functions. This military imbalance was reflected in the casualty figures during the first fourteen days or so of the campaign, when roughly 6,000 Allied service personnel were reported as being either killed, wounded or missing, and of this figure, 80 per cent were British. On 14 February, Crerar issued revised instructions which made the continuing campaign a two-corps affair, with General Guy Simonds' Canadian III Corps operating on the left side of the First Canadian Army and focused chiefly on the capture of the crucial town of Kalkar. Brian Horrocks' XXX Corps, meanwhile, were to operate on the right side of the Allied offensive and swing south-east with the objective of seizing the heavily fortified German-held town of Goch. The dividing line between the two corps was to be the Bedburg–Udem road. Crerar's orders for this new structure became effective on 15 February, and from this time onwards Canadian forces were to be right at the centre of some of the heaviest fighting of the entire campaign. Indeed, the impetus provided by the Canadians in this new and evolving phase of the campaign was shown immediately by Guy Simonds, who proposed that his Canadian III Corps be used in a daring plan to outflank the German forces by crossing the lower Rhine west of Arnhem, and then pushing along the west bank of the Rhine. Both Crerar and Montgomery turned down this plan, preferring instead to carry on with the strategy laid out in Operation Veritable which, of course, gave the Americans the opportunity of outflanking the Germans via a successful prosecution of Operation Grenade.

By the time Simonds was commanding the Canadian III Corps as it advanced towards Kalkar, the overall Allied front established during the Reichswald campaign stretched for some 14 miles. The importance of Kalkar, and the roads that led from it towards the Rhine, had long been recognised by British, Canadian and German commanders, though the German determination to defend the town was consistently underestimated by Allied army strategists. The Germans placed two substantial blocking forces in front of the Allies in order to protect Kalkar – one just to the west in Moyland Wood, and the other to the south, covering the approaches to the town along the Goch–Kalkar road. If the Allies were to succeed in capturing Kalkar, the First Canadian Army had to defeat both blocking forces, and this proved to be a hard and bloody task.

Elements of the 46th Highland Infantry Brigade had been directed to advance on Kalkar at least four days before General Simonds' overall command responsibilities for the Kalkar sector had become common knowledge. The 9th Cameronians, the 7th Seaforths and other 46th Brigade battalions were formed together into what became known as 'Huntforce' and together were tasked with advancing on Kalkar during the evening of 11 February. The actual advance began on 12 February, and was delayed considerably by atrocious weather conditions, which meant that military vehicles were constantly being bogged down in the mud and flood waters which were such a constant feature of the Reichswald campaign. Despite all these delays, a long column of Huntforce Kangaroo vehicles, packed with troops, still managed to advance on Hasselt during the evening of 12 February. The advance had not been an easy one. A wide deployment of forces had not been possible because the Kangaroos had to stick to the road in order to avoid becoming stuck in the ever-present mud and flood water. As a result, Huntforce Kangaroos and other vehicles proved to be easy targets for German shelling and mortar attacks as they progressed along the road to Kalkar in single file. Early on the morning of 13 February, troops from the 15th Scottish Division's Reconnaissance Regiment entered Hasselt and found the village to be empty. The area was subsequently occupied by the 7th Seaforths, who then organised patrols which, by nightfall, reached as far as Moyland Wood. The 46th Brigade's commander then planned an attack against German positions in Moyland for the following day. These attack plans were modified in order to take account of serious flooding in the area but, in the end, it was decided that the 9th Cameronians would advance along the southern edge of Moyland Wood, alongside the 2nd Glasgow

Highlanders, and then swing north to capture the village of Moyland.[2] The attack didn't go well, and both battalions were halted in their tracks by determined German resistance south-west of Moyland village.

Other Allied battalions were increasingly sucked into the bitter attritional battles for Moyland Wood. On 15 February, the 10th Highland Light Infantry (HLI) were concentrated at Bedburg in preparation for a night attack on German positions situated on high ground south of Moyland. The attack was to be launched at 2330 hours, across open ground, aided by the now familiar beams of 'Monty's moonlight'. The 9th Cameronians were also to act in support of the HLI, along with one squadron of tanks from the 4th Coldstream Guards, and there was to be a creeping artillery barrage which would move forward at the rate of 300 yards every twelve minutes. Tank support was withdrawn at the very last minute, probably for reasons to do with the softness of the ground, but the infantry attack still went ahead as planned. All went well for the first few hours, despite heavy German shelling and mortar activity. The fighting did, however, increase in intensity during the very early hours of 16 February. The HLI's D Company beat off two German counter-attacks during this period, and also repulsed one enemy fighting patrol. B Company suffered particularly badly at the hands of the Germans: its positions were completely overrun during one ferocious German counter-attack, and HLI casualties were so heavy that B Company had to be withdrawn from the fighting. Survivors of the German onslaught were so few in number that B Company was later reformed into just one platoon.[3]

While these two companies were fighting for their lives, C Company was ordered to attack Moyland Wood from the west. It did so through a heavy mist, and was hit by enfilade machine gun fire from various German defensive positions. Not surprisingly, the survivors had little option but to retreat. At 0800 hours on the morning of 16 February, yet another German counter-attack on D Company positions was halted by artillery fire, and during the bitter overnight fighting of 15/16 February more than 100 Germans were taken prisoner. The 10th HLI battles in and around Moyland Wood continued on 17 February, when the battalion reported twenty-three killed, wounded and missing personnel. This period of intense fighting for 10th HLI only ended on the evening of 18 February, when its positions were taken over by the Black Watch of Canada, and the battalion retired to Kleve for some much-needed rest and recuperation.

At the cost of a great number of casualties, the HLI, Cameronians, Seaforths and other members of the 46th Highland Infantry Brigade had secured a foothold on the western end of Moyland Wood. From 16 February onwards, however, it increasingly became the job of the Canadian 3rd Division and the 7th Canadian Infantry Brigade to rid the rest of the wood of its stubborn and resourceful German occupants. At midday on the 16th, the Royal Winnipeg Rifles (RWR) advanced to seize high ground in the vicinity of Louisendorf, some 3 miles south of Moyland. They were supported in their attack by the 3rd (Armoured) Battalion of the Scots Guards. On the RWR's left flank, the Regina Rifle Regiment also advanced, supported by one squadron of tanks, to attack German positions in woods closer to Moyland village. The RWR attack, carried out on Kangaroo motorised vehicles, proved to be quite successful, and by 1700 hours the coveted high ground was occupied and 240 German POWs had been taken. The Regina Rifles, however, encountered severe difficulties. Riflemen were cut down by flanking fire from their left, and one C Company platoon was cut off and surrounded on the southern fringes of the wood.

On 17 February, it was the turn of the 7th Infantry Brigade's 1st Canadian Scottish Regiment to take the lead in assaulting German positions. The 1st Canadian Scottish were given the objective of seizing high ground overlooking the hamlets of Heselerfeld and Rosskamp, which were situated roughly half a mile south of the Kalkar end of Moyland Wood. The attack itself took place over open ground and was conducted under heavy fire. Despite this, the battalion seized the high ground, dug in and held on to their gains for the next three days, despite repeated German counter-attacks. Meanwhile, on 18 February, the Regina Rifles attacked from the south and moved in a north-westerly direction through Moyland Wood. Some limited progress was made, though German forces continued to maintain a strong foothold in the area, and Regina riflemen were hit by heavy artillery fire from across the Rhine. During three days of fighting, between 16 and 18 February, the Regina Rifles suffered more than 100 casualties in intensive battles with members of the German 6th Parachute Division, which had arrived recently from northern Holland and rapidly entered the grim battles for control of Moyland Wood. The Canadian Scottish also continued to suffer heavy casualties. On 19 February, C Company of the regiment attacked the south-eastern tip of Moyland Wood. Its initial military objectives were achieved, but the company was soon engulfed by a huge German counter-attack. Sixty-eight men took part in the original C Company attack, but only nine men emerged unscathed from the subsequent fighting – everyone else had been killed, wounded or captured.

By the time that the shattered remnants of C Company had returned to their original battalion positions, Canadian commanders were already planning an integrated assault involving air power, armour, infantry and artillery in order to break the Moyland Wood impasse. On 21 February, divisional artillery pounded the eastern part of Moyland Wood with a variety of high explosives and mortar rounds. In addition, anti-tank guns opened up on the area, and machine-gun rounds were also fired by the Cameron Highlanders of Ottawa. Enemy positions were strafed by RAF Typhoons, and flame-throwing tanks trundled forward into the attack along with two companies of RWR infantry, who entered the woods south-west of Moyland village. This integrated, multi-faceted Canadian attack finally succeeded in ejecting the Germans from Moyland Wood. Two desperate German counter-attacks were repelled during the night, and in the early morning of 22 February the French-Canadian Regiment de Maisonneuve entered the village of Moyland unopposed. German forces had withdrawn, and the road to Kalkar was open. The cost of the fighting had been very heavy for all involved. In addition to British and German casualties, during the five days between 16 and 21 February, nearly 500 soldiers from the RWR, Canadian Scottish and Regina Rifles battalions were reported as being either killed, wounded or missing.

While the Canadian 3rd Division were slogging it out with German forces in the Moyland Wood, General Matthews' Canadian 2nd Division were positioning for an assault on German formations based just to the south-east, along the strategically vital Goch–Kalkar road. This road ran near to the prominent ridge between Udem and Kalkar, which formed an essential feature of the Hochwald defence system. As a result, the Germans were determined to defend the road to the utmost of their capabilities. General Simonds had been reluctant to order a Canadian assault across the Goch–Kalkar road in case German forces in the Moyland Wood area attacked the 2nd Division's left flank. However, on 18 February, Simonds judged that the time was right for an attack on German positions along the road and gave the order for an advance to take place at noon on the following day. The advance was to be led by a battalion of the Royal Hamilton Light Infantry (RHLI) on the left, and the Essex Scottish Regiment on the right. The Royal Regiment of Canada was to act as a reserve. RHLI and Essex Scottish forces moved off from a start line situated at the Louisendorf crossroads, advancing some 2,500 yards eastwards across the Goch-Kalkar road towards an area of high ground roughly 1,000 yards wide and 3,000 yards long, home to the hamlets of Gottern, Brunshof, Schwanenhof and Ebben. The advancing battalions were supported by a heavy creeping artillery barrage provided by two heavy batteries, seven medium and fourteen field artillery regiments.

Rain was a perennial problem during the Reichswald campaign, and the heavens opened yet again during the night of 18/19 February. As a consequence, the open ground along which the Canadians advanced on the 19th was waterlogged and muddy. The RHLI and the Essex Scottish were each provided with support from one squadron of tanks from the Fort Garry Horse, and a number of these tanks were almost immediately bogged down in mud. Kangaroos were used by the 1st Canadian Armoured Personnel Carrier Regiment to transport two companies from each battalion into battle, and some of these vehicles also became bogged down in mud very close to the attack start line. On the RHLI side of the advance, some Fort Garry Horse tanks were destroyed by mines, and accurate fire from 88mm German guns situated along the Goch–Kalkar road knocked out seven personnel carriers. Others were forced to drop the troops they carried far short of their intended objectives.

Despite all the difficulties caused by heavy German fire, mines and mud, leading RHLI companies still managed to occupy buildings in Schwanenhof and Ebben by the early afternoon, and units of the Essex Scottish were also ensconced in Gottern and Brunshof. Things seemed to be going well for both battalions, and by early evening more than 100 prisoners had been taken, mostly from the German 12th Parachute Reconnaissance Battalion. As dusk fell, the Fort Garry Horse were withdrawn from the immediate vicinity of the battlefield in order to refuel and rearm, leaving the Canadian infantry exposed and alone to deal with whatever the Germans threw at them. Some kind of German response was inevitable, and all Canadian commanders expected a counter-attack. Even so, few expected the massive scale and sheer fury of the German counter-attacks which smashed against Canadian positions east of the Goch–Kalkar road during the night of 19/20 February. From about 20.00 hours onwards, twenty-two tanks of the elite Panzer Lehr Division attacked RHLI positions in and around Schwanenhof and Ebben, while units of the 116th Panzer Division moved against the Essex Scottish. New German infantry formations were also thrown into the battle, and both tanks and infantry were given substantial heavy artillery and mortar support. Key units and companies of both the RHLI and the Essex Scottish were simply swamped by the German onslaught. The Commanding Officer (CO) of the Essex Scottish, Lieutenant-Colonel Pangman, along with his entire tactical headquarters staff and facilities, was surrounded by German tanks and infantry. B Company and C Company of the RHLI were surrounded by enemy armour and infantry, and the latter was reportedly overrun in the early hours of 20 February. Elsewhere, A Company of the Essex Scottish simply vanished without trace in the maelstrom of fighting, and some suspected that the unit had been wiped out. The company had in fact been cut off and surrounded by German forces, but they fought off all attacks for thirty-six hours, after which thirty-five dazed survivors managed to return to Canadian lines on the morning of 21 February.

Fighting between the Essex Scottish, the RHLI and German forces continued all night in and around the intersection of the Goch–Kalkar and Bedburg–Udem roads. On 20 February the Canadians launched two counter-attacks to recover lost positions in the village of Verkalt, where Pangman and his HQ staff were rescued from a farmhouse cellar. Further fighting continued throughout the day, until the Germans launched one final attack against RHLI positions, targeting the left side of the Canadian front at around 1800 hours. By this time, however, the Germans were largely a spent force, and with the aid of reserves from the Fort Garry Horse and the Cameron Highlanders of Canada, the Canadian 2nd Division was able to push the Germans back. Fighting ceased within about two hours. The Goch–Kalkar road was now securely in the hands of the First Canadian Army. German forces retired eastwards, and the remnants of the Panzer Lehr Division were withdrawn to an area west of Udem during the night of 21/22 February.

The cost of the bitter fighting along the Goch–Kalkar road had certainly been heavy. On 19/20 February alone, the Canadian 4th Brigade lost over 400 men either killed, wounded or missing. The Essex Scottish Regiment suffered particularly badly, with fifty-one men killed, ninety-nine wounded and fifty-four taken prisoner. The men of the Essex Scottish were awarded a total of eight battlefield awards for bravery for their part in the fighting, including Distinguished Service Orders for Lieutenant-Colonel Pangman and for Major P. W. MacIntyre, who led the trapped A Company back to Canadian lines on 21 February. Company Sergeant Major F. L. Dixon of the Essex Scottish was also awarded a second bar to his Military Medal (MM), originally gained during the 1942 Dieppe Raid. Dixon was one of only thirty-eight Canadian soldiers ever to receive two bars to his MM – effectively meaning that he won the award for gallantry on three separate occasions – and he was the only Canadian to achieve this distinction during the entire course of the Second World War.

10

GOCH: TOWN WITHOUT A FACE

> What is left of Goch is steadily disintegrating under the shelling and mortaring, while house-to-house fighting is levelling even the piles of rubble. This is steadily becoming a town without a face.
>
> *Aberdeen Press and Journal*, 21 February 1945[1]

While Canadian and Scottish troops and armour were hammering away at German positions in the Moyland area during mid-February 1945, General Horrocks was launching a large-scale advance upon the town of Goch, which lay just over 8 miles to the south of Kleve. Goch was an important railroad junction with about 10,000 inhabitants which, along with Kalkar and Kleve, had been deemed as being a 'hold at all costs' sector of the front by German High Command. The town, which fell under the overall command of General Straube and his LXXXVI Corps, was certainly heavily defended. Outer and inner anti-tank ditches ringed the entire town, key land approaches were littered with mines, and concrete pill boxes and stretches of barbed wire formed part of the overall defensive structure. The town of Goch was described by the historian Jorg Friedrich as an 'idyll on the Niers' and a 'farmer's marketplace' prior to the commencement of the Reichswald campaign.[2] Such comments probably exaggerate Goch's pastoral nature. The town certainly sucked in farm produce from the surrounding districts, and it possessed a substantial agricultural warehousing complex in the Thomashof area, which was the scene of heavy fighting once British troops had entered the town. Elsewhere, though, Goch had a substantial industrial area and a large margarine factory, which provided ideal areas for German snipers and ambushes. Bomber Command attacks on Goch during the night of 7/8 February certainly hadn't razed the town to the ground. British soldiers overlooking Goch on the morning of 18 February could see many town chimneys and factory smokestacks still standing. However, much had already been destroyed, and it was the combination of RAF bombing and intense house-to-house fighting within the town itself that resulted in the widespread devastation which so caught the eye of a number of British war correspondents who witnessed the scene.

The attack on Goch was destined to be a massive military and logistical enterprise, involving the 15th Scottish Division, the 43rd Wessex Division, the 51st Highland Division, the 52nd Lowland Division and elements of the 53rd Welsh Division, along with significant armoured and artillery support elements.[3] The overall strategy followed by Horrocks was to launch a two-pronged advance on the town, with the 15th Scottish and 43rd Wessex advancing from the north, and the 51st Highlanders and the 52nd Lowlanders pushing eastwards from the Gennep area. At the end of the advance, it was planned to assail Goch from the north, west and south-west in such strength that the German garrison in the town would soon be overwhelmed. The advance southwards to Goch by the 43rd Wessex Division formed one of the most spectacular episodes of the entire Reichswald campaign. During four days and nights of continuous fighting, between 13 and 17 February, the men of the division advanced over 4½ miles in the teeth of massive German resistance, eventually establishing themselves on the substantial northern escarpment which overlooked the town of Goch. On most occasions during the Reichswald campaign, rain, floods and mud slowed down the pace of military activity. The historian Herman Sligman, for example, quoted a number of Allied veterans of the Reichswald campaign as saying, 'We fought against the Germans and against the weather; hard to indicate which one gave the most problems.'[4] In the case of the Wessex Division, however, climatic difficulties were overcome in a series of speedy forward attacks which, at least in the opinion of General Horrocks, helped turn the tide of battle in the Reichswald campaign.

One of the original Territorial divisions formed in 1908, the Wessex Division spent the first four years of the Second World War training in England. Indeed, in the minds of some cynics the Wessex Division became the most 'overtrained' division in the entire British army. However, a few weeks after D-Day in June 1944, it became involved in its first serious fighting during the Normandy campaign, and it was in the forefront of every major British offensive against the Germans from this date onwards, suffering some 10,000 casualties in the process. By the time of the Reichswald Forest campaign, the Wessex Division, under Lieutenant-General Gwilym Ivor Thomas, was an immensely tough, seasoned formation, and it was no surprise that Horrocks chose it to spearhead the advance southwards to Goch.

In order to start its march to the heavily fortified German citadel of Goch, the division had to push its way through a narrow gap between Kleve Forest and Moyland Wood. The land through which it advanced was fundamentally pastoral, with isolated farming villages and gentle, rolling countryside. It was a convenient eastern exit route from the Reichswald Forest, and the Germans tried to block it by constructing a defensive trench system called the Kellen-Riegel, which ran from Bedburg in the north to the Goch escarpment in the south. It was here, in various parts of the Kellen-Riegel, that the Wessex Division fought a series of running battles with elements of the 47th Panzer Corps and 116th Panzer Division along the entire route to Goch. As the 43rd moved south, it made no attempt to seize Kleve Forest, which was defended in depth by the 156th Panzer Grenadier Regiment. Instead, the north and north-west perimeters of the forest were screened by soldiers of the Wessex's 43rd Reconnaissance Regiment, and the rest of the forest was sealed off by heavy artillery fire and Allied bombing attacks. On 15 February, for example, in one of many instances of effective Anglo-Canadian military cooperation, the 1st Canadian Rocket Unit saturated Kleve Forest by firing 2,400 rockets in support of the Wessex Division. During this particular rocket offensive a number of Canadian 'mattresses' were launched, which involved the simultaneous firing of thirty-two rockets from a single launching system.

On 13 February, the Wessex Division's 129th Brigade began the great advance southwards to Goch by attacking a ridge south-east of Bedburg, which incorporated a few isolated buildings at the tiny settlement of Eselsburg. The initial attack was carried out by the 5th battalion of the Wiltshire Regiment (5th Wilts) and in the afternoon, this attack was continued by the 4th battalion of the same regiment (4th Wilts). Divisional artillery fire was used to support the advancing infantry, and tanks from the 8th Armoured Brigade also moved forward with the infantry, but soon became bogged down in the muddy terrain. Despite the absence of tanks, 4th Wilts persisted with their attack, through heavy German machine gun and mortar fire, and reached the small hamlet of Trippenberg. Here, the battalion dug-in for the night and awaited the inevitable German counter-attack, which came at dawn on 14 February, when 300 infantry and twelve tanks of the 116th Panzer Division, supported by artillery, assaulted 4th Wilts positions. The 4th Wilts war diary recorded the fact that the German shelling during this counter-attack was 'as bad as the worst it had received in Normandy'.[5] Some indication of the severity of the fighting is given by the fact that the 4th Wilts headquarters area was hit by 200 shells in fifteen minutes. One Wiltshire company was overrun during the attack, but the rest of the battalion managed to hang on and eventually halt the German attack.

During the late morning of 14 February, 5th Wilts resumed their advance against German positions, despite the severity of the attacks endured by the 4th battalion. The object of the 5th Wilts advance was to secure a section of high ground south of Bremenkamp farm, and the Wiltshire men continued to move forward despite heavy German mortar and machine gun fire. All the supporting tanks were knocked out during the advance, and virtually every senior battalion officer was killed or wounded during the fighting. The position on higher ground near Bremenkamp was gained, after some desperate hand-to-hand fighting, and during the same night the surviving members of 5th Wilts went on the attack again, without any artillery support, and pushed the Germans back from vital crossroads at Neuenhaus, near the north-east corner of Kleve Forest. These rapid and successful battalion advances came at a heavy price, however. The 4th Wilts lost 200 men killed and wounded during the heavy fighting of 13–14 February, and 5th Wilts lost about the same number of men during the actions near Bremenkamp and at the Neuenhaus crossroads.

The two battalions were increasingly exhausted, but the overall attacking momentum was maintained on 15 February, when the 130th Infantry Brigade leapfrogged 129 Brigade and – supported by tanks from the 13/18th Hussars – continued the advance towards Goch. The newly engaged 130 Brigade incorporated battalions from some of England's finest county regiments within its ranks, such as the 4th and 5th Dorsetshires and the 7th Royal Hampshires. On 15 February, these three battalions continued the pressure on German defences in and around the Kellen–Riegel line by finally clearing the gently sloping Bremenkamp plateau, Eselsberg and the Berkhofel farm area of enemy troops. The 4th Battalion of the Dorsetshire Regiment (4th Dorsets) was involved in particularly heavy fighting at the Eselsberg, where they encountered a newly arrived crack battalion of German paratroopers, who formed what was known as Battle Group Huertz. This new formation of paratroopers contained veterans of the Battle of the Bulge offensive, together with other recruits who were fresh from the German Parachute Training School at Aalten in the Netherlands. Battle Group Huertz proved to be formidable opponents for the two Dorset battalions. Very few Huertz POWs were taken because, by and large, the paratroopers fought to the last man. Inevitably, therefore, the casualties on both sides during the fighting of 15 February were very heavy indeed. B Squadron tanks of the 13/18th Hussars supported 4th Dorsets during their assault on the Eselsberg, and by the end of the day five had been lost in action and only six tanks remained in serviceable order. Twenty-five soldiers from the 4th Dorsets were killed during the same fighting, and forty-five were wounded. Sadly, a number of the Dorset dead during this engagement were teenagers, including seventeen-year-old John Hutchinson. During the Second World War, in Britain, age checks on volunteers were sometimes rudimentary, and in any case males between sixteen and eighteen were still accepted for army service provided parental consent was obtained. Large numbers of teenagers fought in the British, Canadian and German armies during the Reichswald campaign. Many of those who fought in Battle Group Huertz, for instance, were certainly young – particularly those who came straight from parachute training school in Aalten. During its fighting with the Wessex Division, the Huertz battalion was, to all intents and purposes, virtually annihilated. By 20 February, according to a 43rd Wessex Intelligence Summary, the effective fighting strength of the Huertz Battle Group had been reduced to just one company of men.[6]

Early on 16 February, a new advance carried the men of the 130th Brigade on to a ridge between Louisendorf and Kleve Forest. At this point, men of the Wessex's 214 Brigade took over the lead and advanced towards Pfalzdorf and Schroershof, which both lay just a few miles to the north of Goch. The Worcestershire Regiment's 1st Battalion (1st Worcesters) and the 7th Battalion of the Somerset Light Infantry (7th SLI) pushed on throughout the day and night, and their efforts were further supported by night assaults led by the Duke of Cornwall's Light Infantry (DLI) and tanks from the 4/7th Dragoon Guards. By nightfall on 16 February, 7th SLI had actually occupied the eastern part of Pzalzdorf, and 4th SLI were expected to continue the advance on the following day. Much to the surprise of German forces in the area, however, 4th SLI decided to launch an immediate night attack, supported by divisional artillery fire. This surprise attack seems to have finally broken the German will to resist, north of the Goch escarpment. By early morning on 17 February, the two Somerset battalions had occupied a 1,000-yard section of the escarpment overlooking Goch, and with the assistance of tanks from the 4/7th Dragoon Guards, the south-east part of the escarpment was occupied later on the same day. By roughly 1800 hours on 17 February, the 1st Worcesters had also advanced through heavy shelling, cut the southern end of the Goch–Kalkar road, and moved on to the escarpment. The Wessex Division had, as a consequence, established control over a 4,000-yard-wide section of the Goch escarpment after a rapid, determined advance which constituted one of the greatest feats of arms achieved during the month-long Reichswald campaign. The Wessex Division went on to secure seven crossing points across Goch's outer anti-tank defences, but it now became the responsibility of the 15th Scottish Division to actually assault and capture the town.

At the same time as the 43rd Wessex and the 15th Scottish Divisions were massing to the north of Goch, the town was also being enveloped by British forces moving in from the north-west, the west, and the south-west. During the night of 16/17 February, the Welsh 53rd Division emerged from the south-east corner of the Reichswald Forest and assaulted German positions in and around the village of Asperberg, which lay just a few miles to the north-west of Goch. The attack was launched by the 7th Battalion of the Royal Welsh Fusiliers (7th RWF) and the 1st Battalion of the Oxfordshire and Buckinghamshire Light Infantry (1st Oxfords) and was preceded by a substantial thirty-minute rolling bombardment delivered by eight medium and four field artillery regiments. Fighting in the village, and at the nearby site of an already destroyed bridge across the Niers, was severe and lasted into the early morning of 17 February. Eight teenage German paratroopers caused considerable mayhem as they charged around the village mowing down any British soldiers they came across with accurate bursts of fire from their Spandau machine guns. By roughly 7 a.m. all eight German boys were dead, and the village was firmly in the hands of the 7th RWF and the 1st Oxfords, at the cost of over seventy killed and wounded Welsh Division infantrymen.

Further to the west of Asperberg, the town of Gennep was the base from which the western envelopment of Goch could be synchronised with the activities of the 43rd Wessex and 15th Scottish Divisions in the north. The loss of Gennep was rightly seen as something of a strategic calamity by Straube and the senior German officers who planned the defence of Goch, and it was a calamity which they planned to ameliorate at the first available opportunity: on 13 February two companies of infantry, supported by some artillery, were despatched to try and recapture Gennep for the Germans. Any hopes Straube and his coterie of senior officers had of recapturing the town with such a small force were, however, decidedly unrealistic. On the same day as the Germans attacked, the 51st Highland Division was reinforced by substantial numbers of infantry from the 32nd Guards Infantry Brigade, along with the West Somerset Yeomanry and additional artillery, all in preparation for the great advance eastwards to Goch. At least some of these fresh formations were then used to attack the village of Hommershum, 3 miles south of Gennep, on the following day – a task which was completed with little difficulty, other than the loss of a few men to mines. Even so, the small German force sent to attack Gennep performed very well indeed, and nearly overran units of the Gordons, before they were finally forced to retreat to the nearby Broederbosch woods.

A whole new division – the 52nd Lowland Division – was also pulled out of reserve and added to the ranks of the First Canadian Army moving towards Goch. The task of the 52nd Lowlanders was to provide right flank protection for the advancing Allied army. In addition, the new division was given the responsibility of rolling up the left flank of the German forces trying to defend Goch, and then breaking the new defensive line established by Straube's LXXXVI Corps, which ran from just south of the Broederbosch woods, through the small village of Afferden, and terminated at the medieval moated castle of Bleijenbeek. This new southerly defensive line rather mirrored the Kellen–Riegel line established to the north of Goch. For much of its length, the new defensive perimeter followed the course of a small, flooded riverbed which had been enlarged into an anti-tank ditch, and in parts at least, this new Broederbosch–Bleijenbeek line proved to be a difficult obstacle to overcome. On 16 February, the 52nd Lowlanders attacked and captured Afferden. The 5th Battalions of the Highland Light Infantry (5th HLI) and the King's Own Scottish Borderers (5th KOSB) also attacked German positions in the Broederbosch woods on the same day. The fighting in the woods proved to be far more severe than at Afferden, and the advancing Scottish infantry had to cope with accurate and sustained mortar, sniper and machine gun fire. The Broederbosch was finally cleared of German troops only when the 7/9th Royal Scots were brought out of reserve and committed to the struggle.

The moated, brick-built Dutch medieval castle of Bleijenbeek, situated in Limburg province and built at the beginning of the fourteenth century, was really the linchpin of the whole southern defensive line established by Straube's corps. From 17 February onwards, elements of the 52nd Lowland Division made three separate assaults on the medieval citadel, and all were repulsed with heavy casualties. The first direct attack, on the 17th, was made by two battalions of the Highland Light Infantry, who had to withdraw in the face of withering machine gun fire. On 18 February, a combined infantry-and-armoured assault was made across 700 yards of open ground between Broederbosch woods and the castle. The infantry of 4th KOSB, with Churchill tanks from the 34th Armoured Brigade, were again beaten back by heavy fire from the castle, and sustained heavy casualties. Finally, a single company of infantry attempted to storm the Bleijenbeek via a breach in the castle walls, rather like Wellington's British infantry would have assaulted a similar breach during the Peninsular War of the early nineteenth century. The first soldiers through a breach in Wellington's day were often dubbed the forlorn hope, and usually suffered very heavy casualties. Things were no different in February 1945 at Bleijenbeek Castle, where the assaulting company were defeated and virtually wiped out as they attempted to move through the breach. The castle remained in German hands until 21–22 February, when nine 1,000lb bombs dropped by the RAF's No. 84 Group reduced the castle to rubble. Inside the ruins of the castle, the bodies of just fifteen Luftwaffe paratroopers were found. The slogan '*sieg oder Siberien*' ('Victory or Siberia') was found scrawled on one of the remaining castle walls, indicating perhaps that, even in this part of the occupied Netherlands, the spectre of the advancing Russian ogre still motivated at least some German soldiers to keep on fighting to the last.

To the north of the 52nd Lowlanders, the advance of the 51st Highland Division had been proceeding apace. Many key towns and villages had already been seized by the Highlanders during the first phase of Crerar and Montgomery's Operation Veritable masterplan: to the rear of the forces advancing on Goch, the important town of Gennep had been in Allied hands since 13 February. Asperden, just 2 miles from Goch, had been a major objective of Phase 1 of Veritable, and had been in the possession of the Highland Division since 16 February, along with the village of Graefenthal. Hekkens, with its important crossroads, had been cleared of German forces, and during the night of 13/14 February the 7th Argylls had been ferried across the Niers in 79th Armoured Division Buffalos and taken the town of Kessel. On 16 February the village of Hassum was cleared, and the Highland Division's 152nd Brigade advanced down the main road to Goch. As the brigade neared Goch along this main road, German resistance began to stiffen. At 0130 on 17 February, the 5th Cameron Highlanders (Camerons) assaulted German positions in the small townships of Asper and Hervost. The settlement at Asper was cleared with relative ease, but problems were encountered at Hervost, which formed part of Goch's outer defensive perimeter. The Camerons encountered some mines and booby traps as they moved into position, and A Company of the battalion was hit by 'friendly' fire from its own artillery barrage. Three substantial pill boxes, manned by German troops, were encountered in Hervost. The defenders of two of the pill boxes offered no resistance, surrendering at dawn on 17 February. Crocodile flame-throwing tanks from the 1st Fife and Forfar Yeomanry, along with tanks from 107th Royal Armoured Corps, were used to subdue the remaining pill box, and after attacking infantry had dropped grenades down its chimney the surviving Germans came out and surrendered. In all, 125 German soldiers were taken prisoner during the struggles at Hervost. Supporting troops advancing into Hervost behind the Camerons were hit by German Nebelwerfer rockets, but the advance towards Goch continued without much interruption.

The fighting at Hervost really heralded the start of the Highland Division's final assault on the German-held bastion of Goch. Once the Hervost pill boxes had been neutralised, and a nearby anti-tank ditch bridged, elements of the division's 153rd Brigade would pass through and attempt to enter Goch's town centre late at night on 18 February. This rather daring night attack represented just one part of a multi-divisional synchronised assault on the heavily fortified town. Goch was covered by an elaborate network of trenches and dugouts, and all access roads were covered by strategically placed pill boxes. In addition, all parts of the town – other than the south-eastern suburbs – were ringed by a substantial anti-tank ditch. To the north, Goch's defences were even more comprehensive: any armour and infantry moving in from this direction had to circumvent both an outer and an inner anti-tank ditch, placed some 1,000 yards apart, before the town was even entered. Given the extensive nature of Goch's defences, Horrocks and his divisional commanders planned to attack the town at several different points simultaneously, and so split the defending forces controlled by the garrison commander, Colonel Paul Matussek.

As it transpired, the disposition of the German forces in Goch did turn out to be rather unbalanced. The impressive, rapid advance of the Wessex Division towards the Goch escarpment had convinced senior German commanders that the main attack on the town would come from the north, so reinforcements were steered to Goch's northern defences, and as a result there were fewer troops available to counter the surprise night-time attack from the Highland Division when it came during the night of 18/19 February. This initial nocturnal military venture was only the first stage in an overall 51st Highland Division offensive designed to capture the whole of Goch south of the Niers, which bisected the town. The 15th Scottish Division, supported by a brigade of the 53rd Welsh Division, was given the responsibility of seizing the areas of Goch which lay north of the Niers. This latter sector comprised the railway station and its surrounds, together with a significant industrial/commercial district. Despite the brigade-strength presence of troops from the 53rd Welsh Division, the ensuing battle of Goch was fundamentally a Scottish affair. Scottish troops filled the rubble strewn streets of Goch, and this fact was recognised by British war correspondents who wrote about the sometimes savage urban battles for the town in newspapers across Britain. Even so, the heavy fighting to get to and then capture Goch represented a UK-wide military effort made possible, in no small measure, by the Herculean efforts of the men of the Wessex Division, who pushed forward implacably against every German force thrown against them.

Late on 17 February, the 5th Black Watch began to assemble in the Hervost area, and during the early hours of the 19th it began its advance into Goch, in what proved to be one of the most successful and highly publicised battalion actions of the whole campaign. Resistance proved to be remarkably light. B Company captured a prominent road junction and nearby houses on the outskirts of the town with little difficulty, and had reached the town's main square, along with A and C Companies, by around 0500 hours. At least one company had passed Goch's substantial convent hospital building without incident, but D Company encountered small-arms fire as it did so. As a result, D Company's commander, Major Brodie, decided to attack the building. Sporadic gunfire erupted as a D Company squad, led by Sergeant John King, attempted to clear the ground floor. It quickly became apparent that there were Germans present in the hospital cellars. At least one hand grenade was tossed down the cellar steps, and after another brief burst of gunfire a party of Germans began to emerge from the gloomy basement. The first soldier to emerge was a lieutenant carrying a white flag. A major then emerged, followed by a wounded colonel and at least twelve other men. D Company of the 5th Black Watch had in fact just captured the Goch garrison commander, Colonel Matussek, along with his chief of staff, Major Kranz, and numerous other members of the town's military headquarters staff.

The capture represented a considerable coup for the Black Watch, and it was reported in very positive terms by journals and newspapers across the UK. *The London Daily News* of 20 February, for example, claimed that Matussek, a former Luftwaffe officer, and his staff had been caught in bed sleeping at the time of the Black Watch raid.[7] There was some truth in these comments, as Matussek had been resting after staying awake for three days and nights leading the defence of Goch. However, other members of the headquarters staff were certainly awake and working in the hospital cellars, trying to exercise command-and-control functions over their thinly spread forces. Matussek was carried out of the cellar on a stretcher, having been wounded in the leg by one of the hand grenades thrown by D Company. As he emerged into the street, he was apparently saluted by Black Watch soldiers in an unusual act of military courtesy which encouraged some nearby German soldiers to surrender. The military results of the dramatic capture also failed to live up to expectations. A pencilled note from Matussek's superiors was found in the captured colonel's possession, ordering his garrison to fight to the last man. Otherwise, though, little information could be gleaned from Matussek – at least according to the 51st Highland Division's Intelligence Summary, written on 19 February 1945. Moreover, German resistance to the presence of Scottish troops on the streets of Goch failed to collapse after their commander's capture. Indeed, as the Highland Division and the 15th Scottish were to find out, German resistance increased noticeably over the following few days.

On 19 February, 5th Black Watch were given the responsibility of advancing as far as Goch's main town square. After this, it was the job of the 5/7th Gordons to maintain the momentum of the advance by pushing on from the town square to the railway line situated at the eastern end of the town. The 1st Gordons were then scheduled to clear the southern part of Goch. The progress of the 5/7th Gordons through the old town square proved to be painfully difficult, in the face of considerable German sniper and machine gun fire. Although supporting artillery fire could be summoned from sites in the Reichswald Forest and elsewhere, mobile tank support was difficult to obtain in the cratered and rubble-strewn streets of Goch. Essentially, the infantry had to clear the streets, building by building, on their own. Nearby Black Watch infantry, including the redoubtable Thomas Renouf – who survived the street battles of Gennep to fight again at Goch – watched with considerable dismay as one Gordon after another crumpled to the ground after being hit by German gunfire on the streets of the old town. Fighting reached a crescendo on 20 February, when A Company of the 1st Gordons attacked German defensive positions in the cavernous warehousing and agricultural complexes of Thomashof in south-west Goch. With the benefit of hindsight, it was clear to at least some of the Gordons' senior officers that the task of clearing the large Thomashof area was beyond the capacity of just one company of men. Nevertheless, the task was attempted by men from A Company, and virtually all those involved were either killed, wounded or captured during the attempt to take the area. Only when another company – B Company – was thrown into the fight later on did Thomashof finally fall into Allied hands. The 51st Division offensive developed yet further on the evening of 20 February when, as part of a strategy to envelop the entire southern part of the town, 5th Black Watch again advanced to attack German positions, this time in the south-eastern suburb of Slavanien. The battalion's B and C Companies were used in the night attack, which was successful in its entirety, and some eighty POWs were taken. The battalion's war diary records the fact that 'both companies fought really aggressively. Germans were knifed and hit over the head and dealt with in every way.'

Although the fighting in Slavanien had come to an end, the 51st Division still had to subdue pockets of German resistance in other parts of southern Goch throughout 20 and 21 February. The situation was very different in the northern areas of Goch assaulted by forces from the 15th Scottish Division. The 44th Light Infantry Brigade had the primary responsibility for seizing northern Goch, and the Brigade Headquarters war diary recorded that large-scale fighting in the area had ceased by 1800 hours on 19 February.[8] Between 18 February and the evening of the 19th, however, German resistance to the incursions of the 44th Infantry Brigade had been determined and severe. On the 18th, the main assault on northern Goch – and across its two anti-tank ditches – had been led by the

6th KOSB[9] and the 8th Battalion of the Royal Scots Regiment (8RS).[10] Both battalions were supported by tanks. Earlier that day, one company of the Royal Scots had carried out an armed reconnaissance towards Goch, which halted at the outer tank ditch, where no further progress could be made until the ditch was bridged by an AVRE bridge-layer. This bridge, once laid, quickly collapsed, though the Royal Scots company was ordered to stay at the ditch, repulse any German attacks and await the arrival of further bridge-laying vehicles. Twenty German prisoners were taken in sporadic fighting around the anti-tank ditch before two other Royal Scots companies arrived at the scene in Kangaroo vehicles, along with bridge-laying equipment, and the ditch was finally crossed. B, C and D Companies of the Royal Scots advanced into northern Goch during the evening, though increasing fog and poor visibility hampered communications between the advancing soldiers. B Company moved into northern Goch's factory area, but C Company was cut off and surrounded by German forces, and only able to resume communications with other Royal Scots companies early on 19 February.

The 6th KOSB, who had advanced alongside the Royal Scots on 18 February, were also halted by the collapse of the first bridge over the anti-tank ditch. Two companies moved round the side of the substantial ditch, and continued to advance on foot until they were held up by heavy German machine gun fire. A third company – B Company – also advanced on foot late into the evening, in the face of considerable German resistance. Once the anti-tank ditch had finally been bridged, only D Company had the luxury of being transported into battle on Kangaroos, and even they dismounted from their vehicles to enlarge the divisional bridgehead across the ditch on foot. On 19 February, there was heavy fighting at various locations across northern Goch. According to the 44th Brigade Headquarters war diary, heavy reliance was placed on support from flame-throwing Crocodile tanks. Evidence of the strong link between armour and infantry in this northern sector of the Goch battlefield can be seen in individual battalion war diary entries. From 0630 onwards, for example, one troop of tanks was allotted to each company of the 6th KOSB, as they moved south through Goch towards the Niers. By the end of the day, the Borderers and their supporting tanks had managed to clear their allocated sectors of Goch all the way down to the river, despite heavy and sustained shelling from the Germans. Elsewhere, 8RS were involved in heavy fighting along Goch's railway line but cleared other areas of the town with support from various tank units.

During the early morning of 19 February, the 6th RSF was thrown into the battle for northern Goch. The battalion was ordered to secure the line of the Niers in central Goch, and almost immediately came under heavy shelling and mortar fire from German positions situated in the south. This heavy shelling and mortar fire continued throughout the day, causing 'fairly heavy casualties' according to the battalion's war diary.[11] Despite these casualties, the battalion still managed to achieve its objective of clearing the central river area of German troops, and it continued with its mopping-up operations on 20 February, supported by a squadron of tanks from the 4th Grenadier Guards. During these latter operations, 6th RSF encountered some small-arms fire which came from unknown locations in south-east Goch, but German resistance was clearly at an end in the north. Desultory fighting lingered in the Highland Division's southern areas for another twenty-four hours, but on the evening of 21 February the guns finally fell silent. The savage battle for the ruined town of Goch was at an end.

11

ANTHEM OF DEATH

> Thoroughness is his motto. Like Montgomery, with whom he works so well, General Simpson is gaining ground with the minimum loss.
>
> *Sunday Sun*, 1 April 1945

On 23 February 1945, U.S. Lieutenant-General William Hood Simpson finally launched the much-anticipated Operation Grenade, which had been delayed for over two weeks by rain, floods and the German destruction of the massive Schwammenauel dams.[1] Grenade was part of Montgomery's grand strategic plan to encircle German armies fighting on the northernmost part of the Third Reich's West Wall defences. Crerar's First Canadian Army was to move in from the north while Simpson's forces pushed north-east from the Roer, leaving the outnumbered German army trapped between them. As it turned out, Crerar's Anglo-Canadian offensive had taken place on its own, and British and Canadian forces had fought the German armies assembled in the Reichswald, at Gennep, Kleve, Goch and Moyland Wood in a series of increasingly bloody engagements which had sucked in many of the enemy's precious armoured and infantry reserves. Now that the flood waters of the Roer had receded to the extent that Simpson's men could cross and then pivot north-east to link up with the British and Canadians, the whole context of the Reichswald campaign was changed immediately. German armour and infantry had hurled itself at the British and Canadians in increasing numbers and with considerable determination, denuding itself of the men and resources needed to cope with huge simultaneous attacks from the Americans. Horrocks, Crerar, Montgomery and other senior commanders therefore became increasingly optimistic that the Veritable campaign begun in the Reichswald Forest could now be brought to a successful conclusion, with British and Canadian armies standing astride the Rhine, having destroyed substantial German forces on the river's west bank.

The optimism engendered by the late intervention of Simpson's U.S. 9th Army, which had been under Montgomery's command since the time of the Battle of the Bulge, certainly came at an opportune time. Following the sometimes desperate fighting in Goch, there had been a general lull in the Anglo-Canadian offensive. The 51st Highland Division certainly needed a rest, and its men were told that there would be no significant offensive operations for the next forty-eight hours. There was a feeling amongst at least a few of the veterans that if the Germans fought as hard for every town as they had done for Goch, then few of the Highlanders would live to see the end of the war. However, the intervention of the U.S. 9th Army offered these soldiers, along with their commanders, some hope that the campaign might soon be over. This optimism was shared by many on the Home Front who read the censored British press reports of Simpson's passage across the Roer. There was a news blackout on specific details concerning the 9th Army's activities, but general comments could still be made, and they were all very positive. A Reuters correspondent, for example, was quoted in the *Evening Despatch* of 28 February 1945 as saying, 'The whole front is aflame, and an anthem of death is sounding along the Rhine.' The death alluded to was that of German armies still to the west of the Rhine, and it was to be brought about by Simpson's crossing of the Roer. The same correspondent went on to claim that 'General Simpson is striking a shattering blow'.

Newspapers and correspondents weren't entirely engaging in hyperbole when they highlighted the significance of the U.S. 9th Army's attack across the Roer, and its impact upon the on-going Anglo-Canadian offensive in the north. The beginning of Simpson's move forward was indeed a hammer blow to the Germans. At 02.45 on 23 February, more than 1,000 U.S. guns and mortars opened up on German positions across the Roer in a forty-five-minute flurry. Enemy strongpoints, headquarters and supply dumps were all hit. Following this, six assault infantry divisions crossed the Roer in a mixture of small boats, ferries, amphibious tractors and motorised double-boat ferries. Simpson had a total of 375,000 men at his disposal, divided into fifteen divisions and four corps. In addition, the 9th Army could call upon the direct support of five groups of fighter-bombers, totalling 375 planes, which were part of the U.S. XXIX Tactical Air Command. This was by any standards a massive force, and it was initially faced by just 30,000 men of General Gustav Adolf von Zangen's Fifteenth Army, which had only limited artillery and armoured capability. Allied intelligence suggested that the Germans could also muster 400 fighters and fighter-bombers, including perhaps seventy-five new Luftwaffe jets, along the section of the front being attacked by Simpson's 9th Army.

By the end of 23 February, all six of Simpson's assault divisions were across the Roer, and seven bridges were in place, and all this had taken place at the cost of 1,447 American casualties.[2] The build-up of troops and supplies was remorseless, so that within two days of the crossing, a bridgehead of forty-eight battalions of infantry, seven tank and tank destroyer battalions, and eight field artillery battalions had been established. The Germans had sent their mobile reserves to deal with the Anglo-Canadian offensive through the Reichswald, so they simply didn't have the resources in place to launch vigorous counter-attacks to throw Simpson's men back across the Roer. Despite being so outnumbered, however, von Zangen's Fifteenth Army put up a tenacious defence. German artillery fire, for example, proved to be particularly accurate in destroying at least some of the bridges constructed across the Roer during the first day of the U.S. offensive, and out of 400 VII Corps bridging engineers involved in the initial assault, 153 were killed or wounded. Two of Simpson's four corps – XIII and XIX – were given the main responsibility of driving to the north-east and linking up with Crerar's First Canadian Army, and during the period 25–26 February these corps were advancing at a rate of just 2 to 3 miles a day, such was the intensity of the German resistance. Thus, a link-up with the British and Canadians to the north was not likely to be achieved immediately. Even on 28 February, some British newspapers were reporting that 9th Army spearheads were still some 30 miles away from linking up with leading Anglo-Canadian forces.

The implications of the launch of Operation Grenade were discussed by General Crerar in a conference held with his corps and divisional commanders on 21 February.[3] Crerar met with his subordinates on a very regular basis, as did Horrocks, and the conference on 21 February was particularly significant because it was here that plans for a revitalised Anglo-Canadian offensive were spelled out. It was entirely logical and predictable that new attacking plans would be developed in order to take advantage of the U.S. 9th Army's advance across the Roer, and on the day after Crerar's conference these new plans were given the codename of Operation Blockbuster. It would be wrong to see Blockbuster as an entirely new military operation. In many ways, Blockbuster simply represented the completion of aims and objectives originally included in the second and third phases of Operation Veritable. Veritable's Phase Two had involved the seizure of Weeze, Udem and Kalkar, and these three towns were again prominent objectives in Operation Blockbuster. Similarly, Veritable's third and final phase centred upon the destruction of the German Hochwald defensive system and an advance to

Xanten and Geldern. These objectives were also at the core of Blockbuster. Although Blockbuster was in many respects just Veritable under a different name, there were some changes and enhancements to the original Veritable masterplan. To begin with, two new divisions were added to the fray: the 4th Canadian Armoured Division and the 11th British Armoured Division. The 4th Canadian Division would prove to be a particularly significant addition to Blockbuster forces, playing a major role in the forthcoming battles. In many respects, the formation had a background similar to that of the British 43rd Wessex Division. It spent nearly two years training in the UK before being deployed on active service during the latter stages of the 1944 Normandy campaign, and by the time of the Reichswald battles the division was being commanded by the tough, vastly experienced and occasionally outspoken Major-General Christopher Vokes. The 159th Infantry Brigade was at the core of the 11th British Armoured Division and had seen a considerable amount of fighting in north Africa and western Europe since its formation in June 1942. The 3rd Battalion of the Monmouthshire Regiment, along with the 75th Anti-Tank Regiment, was also added to the 11th Armoured Division before it commenced its role in the Reichswald campaign, under the command of the very experienced and talented thirty-eight-year-old Major-General George Bradley Roberts.[4]

Other changes in approach between Veritable and Blockbuster were also discernible. Horrocks' XXX Corps had taken centre stage during the initial campaign through and around the Reichswald Forest, while Canadian divisions had provided flank protection and other vital but largely secondary services. At the commencement of Blockbuster these roles were somewhat reversed, with the Canadians right at the centre of the planned offensive while British divisions, such as the 15th Scottish and 53rd Welsh, pushed south towards Weeze and guarded the southern flank of the First Canadian Army against possible German counter-attacks. The 43rd Wessex Division initially fulfilled much the same role of flank protection in the north, while the recently deployed 11th Armoured Division was positioned centrally in order to probe and exploit German weaknesses wherever they occurred on the battlefield. The major offensive eastwards through the Hochwald – the centrepiece of Blockbuster, with the seizure of the towns of Xanten and Wesel as its ultimate objectives – was largely planned by Canada's General Guy Simonds. Once Xanten and Wesel had been occupied, and a link-up with the Americans achieved, then the First Canadian Army and the U.S. 9th Army could begin to plan the crossing of the Rhine. The process of getting to the Rhine, however, proved to be complex and exhausting, and the First Canadian Army still had a number of bloody battles to fight before Veritable/Blockbuster and the overall Reichswald campaign could be drawn to a close.

12

OPERATION LEEK AND THE DEPARTURE OF THE 15TH SCOTTISH DIVISION

> During the last weeks of World War II, over 10,000 young men from all over Germany lost their lives here in the Goch–Weeze–Udem triangle.
>
> Liberation Route Europe, 2023

Even before fighting had ceased in southern Goch, elements of the 15th Scottish Division had moved eastwards to help clear a triangle of land which lay between the towns of Udem, Goch and Weeze. This was a rural area, composed of woods, streams and some marshes, together with isolated villages and farmsteads, and it was defended in some depth by German infantry, armour and artillery. These German forces presented an obvious threat to the right flank of the First Canadian Army as it prepared to cross the Kalkar–Udem ridge and advance through the Hochwald. The triangle also had to be cleared if an advance to the town of Weeze was to take place. As a result, on 20 February elements of the 15th Scottish began an advance which had as one of its ultimate objectives the seizure of Schaddenhofbrucke and its strategically placed bridge, which dominated the eastern approaches to the town of Weeze.

The second battalions of both the Argyll and Sutherland Highlanders and the Glasgow Highlanders were in the vanguard of this push towards Schaddenhofbrucke, with the second battalion of the Gordon Highlanders acting as a reserve. These battalions from the 15th Scottish Division were faced, initially at least, by three battalions of German troops, composed of remnants from the battered 84th Infantry Division, the 11th Panzer Regiment and the 115th Panzergrenadier Regiment commanded by Wolfgang Mauck. The first day of the 15th Scottish's advance proved to be a successful one, with the Glasgow Highlanders seizing the southern part of Buchholt while the 2nd Argylls went on to capture northern Buchholt and the nearby settlement of Bremershof. Between them, the 2nd Argylls and the Glasgow Highlanders took nearly 350 POWs. The 2nd Gordons then moved ahead and attacked German positions in the vicinity of Schloss Kalbeck and its gardens. This action was supplemented by the advance of the 6th RSF towards the castle's nearby foresters' lodge, known as the Forsthaus Kalbeck. From this point onwards, the castle, grounds and lodge became the scene of heavy and confused fighting.

The castle itself was relatively new, having been built between 1906 and 1910 after a devastating fire destroyed the original, which had existed nearby since the fourteenth century.[1] Much of the newer building was destroyed in the fighting of February 1945, though parts of the first floor did survive the depredations of both the Scottish and German soldiery. German commanders rushed an extra company of men into the area around the lodge, and new defensive lines were formed to link the villages of Hovesaat and Schlubeckshof, Fasanenkath and Saarbrockshof, and Bussenhof and Vasenhof. In all, some three battalions of German infantry were fed into these new defensive lines, with an extra company also allocated to the Fasanenkath area.

During the course of 21 February, fighting developed along the entire length of these newly defended village lines, and on 22 February the fighting intensified, particularly around the castle and the lodge. Heavy German artillery and mortar fire rained down on 227 Brigade. Four Bren carriers were hit by German shells, and a deafening explosion rent the air when a Bangalore torpedo carrier received a direct hit. The 2nd Gordons managed to capture the small settlements of Schlubeckshof and Pleesenhof but were immediately counter-attacked by German forces, and reinforcements, supported by tanks, had to be brought in to prevent the 2nd Gordons from being overrun. Meanwhile, German troops were steadily infiltrating the woods around the castle and the lodge.

As the fighting intensified, the Scottish Division's 46th Brigade was brought in from Kleve to aid in the struggle, and to assist in the capture of the settlement at Saarbrockshof. Even removing the wounded from the battlefield became a very difficult process. The 46th Brigade's 193rd Field Ambulance Unit had established an Ambulance Car Post at the castle, but this had to be withdrawn when two cars were hit by shelling and mortar fire. Slowly, despite determined resistance, German forces were being pushed back, and their commanders had little option but to retreat and establish a new defensive line between the villages of Geurtshof and Bussenberg. In reality, 22 February marked the high-water mark of German resistance in the Udem–Goch–Weeze triangle. On the following day, the German position in this much-contested area began to collapse. The 6th KOSB captured Fasanenkath, then went on to occupy Heishof and Vasenhof, which had both been abandoned by their German defenders. Meanwhile, the 8th Royal Scots finally captured the farm complex at Saarbrockshof, and the village of Rottum was in 15th Division hands by the end of the day. At this stage, after four days of fighting, the 15th was relieved by the British 3rd Infantry Division and its role in the Reichswald campaign came to a close. Its contribution to the overall campaign had been a distinguished one, perhaps best summed up by the official history of the division's 46th Brigade when it says: 'We had been told to fight ourselves to a standstill, and we had done so. The limit of human endurance is an unknown quantity and can only be gauged by experiment. We had nearly reached this limit in Operation Veritable.'[2]

Once the villages and farmsteads north of Weeze were cleared of German troops, the 53rd Welsh Division was given the job of assaulting and seizing the fortified town itself. The assault began at 0600 hours on 24 February and was supported by all the artillery and armoured firepower that XXX Corps could muster. In sum, thirteen forward regiments, six medium regiments, two HAA regiments and one heavy regiment hurled all the ordnance they could at German defensive positions in Weeze. Considerable armoured support was also made available from the 8th Armoured Division, and from the Flails, Crocodiles, AVREs and Kangaroos of Hobert's 79th Armoured Division. The initial attack was to be made from the north, across a stream and an anti-tank ditch, by two infantry battalions of the division's 160th Infantry Brigade. Once a bridgehead over the stream and anti-tank ditch had been achieved, it was then intended to move the 71st Infantry Brigade through in order to capture Weeze itself. Ancillary objectives such as the seizure of nearby villages at Hees and Wemb would be tackled by the 158th and 160th brigades. German resistance to the northern assault on Weeze was ferocious from the very start. After six hours of fighting, the 160th's two infantry battalions had advanced across the anti-tank ditch and stream in Kangaroos, but only managed to advance to the Goch–Weeze road, which was some 4,000 yards short of the town itself. There was slightly better news from some of the smaller villages surrounding Weeze, such as Hohenhoff and Horst, which were cleared that afternoon with the aid of flame-throwing Crocodile tanks. The 71st Brigade was on the point of moving ahead to try and capture Weeze, but this advance failed to materialise because of the sheer ferocity of the fighting across the whole length of the Welsh Division's front. German forces launched wave after wave of counter-attacks, causing heavy casualties among the 53rd Division infantry and the loss of numerous tanks in the 8th and 79th Armoured. On the positive side, however, 53rd Division troops and armoured units still managed to take at least 300 German POWs, and wooded areas west of the Weeze railway line were cleared despite heavy enemy artillery and mortar fire.

The severity of the fighting on the northern boundaries of Weeze had considerable strategic ramifications. General Crerar even contemplated scaling back the imminent offensive through the Hochwald until the Weeze problem was resolved, and at some point during 24 February it also became clear to General Horrocks that an immediate infantry and armoured breakthrough into Weeze, via the bridgehead in the north, was highly unlikely. He made it clear to the on-the-spot commanders that no forced entry into Weeze should be attempted on 25 February unless the town could easily be cleared of German troops. Horrocks' unease about the assault on Weeze was understandable: the Canadian-led offensive across the Hochwald was due to begin on 26 February, and XXX Corps artillery was required to support this particular offensive as an absolute priority. Thus, unless Weeze could be seized very rapidly, the Welsh Division would have to fight without proper artillery back-up. Having received no reassurances about the speed with which Weeze could be cleared, at 0515 hours on 25 February, Horrocks ordered the Welsh Division to advance no further. For the time being, at least, the northern assault on Weeze had come to an end, with Welsh Division troops digging in about a mile short of the town.

The temporary pause to the Weeze assault had only a limited impact, though it did allow the 51st Highland Division and the 3rd Infantry Division to move up and cover the exposed left and right flanks of the northern bridgehead facing towards Weeze. On 26 February, the Welsh Division's 71st Brigade moved into the front line just north of Weeze and continued to probe German defences in the area. One of the most notable casualties of the Weeze fighting that day was Lieutenant Anthony Paget, who was an officer in the 1st Oxfords. The battalion was part of 71 Brigade, which was at the forefront of the Welsh Division's attempts to capture the town. On 26 February, Paget was badly wounded on the battalion's front line, and he succumbed to his wounds on 5 March. Paget came from a distinguished military family. At the time of the Reichswald campaign, his father, Sir Bernard Paget, was Commander-in-Chief of Britain's Middle East Command. Anthony Paget's elder brother, Julian, was also an officer in the Coldstream Guards, and had served during Operation Market Garden as part of the Guards Armoured Brigade. After leaving Radley College, Anthony Paget was commissioned as a second lieutenant in the 1st Oxfords during July 1943, where he proved to be a dedicated and courageous officer from the very start. In July 1944 he was mentioned in dispatches for his actions at the battle of Cahier, and he was later awarded the Croix de Guerre by the French. Shortly afterwards, he was wounded and invalided back home to England. He rejoined his regiment in December, and subsequently played an exemplary role in the Reichswald campaign. On 16 February he won the Distinguished Service Order (DSO) for 'his undaunted leadership and sheer bravery and skill' during fighting at Asperberg, near Goch. Commenting on Anthony's death on 5 March, a fellow officer wrote that 'those who knew him will never forget him, his happy and charming personality, and his dauntless courage'.[3] Paget's mother collected her son's posthumous DSO from King George VI in a ceremony held at Buckingham Palace on 24 November 1945. At the time of his death, Lieutenant Paget was just twenty years old.

The very strong German resistance to attacks on Weeze from the north led to a refinement in XXX Corps' tactics at the end of February. Rather than focusing on breaking into Weeze solely from the north, attempts were made to envelop the town from three sides at once. On the night of 28 February, the 7th RWF, supported by two squadrons of tanks from the Sherwood Rangers Yeomanry (SRY), attacked German positions in woods to the east of Weeze.[4] Another SRY squadron joined with the 53rd Reconnaissance Regiment and a company from the King's Royal Rifle Corps (KRRC) to create a formation known as Robin Force, which was commanded by Major Ringrose. Robin Force captured the village of Tilshof, together with some nearby farm buildings, which were also to the east of Weeze. Large concentrations of German infantry in the vicinity were also cleared by B Squadron of the SRY, together with a battalion of infantry from the East Lancashire Regiment. Once enemy forces were pushed out of these eastern areas, 53rd Division formations were hoping to cross the Niers, which ran in a north–south direction east of Weeze, and then surround the town from the east, and possibly from the south as well. Fighting in the woods to the east of the Niers was severe, lasting throughout 1 March. Twenty-year-old Lieutenant Donald Addison, from Blythe in Northumberland, won the Military Cross for leading a dismounted Reconnaissance Squadron party, supported by tanks, in an assault on Germans concealed in wooded areas and farm buildings. Once the enemy were cleared from these areas, Addison organised another immediate attack against Germans located in a smaller nearby wood. By the end of the day, Addison and his small band of men had taken over seventy German prisoners. The SRY lost a total of nine tanks during the fighting, but also managed to destroy two German Panther tanks. By nightfall, seven German tanks were still preventing Welsh Division forces from crossing the Niers, but the 1st Oxfords, together with 4th RWF and supporting tanks, were also attacking from the north. This combined pressure finally caused the Germans to retreat. During the evening of 1 March, Weeze was surrounded on three sides and XXX Corps patrols ventured somewhat hesitantly into the outskirts of the town. At approximately 1000 hours on 2 March, it was finally established that German forces had abandoned Weeze. After sustaining approximately 900 casualties, XXX Corps' hard fight for Weeze was at an end.

13

AUBREY COSENS, MOOSHOF, AND THE FIGHT FOR THE UDEM–KALKAR RIDGE

So it's sergeant now, and what a lot of work to do, and do I ever have a lot of dirt flung at me from all angles. But I'll beat it if it kills me.

Aubrey Cosens VC (in a letter written to his girlfriend in Canada) before Operation Blockbuster[1]

While Horrocks' British forces were pushing the Germans back in the south, and thereby protecting the First Canadian Army's right flank, the rest of the Allied infantry and armour hurled itself against the Germans at the start of Operation Blockbuster. The overall aim of Blockbuster was to seize the Hochwald area, punch through the so-called Hochwald Gap between the Hochwald and its smaller neighbour the Balberger Wald, and then drive on to the Rhine-based towns of Xanten and Wesel.

Guy Simonds, commander of the Canadian II Corps, was mainly responsible for planning the offensive, and one of the first crucial choices Simonds had to make as commander was the selection of routes – the axes of advance – for the intended drive eastwards to the Rhine. A southern route was really out of the question, because the roads would need to be shared with Horrocks' XXX Corps vehicles pushing south from Weeze in order to link up with Simpson's U.S. 9th Army. A northern axis of advance, along the roads between Moyland, Kalkar and Xanten, had much to commend itself. Indeed, a German High Command intelligence memorandum of 24 February predicted that this would be the route the First Canadian Army used to advance towards the Rhine.[2] The sheer predictability of this northern axis of advance was probably enough of a reason for Simonds to reject it. Instead, the axis of advance chosen was further to the south, along the Goch–Xanten railway line, which lay between solid embankments free of mines, and went through the gap between the Hochwald and the smaller Balberger Wald. Allied planners proposed tearing up the railway track and creating a new, solid roadbed which could withstand the weight of heavy military traffic.

The great Hochwald offensive, led by the Canadians, was launched on the early morning of 26 February, and the first phase of the attack involved an assault on German defensive positions spread across the substantial ridged plateau which ran in a south-westerly direction from Kalkar to Udem. Once Allied forces were ensconced securely on this strategic plateau to the north-west of the Hochwald, the Germans would find it difficult to launch major counter-attacks from the east, and Allied armour would have a solid base from which to move on to the low-lying Hochwald. A thrust along the plateau might also induce the Germans to move reinforcements northwards from the Udem area, and thereby weaken their defences in the southern sector of the front. Even before Allied infantry and armour moved off eastwards across the ridged plateau, at least eighteen German defensive positions had been attacked by Allied fighter-bombers, and medium bombers flew sorties against German targets near Kervenheim, Kehrum, Marienbaum and Sonsbeck.[3] A huge artillery barrage preceded the advance of the 2nd and

3rd Canadian divisions on to the Kalkar–Udem ridge. At 0345 on 26 February, the guns of twelve field, six medium and three heavy artillery regiments opened up in support of the 2nd Division, and seven field and two medium regiments fired off salvoes in support of the 3rd Division.

Five infantry battalions of the 2nd Canadian Division lined up on their start lines just to the west of the Goch–Kalkar road, during the early morning of 26 February. Conditions were wet and overcast, and the ubiquitous Monty's Moonlight was again used to provide extra visibility. Tensions mounted as the time for the attack drew closer and, somewhat ironically, it was the Germans who struck first, when paratroopers and six tanks assaulted the waiting Canadian forces. This decidedly unexpected initial burst of fighting only ended when a company from the Royal Hamilton Light Infantry, supported by tanks from the Fort Garry Horse, drove off the attacking Germans just fifteen minutes before the commencement of the massive bombardment heralding the start of the Hochwald offensive. At 0430, 2nd Division Canadian armour and infantry began to move forward along a 3,000-yard front. On the whole, the advance went well. Objectives were achieved and casualties were comparatively light, though Canadian armour had severe problems moving through the muddy and waterlogged fields south-west of Kalkar. At least ten tanks became bogged down in the mud, and one further tank was blown to pieces by a German mine. The Cameron Highlanders of Canada had the greatest difficulties. Their objectives were some 2 miles to the east of the original start line, and mines and soft ground soon forced them to make a detour northwards behind the French-Canadian Les Fusiliers Mont-Royal Regiment. The Camerons' commanding officer was shot dead by a sniper, and the fact that the battalion achieved its objectives owed much to the martial endeavours of one of its senior officers, Major D. M. Rogers, who won a DSO for his actions on the Udem–Kalkar plateau. Rogers cleared two houses full of German snipers and then went on to attack another building full of Germans who were firing on the Camerons' headquarters facilities.

While the infantry of the Canadian 2nd Division were tackling the Germans just east of the Goch–Kalkar road, men of the 3rd Canadian Division were responsible for securing the high ground immediately north of the important settlement of Keppeln, which formed a key link in the overall German defensive system along the Udem–Kalkar ridge. Progress in these endeavours proved to be quite slow, hampered by a noticeable absence of tank support. The Black Watch of Canada, for example, had to seize an important crossroads a mile south of Kalkar, even though half the Hussar tank squadron allocated for their support had become bogged down irretrievably in acres of mud right at the start of the offensive. The advance of the French-Canadian Le Regiment de Maissonneuve towards a wooded area near the junction of the Goch and Kleve roads also came to a shuddering halt when they were hit by ferocious fire from German defensive positions. Without tank support, Le Regiment simply had to dig in and hang on until mechanised back-up arrived later in the morning. Once it arrived, the infantry advance resumed and the Germans were ejected from the woods after some bitter close-quarters fighting in which many of the defenders chose to fight to the death rather than surrender.

The heavily defended hamlet of Mooshof, 8 miles north of Keppeln, was assaulted by two companies of the Queen's Own Rifles of Canada during the morning of 26 February. The sodden nature of the ground again prevented much in the way of tank support, as the Canadian riflemen advanced up an open slope towards the farm buildings of Mooshof. Two Allied tanks do seem to have made it into the battle for Mooshof, but the Canadians were still beaten back on at least two occasions, suffering heavy casualties. It was at this point that a very singular, courageous and professional Canadian soldier, Sergeant Aubrey Cosens, emerged to take control of the situation. Cosens, born in 1921, had had a tough upbringing in one of the more remote areas of northern Ontario. The only son of a widowed railway worker, Aubrey had also found work on the Canadian National Railways before enlisting in the Canadian Army during 1940. Promoted to the rank of corporal, he had fought through much of the 1944 Normandy campaign and the battles for the Scheldt before participating in the Reichswald fighting of February 1945. By the time he advanced up the rain-sodden slopes towards the farm buildings of Mooshof, he had risen to the rank of sergeant, and had previously commanded platoons of men in action. He was already the epitome of a dedicated, professional soldier. His letters to his girlfriend back home in Canada illustrate his total lack of concern for his own personal safety. Instead, Aubrey seemed totally focused on fulfilling the responsibilities he had as a sergeant. Responsibility was the key factor and motivator for Cosens – responsibility for carrying out tasks to the best of his abilities, whatever the consequences, and responsibility for ensuring that he did the best for his men.[4]

During the battle for Mooshof, two failed attacks on German positions left only four of Cosens' platoon alive and fit to fight. The platoon commander was among those killed, and Aubrey Cosens therefore set about trying to capture the Mooshof settlement on his own, with the aid of covering fire from the surviving members of his platoon and directed fire from one Canadian tank. The Queen's Own sergeant ran across 25 yards of open ground, under heavy fire, leapt on to the front of an Allied tank, and then directed its fire so effectively that startled German paratroopers were halted from launching another counter-attack against Canadian positions. After urging the tank on to ram the front of a farmhouse full of German soldiers, he leapt off and disappeared into the building, where he fought and subdued enemy troops in every room, before emerging with prisoners. Cosens then repeated these almost superhuman martial endeavours in two further farmhouses before ensuring that reinforcements were brought up to consolidate the Canadian hold over Mooshof. The battle for the strategically placed hamlet was at an end, largely thanks to the efforts of one man, and two reserve Queen's Own Rifles companies were moved forward to occupy the nearby villages of Steeg and Wemmershof.

Cosens' spectacular actions certainly saved the lives of other Allied soldiers, but there was to be no glorious, rose-tinted future for the Queen's Own sergeant. As Cosens attempted to return to Canadian lines to report what had happened to his commanding officer, he was shot in the head by a German sniper and died instantly. Aubrey Cosens' body was interred at the Groesbeek Canadian War Cemetery in September 1945, by which time he had become the deserving recipient of a posthumous Victoria Cross, Britain and Canada's highest possible award for gallantry in the face of the enemy. The original citation which led to Cosen's being awarded the VC really sums up the significance of the man's actions:

> The outstanding gallantry, initiative and determined leadership of a brave NCO, who himself killed at least twenty of the enemy, and took an equal number of prisoners, resulted in the capture of a position which was vital to the success of future operations of the brigade.[5]

Aubrey Cosens' VC was the first to be awarded during the Reichswald campaign, but it would not be the last.

The capture of Steeg and Wemmershof essentially marked the end of the first phase of the battle to eject all German forces from the Kalkar–Udem ridge and plateau. The second phase involved an advance over flat, open country towards the village of Keppeln, situated just over 4 miles south-west of Kalkar. Keppeln was a key anchor point in German defences along the northern plateau, and occupied by elements of the 116th Panzer Division, which had just been reinforced by troops from the Eifel region of western Germany. Two Canadian battalions, from the North Shore (New Brunswick) Regiment and the Regiment de la Chaudiere, advanced in a south-easterly direction to seize Keppeln.

The speed of the advance upon Keppeln was really dictated by the presence or absence of tank support. During the early part of their advance, the North Shores had no tank support at all and were halted by heavy German machine gun and mortar fire. The demands made upon the Canadian 2nd Armoured Brigade, and other armoured units, were simply too great for tanks to be committed to every individual battle. Even when tanks were committed, soft ground often limited their mobility and usefulness during key stages of the overall Reichswald campaign. References to tanks and other vehicles being 'bogged down' were common in war diary entries throughout the entire First Canadian Army. Such problems weren't emphasised by either British or Canadian commanders, and war correspondents at both Montgomery's and Crerar's command headquarters were encouraged to promote the power and efficacy of the First Canadian Army's armoured capabilities. The experienced war correspondent Doon Campbell, for instance, reported from Canadian Army HQ that Crerar's tanks were 'swanning about – a most healthy expression. The Canadian Army commander has fed scores of tanks into the battle.' These comments were picked up and used by countless British newspapers. While based at Montgomery's headquarters, Campbell also made similar comments to the effect that 'a stupendous weight of armour is at the call of the Allied commanders'.[6] There was indeed much armoured support at the disposal of the First Canadian Army, but it couldn't always be used that effectively in the Reichswald, nor in the adjacent towns and countryside west of the Rhine.

Although the advance on Keppeln had stalled during the morning of 26 February, that afternoon the French-Canadian Chaudiere battalion captured the small village of Hollen, half a mile to the west of Keppeln, aided by a squadron of 1st Hussars tanks. The fight for the tiny village was a hard one, the Germans using three of their technically impressive Panther tanks to mow down small groups of Canadian infantry. The North Shores were eventually given the support of thirteen tanks from C Squadron of the 1st Hussars during the early afternoon, and subsequently resumed their advance on Keppeln alongside the Chaudieres. By early evening, the two Canadian battalions had secured the village at the cost of twenty-eight men killed and fifty-three wounded. During small-scale tank battles in and around Keppeln, German tanks had also managed to destroy three Canadian Shermans, and by the time fighting finally died down a total of nine Canadian tanks had been destroyed in action, while four had become hopelessly 'bogged down' in the glutinous terrain of the area. At the same time as the Canadians were fighting hard in Keppeln, a combined infantry and armoured battlegroup of Robert Moncel's 4th Armoured Division was pushing eastwards in order to extend Canadian control over as much of the plateau as possible. As ever, the advance was slow and laborious. Soft ground restricted many of the tanks to a mere crawl, and only 500 yards were gained during the first two hours of the drive eastwards. German hand-held Panzerfausts, which fired single-shot high explosive missiles from their launch tubes, also destroyed numerous Canadian tanks. Nevertheless, by the late afternoon the battlegroup had still managed to seize control of the area around Todtenhugel, a few miles to the north-east of Keppeln.

Once Keppeln and the Todtenhugel area was safely in Canadian hands, only the major German road centre and strongpoint of Udem remained as an obstacle to the launching of the Simonds/Crerar offensive through the Hochwald. This culminating Canadian attack on Udem contained two key elements. Firstly, the high ground around the fortified town had to be captured, and this task was given to Smith Force, named after its leader, Lieutenant-Colonel E. M. Smith, who was the commander of the Governor General's Foot Guards. Attacks on the high ground at Paulsberg and Katzenberg began during the evening of 26 February. Paulsberg was occupied with some ease, initially at least, by a company of the Lake Superior Regiment. However, the inevitable German counter-attacks soon followed later in the evening, and it was only when these assaults had been beaten off that the position fell finally and irrevocably into the hands of the Canadians. The Katzenberg was then seized with less fuss during the early hours of 27 February.

Once the strategic high ground on the plateau was occupied by Canadian forces, the final attack on Udem was launched with considerable speed. The difficult task of storming the town, surmounting its substantial anti-tank ditch and overcoming its garrison of paratroopers from the 7th Parachute Regiment, was given to three battalions of the 3rd Canadian Division. The Highland Light Infantry of Canada (HLIC) and the Stormont, Dundas & Glengarry Highlanders (SDGH) were ordered to attack the northern outskirts of Udem, and then the Nova Scotia Highlanders would move ahead of the other two battalions and seize the rest of the town. The assault was launched at 2100 on the evening of 26 February, after a brief artillery bombardment. Each battalion was allocated a squadron of Fort Garry Horse tanks to support them, but such were the commitments of this Winnipeg-based armoured formation elsewhere on the plateau that no Fort Garry tanks actually took part in the final assault on the town. Despite the absence of tank support, the HLIC and the SDGH moved into the northern parts of Udem without much difficulty. Fighting intensified as the Canadians moved into the central part of Udem, but by late afternoon on 27 February all was quiet in the town.

While the Canadians consolidated their hold on the former German stronghold of Udem, Lieutenant-General George Roberts' British 11th Armoured Division moved on to attack and subdue the remaining German positions on the southern tip of the much-contested Kalkar–Udem ridge and plateau. These actions helped secure the right flank of the Canadian armour and infantry massing to the west of the Hochwald. The 43rd Wessex Division were also providing some flank protection to the Canadians in the north. On the afternoon of 27 February, the 5th Wiltshires entered Kalkar unopposed, though all bridges in and around the town had been destroyed by German forces – principally from the 17th and 18th Parachute Regiments – as they retreated eastwards. The capture of Kalkar, like Udem, had been a major objective of the second phase of the original Operation Veritable masterplan, following the breakout from the Reichswald Forest and the crossing of the Materborn Gap. Finally, after considerable delays and nearly three weeks of intensive fighting, the two towns were in the hands of the First Canadian Army. The Wessex Division continued to probe eastwards towards Marienbaum, with Gloucestershire Regiment squadrons at the absolute apex of the division's reconnaissance activities, To the south, the 11th Armoured Division pushed onwards towards Gochfortzberg and Sonsbeck, and in the centre, with both flanks apparently secure, the Canadians could at last launch their major offensive through the Hochwald.

14

THE BATTLE FOR THE HOCHWALD

> I spent the whole morning there [28 February, in the Hochwald Gap] where I could see what was happening. The Argylls had been pushed back and had withdrawn and this shell fire was coming down. I didn't move and I told the wireless operator that I was out to lunch if anyone called. I wasn't going to take any calls.
>
> Lt-Col Rowan Coleman, reminiscing about the Hochwald battle during a 1984 interview[1]

Nineteen days after the Reichswald campaign was launched from the muddy fields of Groesbeek, the First Canadian Army launched one of its largest and bloodiest operations of the entire Second World War. The objective was to punch a sizeable hole through the Hochwald Layback, the last major German defensive line west of the Rhine, and then seize the key town of Xanten. In order to break through these substantial German defences, sometimes referred to as the Schlieffen Line, the Canadians assembled a massive infantry and armoured force boasting at least three divisions. The Canadian 2nd Infantry Division was ordered to attack the Hochwald from the north, and then move through the forest to outflank German positions in the Hochwald Gap. This gap lay between the Hochwald to the north and the smaller Balberger Wald to the south, and right at the northern extremity of the Balberger lay the even smaller Tuschenwald. The 4th Canadian Armoured Division, led by Major-General Christopher Vokes, was given the daunting task of attacking straight through the Hochwald Gap, while the 3rd Canadian Division was ordered to move through the Balberger. Beyond this, the British 11th Armoured Division was positioned to provide some flanking protection for Vokes' men as they plunged through the gap, and the 43rd Wessex Division guarded the Rhine flank to the north of the Hochwald.

These military dispositions were of course the exact opposite of those pertaining at the start of the campaign, when British divisions pushed into and around the Reichswald Forest area while Canadians provided crucial flank protection. This new balancing of Anglo-Canadian forces certainly made strategic sense in light of Montgomery's professed objective of lining up British forces next to the Americans on the banks of the Rhine; such a linkage could be more easily obtained by Horrocks' XXX Corps punching south-east of the Hochwald, towards Simpson's Americans, who were, of course, also commanded by Montgomery. This left the Canadians, aided by the British on the flanks, to fight through the Hochwald, and the battle of the Hochwald proved to be a defining, if understated, moment in the evolution of Canadian nationhood. Its infantry and armour became embroiled in murderous battles with German forces and sustained very heavy casualties indeed, particularly in the Hochwald Gap itself. Despite an overwhelming superiority in both men and tanks, Canadian advances were sometimes brought to a standstill by German infantry counter-attacks, well-placed artillery barrages and the actions of scarce but technically superior Tiger and Panther tanks. Canadian Sherman tanks often advanced along narrow, easily ambushed Hochwald roads and tracks where small numbers of German tanks could execute the so-called Wittmann manoeuvre, which involved destroying the first and last tanks in a column before picking off the trapped tanks in between.[2]

The 4th Canadian Armoured Division formation selected to launch the central assault on the Hochwald Gap was Lion Force, a small battlegroup led by Brigadier J. C. Jefferson.[3] The spearhead of this small force was made up of the 29th Armoured Reconnaissance Regiment (the Alberta Regiment) together with assault companies from the Algonquin Regiment. Lion Force began its advance towards the gap on the evening of 26 February, but only arrived at its start line for the attack at around 0500 on 27 February, having been delayed by the predictable chaos of muddy roads. Some of Lion Force's Algonquin sub-units were also late in joining the advance towards the battlegroup's start line. In order to maximise its chances of success, Lion Force had to advance as far as it could during the hours of darkness, so time was running short. The battlegroup's first objective was a hill, codenamed 'Albatross' and sometimes referred to as Point 73, which filled the western part of the Hochwald Gap. A small diversionary attack was also launched by a South Alberta reconnaissance squadron, supported by an Algonquin carrier platoon, which headed to the right of the gap, crossed the Goch–Xanten railway line and attempted to capture the small village of Udemerbruch, which was situated close to Point 73. The advance of Lion Force towards Albatross was supported by a two-hour bombardment from eight artillery regiments and, initially at least, all seemed to be going well for the small battlegroup as it moved towards enemy territory in the gap. German anti-tank ditches were surmounted, a minefield was successfully negotiated, and knee-high barbed-wire belts were circumvented. A first line of German defensive trenches was also encountered and overcome. Even so, as daylight emerged, Lion Force was in an increasingly exposed and dangerous position. The usual pattern throughout the Reichswald campaign was for German forces to cede some ground initially, only to return later on with concerted, often ferocious counter-attacks. This pattern was being repeated at the Hochwald Gap, where German counter-attacks against Lion Force grew in intensity as the day progressed. Indeed, the

Germans had considerable resources to throw into these counter-attacks: three parachute battalions, plus anti-tank guns, had been deployed to defend the area.

Lion Force's position was made even more isolated by the failure of supporting Canadian flank attacks. The diversionary attack across the Hochwald Gap railway line met with disaster before it could seize the village of Udemerbruch. The assault squadron, comprising eleven tanks and thirteen Algonquin troop carriers, was virtually annihilated as it made its way south-east from Kirsel, just to the north of Udem. In the wet, pitch-black night of 26/27 February, the force took the wrong route to the Hochwald Gap and crossed the railway line to Xanten much further west than was intended, and in an area still occupied by the Germans. Canadian tanks were hit by accurate fire from German anti-tank guns, and German infantry also advanced to fire their Panzerfausts at both tanks and carriers. All eleven tanks involved in the attempted diversionary attack were destroyed, along with twelve out of thirteen of the accompanying carriers. Stunned survivors of the slaughter had little option but to pull back immediately towards Kirsel.

Elsewhere on the Canadian right flank, 'Pip' Roberts' British 11th Armoured Division was increasingly mired in boggy ground, and unlikely to be able to provide much in the way of immediate mobile flank support to the Canadians at the Hochwald. More significantly, perhaps, the Canadian 3rd Division, who were intending to outflank enemy positions at the Hochwald Gap via a thrust to the south of the Balberger Wald and Tuschenwald, were still embroiled in the struggle for Udem on the night of 26/27 February. On the northern side of the gap, the 2nd Canadian Division had at least started their advance towards the Hochwald, which might outflank German positions in the gap, but their attack had progressed no further than the village of Schmachdarm, which was seized at around 2200 on 27 February. Heavy German shelling meant that 2nd Division formations could move no further that night, so Lion Force was on its own.

Halted in their tracks by withering German fire, Lion Force made one last attempt to prise open the Hochwald Gap during the late afternoon of 27 February, and the Argyll and Sutherland Highlanders of Canada were sent on through the Algonquins to try and capture the entry to the gap. This attempt also failed due to extremely heavy enemy mortar and artillery fire, and the Argylls were forced to a halt some 500 yards to the west of the Hochwald Gap entrance. The isolated battlegroup was hit by German shell and mortar fire from the north, south and east, and even from the northern banks of the Rhine. In the circumstances, Lion Force could only dig in and hope to survive the maelstrom of shell and shot that came their way.

Clearly, by the end of 27 February, Lion Force was in a desperate situation, and a reappraisal of Canadian tactics was needed. At an urgent conference held during the evening, Christopher Vokes, general in charge of the 4th Canadian Armoured Division, had some difficult choices to make. He could, of course, have ordered a retreat from the gap, and come up with a revised plan for the Canadian offensive in the area. Such a solution, however, was never likely to be considered in depth. Vokes, like almost all the other Canadian, British and American generals in early 1945, was wedded to the concept of speed and 'pressing on'. He, like Eisenhower, Montgomery and Crerar, believed that the Germans were on the brink of total collapse. All that was needed to bring the Germans to their knees on the Western Front, he felt, was relentless pressure. Indeed, just before the Hochwald battle commenced, he told his officers, 'The troops must be impressed with the vital necessity to get on and destroy the enemy ... Do not sit on the objective if you can press on.'[4] Thus, it was no real surprise that Vokes and his superior officer, Guy Simonds, ordered reinforcements into the gap in order to continue the fight on 28 February, whatever the level of German resistance. This commitment to 'pressing on' in the Hochwald Gap was controversial, and has been criticised ever since by many veterans and historians. It was also a risky decision, because the absence of immediate support on the flanks meant disaster could strike at any time. In the event, however, 'pressing on' worked, and the Canadians did batter their way through the gap, albeit at a considerable cost.

The strategy planned for 28 February involved far more than just a focus on the Hochwald Gap. Vokes also sought to make the route from south of Udem to the Hochwald safe and secure, so that disasters such as that which befell the diversionary force advancing on Udemerbruch never happened again. The axis of advance along this route was then to be improved by engineers so that a 4th Armoured Brigade battlegroup could pass along it and seize a wooded area roughly a mile inside the western edge of the Hochwald Gap. During the early hours of 28 February, after a preliminary bombardment, the Argylls moved off Point 73 and advanced towards a strategically important lateral road which ran along the western tip of the gap. The Argylls' leading role in this second day of fighting at the gap was no real surprise, as its new commanding officer, Lieutenant-Colonel Frederick E. Wigle, had a strong personal and professional relationship with Vokes that went back to student days at McGill University in Montreal, and he backed the general's strategy at the Hochwald Gap to the hilt. Indeed, Wigle didn't anticipate a serious struggle for his men on this second day of fighting, because he believed that the Germans had taken 'a sound drubbing on the first day' and were probably focused upon pulling back to the Rhine.[5] Such comments proved to be unfortunate, and very wide of the mark, because during the course of the day the Argylls came under the heaviest fire they'd experienced during the entire war. By daylight, Wigle's men had seized the key lateral road on the western edge of the gap, but afterwards they endured repeated counter-attacks from German infantry and tanks. The Argylls dug in and hung on tenaciously during the day, but by nightfall Wigle's own B Company had been reduced to just fifteen men.

The next stage in Vokes' plans for 28 February involved launching the Lincoln & Welland Regiment towards the railway line that ran through the Hochwald Gap, and then onwards to the Tuschenwald at the north-west end of the Balberger Wald. This particular advance ended in abject failure when the Wellands were halted by a German bombardment so intense that their commanding officer, Lieutenant-Colonel Rowan Coleman, felt it was impossible to move at all in the gap, let alone advance across the railway line and secure the Tuschenwald. Sensibly, the attack was abandoned. Elsewhere in the gap, the Algonquins finally managed to secure the village of Udemerbruch, but other planned attacks were cancelled and the Wellands, Algonquins and Argylls were again placed in the difficult position of having to hold out until the military position improved.

Though the position in the Hochwald Gap was undoubtedly grim on 28 February, there were developments on the Canadian flanks which showed some promise. On the southern flank, the British 11th Armoured Division was beginning to probe the outlying defences of the Hochwald Layback, despite the perennial problems of mud and soft ground, and in the north the Essex Scottish Regiment was attacking German positions right at the edge of the forest. If these flank attacks to the north and south continued to make progress, then German forces in the Hochwald Gap might be forced to withdraw from their strong defensive positions to avoid the risk of being encircled. Finally, the weather began to improve on 28 February, and as a result the RAF's No. 84 Group was able to fly a total of 602 sorties, including attacks on German gun positions and troop concentrations in the Hochwald. On 1 March, Allied fighter-bombers and bombers went on to conduct numerous further strafing sorties against German positions at or near the gap.

On 1 March, fighting resumed with maximum intensity. In the northern Hochwald, Bruce Matthews' Canadian 2nd Division began to punch its way into the forest. German paratroopers resisted the Canadian attacks with grim determination, and the battles were particularly ferocious in the areas allotted to the Essex Scottish Regiment. In this sector of the northern Hochwald battlefield, the Essex Scottish had to cross 500 yards of open, muddy ground and make their way through 10-foot-thick barbed wire entanglements before they even arrived at the first line of German defensive trenches. Tanks from the Sherborne Fusiliers were allocated to support the advance, but the ground was simply too soft and waterlogged for armour to be of much use. The infantry, not for the first time in the overall campaign, was on its own. It was in these inauspicious, intimidating circumstances that the bravery and leadership capabilities of one particular soldier, Major Frederick Tilston of C Company of the Essex Scottish Regiment, came to the fore. Tilston was a thirty-eight-year-old former pharmaceutical salesman from Toronto who entered the Canadian Army as a private but had risen to the rank of acting major by the time of the Reichswald campaign. On 1 March, he led his company, and battalion, with considerable panache. He was the first man across the open ground, through the barbed wire, and into the German trenches, despite a serious head wound. He then proceeded to knock out an enemy machine gun post, before leading his men in a successful assault on the second line of German defences. During this second attack, Tilston received a severe thigh wound. Even so, he still managed to prepare his men for the inevitable German counter-attack. Once this attack was in progress, Tilston managed to hobble along the entire length of the Essex Scottish line, delivering ammunition and providing advice and guidance wherever it was needed, and he was wounded yet again while engaged in these activities. The regiment held on to its hard-won territorial gains, and a base was provided from which the Canadians could go on to clear the rest of the northern Hochwald. Once the battle was over, Frederick Tilston was found, barely alive, in a shell hole. His injuries were extensive; both his legs needed to be amputated, and he also lost an eye. The Essex Scottish major was awarded a much-deserved VC for his many acts of gallantry on 1 March, and on 22 June 1945, during a special ceremony at Buckingham Palace, he was led up a specially installed ramp to receive the coveted medal from King George VI in person.[6]

Although the Tilston-led Essex Scottish heroics had secured a foothold for the Canadians in the northern Hochwald, to the south Le Regiment de la Chaudiere were pushed back after a failed attempt to seize the Tuschenwald during the evening of 1 March. On the following morning, however, the Chaudieres – with armoured support – did manage to clear the rest of the Tuschenwald, and it was left to battalions of the North Shore Regiment and the Queen's Own Rifles to begin the arduous task of pushing the Germans out of the larger Balberger Wald. This particular task was only achieved by the end of 4 March, after two days of tense, low-key but deadly forest fighting in which small-scale ambushes, counter-attacks, booby traps and anti-personnel mines ensured a steady stream of Canadian casualties. North of the gap, on 2 March, the Royal Hamilton Light Infantry advanced from positions won at great cost by the Essex Scottish and attacked in a north-easterly direction towards Marienbaum. This particular advance was halted by German resistance after only 500 yards had been gained. Nevertheless, the eastward push was resumed on the following morning by formations of the Canadian 2nd Division, and by nightfall all forest areas west of the Marienbaum road had been cleared of German infantry and armour.[7] The German position in the Hochwald Gap, and the forest as a whole, had become increasingly untenable during the first few days of March. To its front, Alfred Schlemm's First Parachute Army had been battered and bludgeoned by dogged First Canadian Army attacks in the Hochwald. Also, equally alarmingly, his left flank was under severe threat from Simpson's massive U.S. 9th Army, which was advancing rapidly from the south-east. Britain's XXX Corps was moving around the German left flank in the meantime, and Schlemm and the German High Command rightly suspected that these Allied forces would advance along the left bank of the Rhine and attempt to encircle the German armies facing the First Canadian Army in and around the Hochwald area.

For much of the time since the launching of the Reichswald offensive on 8 February, the Germans had been able to draw on their forces facing Simpson's immobilised 9th U.S. Army in order to reinforce formations ranged against the First Canadian Army. The detonation of the Schwammenauel dam, and the consequent increase in water levels along the Roer, had been a strategic German masterstroke which utterly changed the nature of the Reichswald campaign. However, once the flood waters had subsided enough for the Americans to launch Operation Grenade, the German military position became severely overstretched. German forces now had to be transferred away from the sector facing the British and Canadians to fend off the Americans. In these circumstances, a German withdrawal from the Hochwald, and the hotly contested Hochwald Gap, became a vital strategic necessity. Despite this, however, there was still time for the Canadians and the Germans to fight one last savage battle in the Hochwald Gap.

During the early dawn of 2 March, three companies of infantry from the Lake Superior Regiment and a company of men from the Algonquins, supported by tanks from the Canadian Grenadier Guards and the Governor General's Foot Guards, took part in a staggered two-stage offensive along the gap. The first stage of the attack involved a 1,000-yard push eastwards to seize farm buildings which stood astride the Marienbaum–Sonsbeck road. The Algonquins would then move ahead for another 1,000 yards, carried on Foot Guard tanks, and secure a bridgehead across the Hohe Ley stream, which lay at the extreme eastern edge of the Hochwald Gap. The objectives of the intended attack were certainly ambitious, but the Canadian battlegroup's commanding officer, Brigadier Moncel, who felt that the Germans were on the point of collapse, was another advocate of the 'pressing on' policy. In the event, the attack proved to be a costly failure. Moncel himself had to be replaced at the last moment due to illness, and Kangaroos used to ferry troops forward to their objectives also arrived late at their assembly points because of the lakes of mud that engulfed much of the Hochwald area. Once the attacking force began its advance eastwards along the deadly gap, it was assaulted on all sides by German infantry, tanks and artillery fire, and the Algonquins never reached the Hohe Ley stream. Indeed, five out of the eight tanks used to carry the Algonquins into battle were destroyed, and the remaining three had to beat a hasty retreat under intense German artillery fire. Forward platoons of the inadequately resourced Canadian force were completely overrun by German infantry and armour. The commanding officer of the Lake Superior Regiment, and all the officers of C Company, were either killed, wounded or captured; only eight men from the entire company were able to rejoin Canadian lines after the battle.

This last clash in the Hochwald Gap might have ended in a German victory, but the Canadians were soon in control of the battlefield. When patrols moved through the gap on 4 March, they found that the Germans had departed. All that was left was a landscape littered with the inevitable detritus of war – the smouldering ruins of buildings, burned-out tanks and military vehicles, wrecked artillery pieces, and countless corpses. The Hochwald had been a vital hinge point in German defence lines, allowing troops on either side to retreat in reasonably good order back towards the Rhine. By 4 March, however, the Germans and Canadians had fought themselves almost to the point of exhaustion along the entire Hochwald front, and German forces had no real option but to withdraw. The battle lines now moved onwards, inexorably, towards the banks of the Rhine.

15

RENDEZVOUS WITH THE AMERICANS

> You have broken through the Siegfried Line and drawn on to yourselves the bulk of the German reserves in the West. A strong U.S. offensive was launched over the Roer at 0330 hrs this morning against positions which thanks to your efforts are lightly held by the Germans. Our offensive has made the situation most favourable for our Allies and greatly increased their prospects of success. Thank you for what you have done so well. If we continue our efforts for a few more days the German front is bound to crack.
>
> General Horrocks to his troops,
> 23 February 1945[1]

While the Canadians were attempting their eastwards thrust through the Hochwald, General Horrocks' XXX Corps advanced in a southerly direction towards Geldern, where they planned to link up with Simpson's U.S. 9th Army. Once this junction with the Americans had been achieved, the entire focus of the advance shifted eastwards towards the key towns of Wesel, Alpen and Xanten, situated on the banks of the Rhine. There were a number of elements in this Horrocks-led thrust to the south and the east.

The 11th Armoured Division were nearest to the Canadians, and moved along the southern flank of the Hochwald area. To the south of the 11th Armoured were the British 3rd Division, and the Guards Armoured Division, who advanced towards Kervenheim, Winnekendonk and Bonninghardt. The most southerly element of the XXX Corps offensive to the south and east was made up of the 53rd Welsh Division, and the 52nd Lowland Division. The 1st Commando Brigade was also attached to 52 Division, and this particular formation advanced along the line Langstraat to Well, close to the flooded eastern banks of the Maas.

The 51st Highland Division's role in this renewed XXX Corps advance was brief, ending on 28 February when the division was withdrawn to train for Operation Plunder – the crossing of the Rhine. In the few days prior to their withdrawal, however, the Highlanders were given the significant task of clearing areas to the south-west of Goch which were still in enemy hands. These were essentially small-scale but still important tasks, necessary to ensure the security of the right flank of the intended XXX Corps sweep south and east towards Geldern, Xanten and Wesel. The villages still occupied by German forces included Mull, Hassum, Tarpauten, Gaesdonk and Groote Horst. In effect, a small German salient had been formed, and on 21 February the 3rd battalion of the Irish Guards, which formed part of the 32nd Guards Brigade, tried to neutralise at least one part of this salient by launching an attack on Haus Terpoten. The attack proved to be a costly failure, as the Irish Guards war diary of 21 February makes clear when it says the Guards were 'very heavily opposed and driven back by enemy many times their number'.[2] Irish Guards casualties were predictably high, with 138 guardsmen wounded, and thirty-seven killed, including two company commanders.

Thus, the 51st Division had no easy task when it was ordered to attack this small German salient during its last campaign operation, which took place over two nights, between 25 and

27 February, and involved the 152nd, 153rd and 154th Brigades. Basically, all three brigades were involved in clearing territory north and south of the Kendel Brook, which lay south-west of Goch. On the night of 25/26 February, 152 and 153 Brigades cleared areas north of the Brook with little problem. South of the Brook, however, things were rather different. The 2nd and 5th Seaforths, who were part of the 152nd Brigade, encountered some heavy opposition as they pushed forward. The 2nd Seaforths were unsuccessful in their initial attempts to seize strong German defensive positions at Blumenthalshof and decided to wait for artillery support before renewing their attacks on farm buildings in the area. Artillery fire was also used to soften up German targets in the hamlets of Jenkenshof and Haus Terpoten before infantry from the 2nd and 5th Seaforths moved forward to attack. The tactic obviously worked, because although the 2nd Seaforths encountered heavy small arms fire before they captured Jenkenshof early on the morning of 27 February, both Blumenthalshof and Haus Terpoten were deserted by the time the Seaforths arrived on the scene. Siebengewald was also ceded to the 5th Seaforths without any further fighting by an enemy seemingly intent on abandoning the area.

The 153rd Brigade had a more difficult task in capturing German positions in the small farming hamlets of Robbenhof and Angstforth. The 5th Black Watch attacked the hamlets late on 25 February, and had secured both by early on 26 February, but only at the cost of twelve killed and fourteen wounded. The hamlet of Robbenhof proved to be particularly difficult to subdue. A large German pill-box, disguised as part of a barn, was at the centre of Robbenhof's defences, and this particular obstacle was only overcome when a Black Watch sergeant, Frederick Maxey, took the sensible decision of bursting into the pill-box via its lightly guarded back door. Once inside, Maxey overcame all those nearby with judicious use of smoke grenades and a Sten gun. For this activity, and for capturing a nearby farmhouse occupied by enemy troops, the redoubtable sergeant received an immediate DCM. Three companies of the 7th Argylls, along with the 1st Black Watch, also crossed the Kendel during the night of 25/26 February as part of the division's 154th Brigade. Despite encountering some light small-arms fire and heavy mortaring during their advance, the small farming villages of Hulm and Winkel were captured with considerable speed. The assembled Highlanders were then asked to capture the additional villages of Boyenhoff and Kerkenhoff during the night of 26/27 February. These additional objectives were taken by the Argylls and the Black Watch during the early hours of 27 February, but only after some heavy fighting. During these last actions at or around the Kendel Brook, between 25 and 27 February, forty men from the 154th Brigade were listed as killed, wounded or missing.

Following the battles at the Kendel Brook, the Highland Division as a whole remained in the Reichswald area until 6 March. Although the 51st was no longer in the front line, it still had one significant duty to perform, because on 4 March, Winston Churchill visited the battlefields of the Reichswald, and as part of his visit he stopped off at the division's headquarters at Kloster Graefenthal. Churchill's visit began at the Reichswald Forest, where the campaign began, though fear of mines and unexploded ordnance somewhat restricted the Prime Minister's movements. Prior to Churchill's arrival, dogs and handlers from the Mine Platoon of the Royal Engineers were deployed to hunt for undetected mines in the forest. Lieutenant Peter Norbury and his black Labrador sniffer dog Rex were one of the principal teams used during this exercise. Norbury and Rex had already saved many lives by detecting forest mines planted by the Germans, but no further devices were detected to impede Churchill's visit. After the war ended, Rex was awarded the Dickin Medal for animal bravery for his life-saving activities, but sadly this was a posthumous honour. Rex was a rescue dog with no registered owner back in the UK and, as a consequence, the Ministry of War ordered that the mine-detecting, life-saving dog be destroyed. Many other 'ownerless' dogs, among the 3,300 dogs of war used by the British during the Second World War, were also treated in a similar fashion. This was certainly one of officialdom's more callous, thoughtless acts, reminiscent of Britain's poor treatment of horses on the Western Front after the end of the First World War, when large numbers were destroyed once they were deemed to be of no further use. Reichswald Rex, however, was never forgotten by his former handler, Peter Norbury. In 2016, the elderly former Royal Engineer brought Rex's case to public attention, and the dog was posthumously recommended for that year's *Daily Mirror* Animal Hero Award.[3]

After Churchill's somewhat restricted visit to the Reichswald Forest, he and his VIP party progressed rapidly via Materborn, Goch, Asperden, Hekkens and Gennep to the 51st Division's Kloster Graefenthal headquarters. Here, the Prime Minister and his VIP entourage, which included Sir Alan Brooke, the Chief of the Imperial General Staff, Crerar and Montgomery, listened to the massed pipes and drums of the Highland Division and the 79th Medium Regiment, Royal Artillery. Churchill, ever a sentimentalist, seemed to be visibly moved by the stirring sounds. Many of the Highlanders involved in the last few weeks' fighting were at the afternoon event at Kloster Graefenthal, and with typical military efficiency and discipline the 51st Highland Division Headquarters ordered that 'troops on this route not attending pipes and drums will line roads and cheer'.[4]

Once Churchill had gone, the 51st Division could intensify its training and preparations for crossing the Rhine. In the meantime, the 52nd Lowland Division took over the 51st's sector and advanced eastwards as part of XXX Corps' great push to link up with Simpson's U.S. 9th Army. Once the 51st Highlanders had removed the annoying German salient around the Kendel Brook, and the 52nd Lowlanders were in place, Horrocks' XXX Corps could advance southwards with its

Above: Allied commanders at Maastricht discussing the response to the German Ardennes Offensive, December 1944. From left to right: Omar Bradley, Commander of the U. S. 12th Army Group; Arthur Tedder, Deputy Supreme Commander of SHAEF; Dwight Eisenhower, Supreme Commander of SHAEF; Bernard Montgomery, Commander of the 21st Army Group; William Hood Simpson, Commander of the U. S. 9th Army. (Courtesy of Regionnal Historisch Centrum, Limburg)

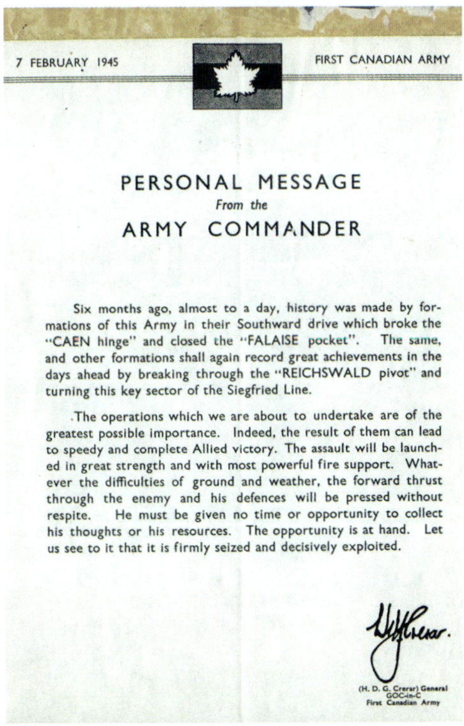

7 FEBRUARY 1945 FIRST CANADIAN ARMY

PERSONAL MESSAGE
From the
ARMY COMMANDER

Six months ago, almost to a day, history was made by formations of this Army in their Southward drive which broke the "CAEN hinge" and closed the "FALAISE pocket". The same, and other formations shall again record great achievements in the days ahead by breaking through the "REICHSWALD pivot" and turning this key sector of the Siegfried Line.

The operations which we are about to undertake are of the greatest possible importance. Indeed, the result of them can lead to speedy and complete Allied victory. The assault will be launched in great strength and with most powerful fire support. Whatever the difficulties of ground and weather, the forward thrust through the enemy and his defences will be pressed without respite. He must be given no time or opportunity to collect his thoughts or his resources. The opportunity is at hand. Let us see to it that it is firmly seized and decisively exploited.

H.D.G. Crerar.

(H. D. G. Crerar) General
GOC-in-C
First Canadian Army

Right: General Crerar's message issued to all Allied troops in the First Canadian Army on 7 February 1945. With its references to the forthcoming offensive being 'pressed without respite', the message set the tone for the entire campaign. (Courtesy of the Canadian War Museum, Ottawa)

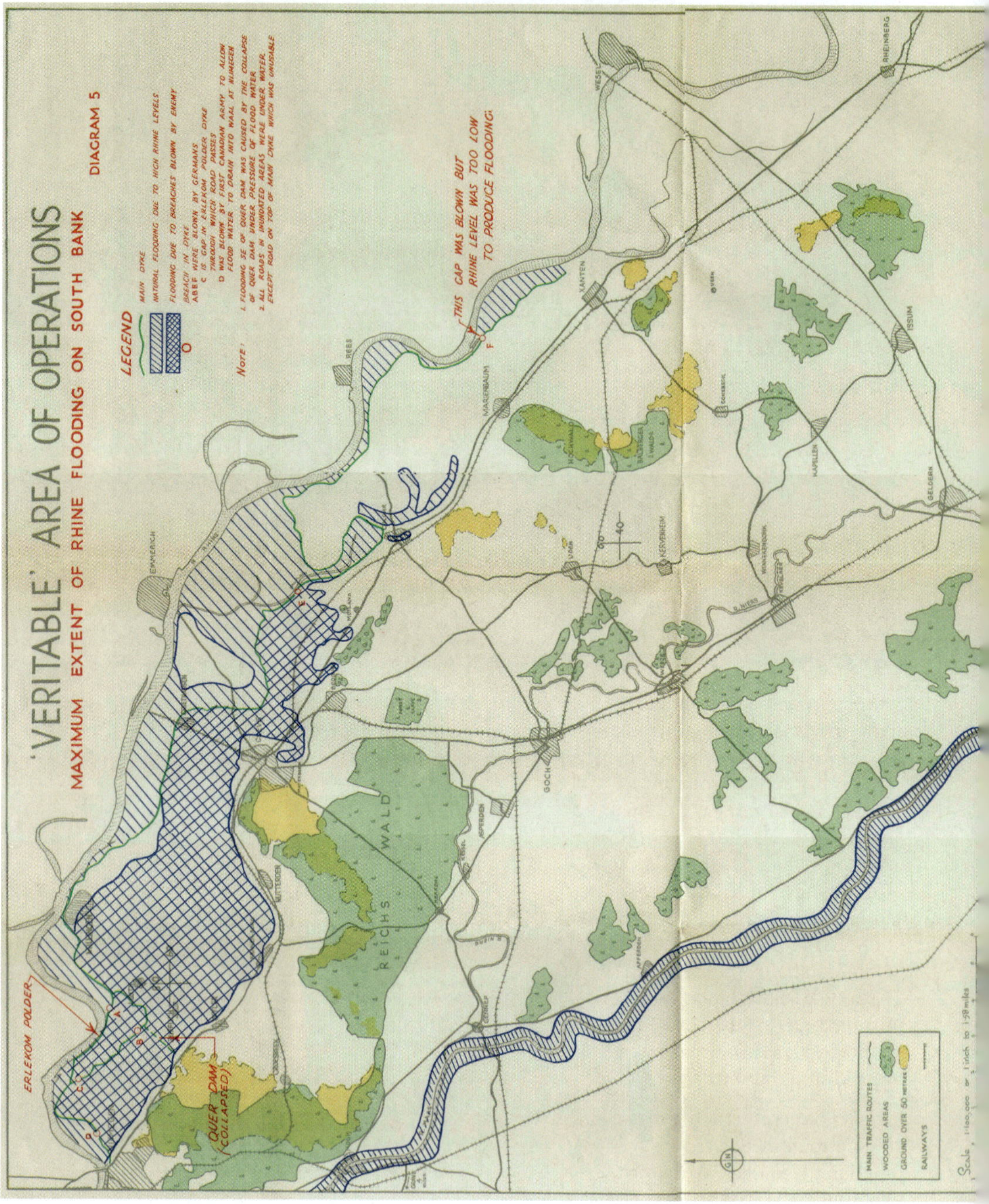

Operation Veritable area of operations: the extent of flooding. Compiled by G. Ops. 21st Army Group, February 1945.

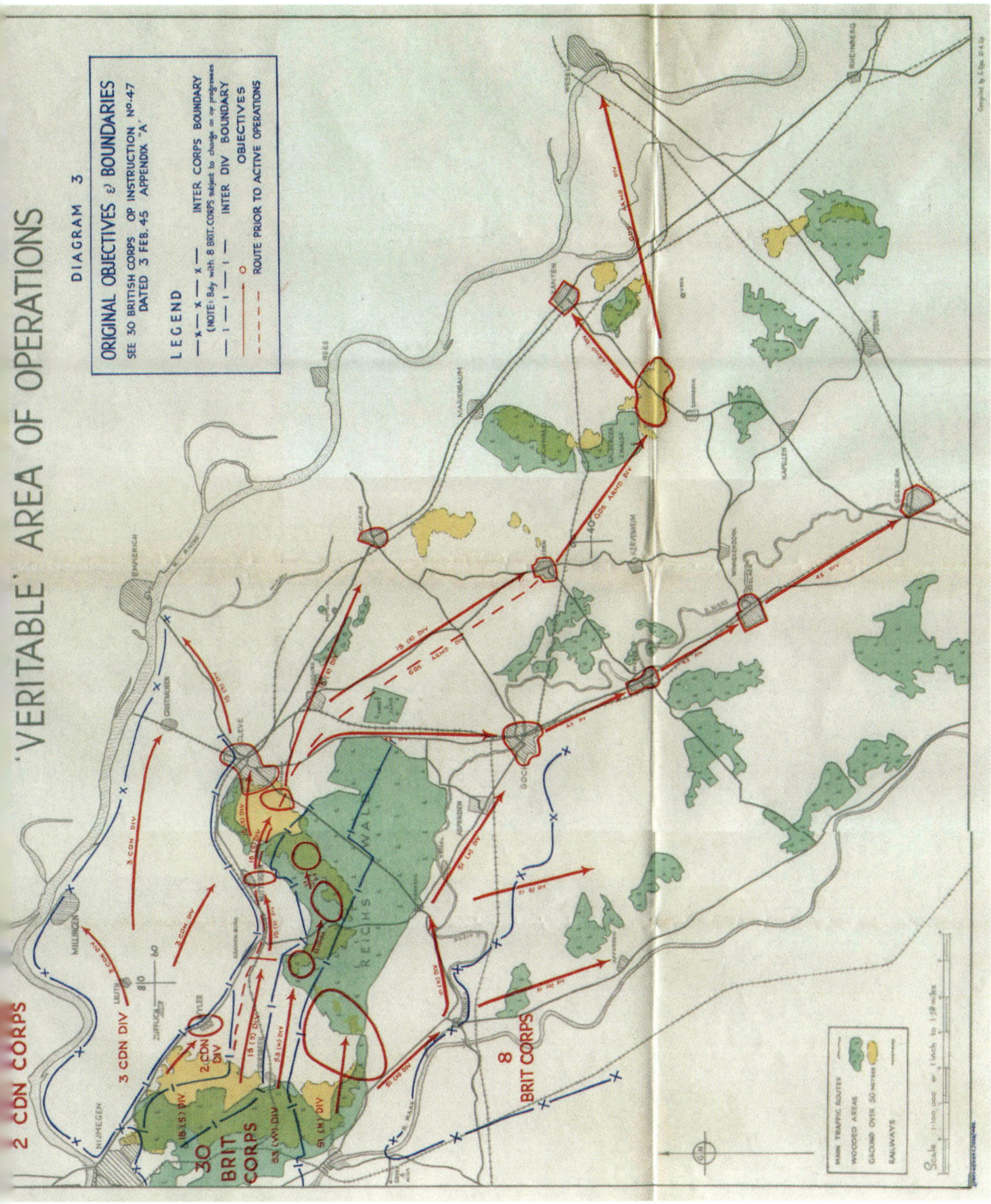

Operation Veritable: original objectives. Compiled by G. Ops. 21st Army Group, February 1945.

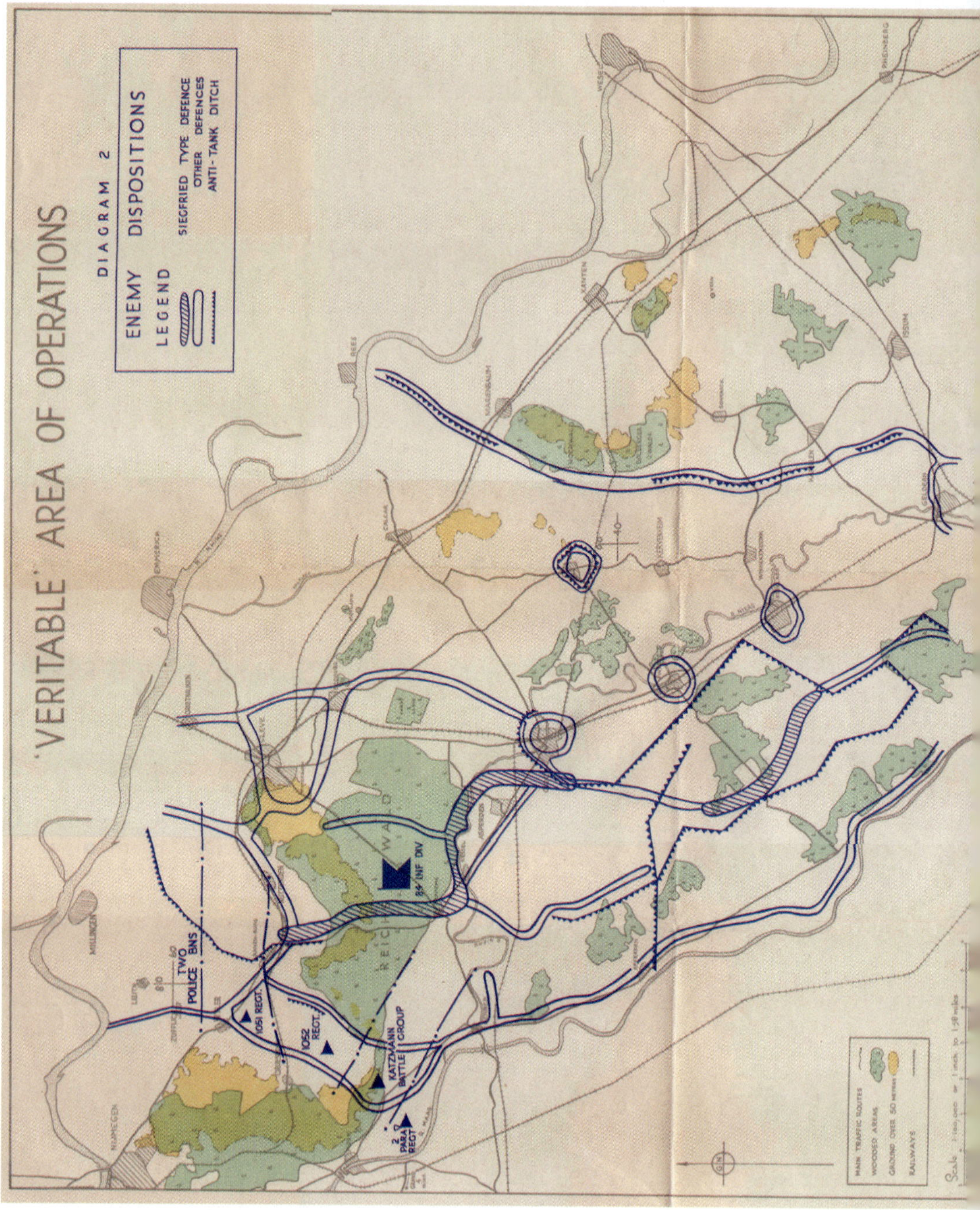

Plan of enemy dispositions, 8 February 1945. Compiled by G. Ops. 21st Army Group, February 1945.

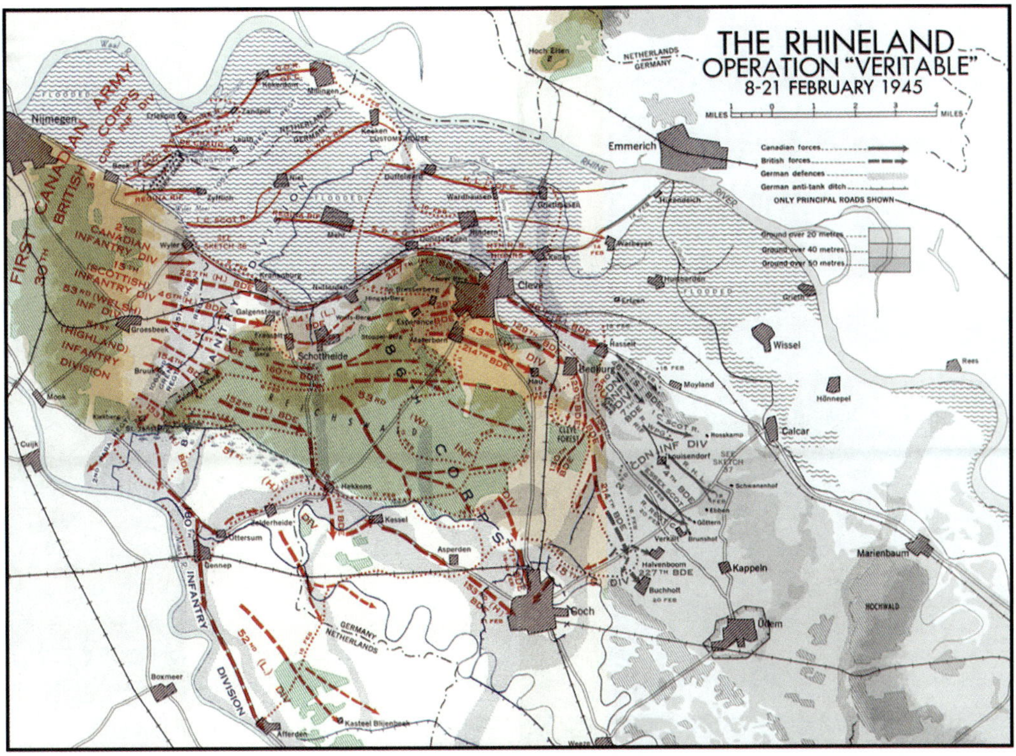

Operation Veritable, 8–21 February 1945. (Courtesy of Paul Klinkenberg)

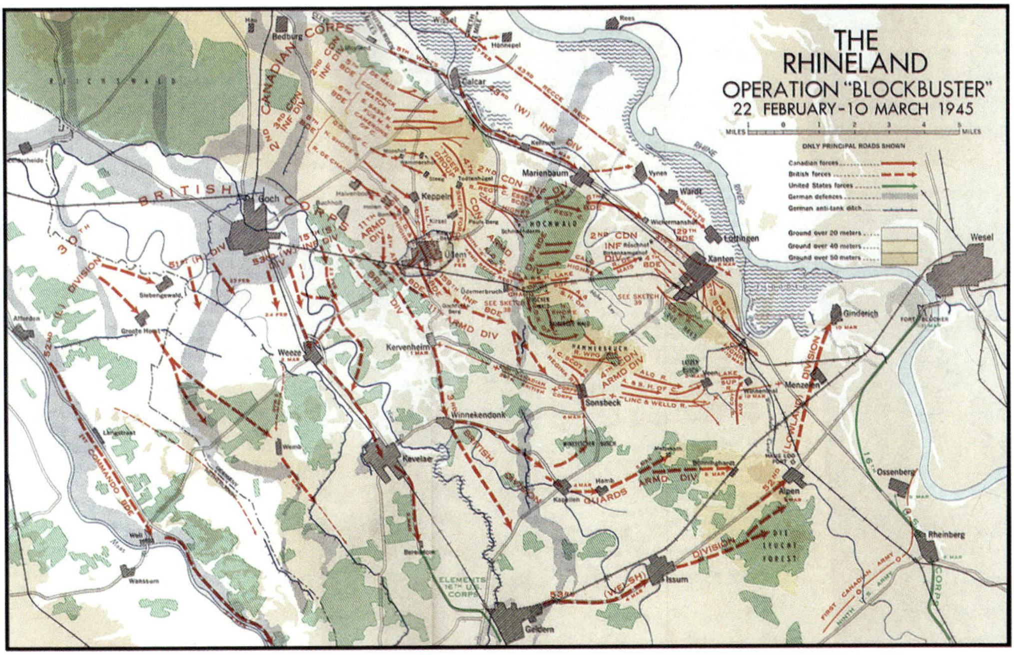

Operation Blockbuster, 22 February–10 March 1945. (Courtesy of Paul Klinkenberg)

Above: A British column of Churchill tanks moving along a surfaced road on the opening day of Operation Veritable, 8 February 1945. Such roads – not covered by flood water and mud – were a rarity during the course of the campaign. (No. 5 Army Film & Photographic Unit, 1945)

Left: British troops advancing through the Reichswald early in the campaign. Fighting in the forest proved to be a brutal affair of ambushes and hand-to-hand combat. (Courtesy of the Canadian War Museum, Ottawa)

Abandoned British Valentine tank in Kranenburg, north of the Reichswald. The extent of flooding in the area can be clearly seen. (Courtesy of the National Army Museum, London)

Amphibious vehicles, led by a Weasel, move through flooded Kranenburg, February 1945. (Courtesy of the National Army Museum, London)

Modern reminders of the fighting in 1945. This tree bark, with burn marks and pieces of shrapnel embedded in the wood, was removed from the Reichswald in recent times. Unexploded ordnance from the period of the 1945 campaign can still be found in the forest. (Courtesy of the Freedom Museum, Groesbeek, the Netherlands)

Post-war image of the remains of a German defensive position in the Reichswald. (Courtesy of the Freedom Museum, Groesbeek, the Netherlands)

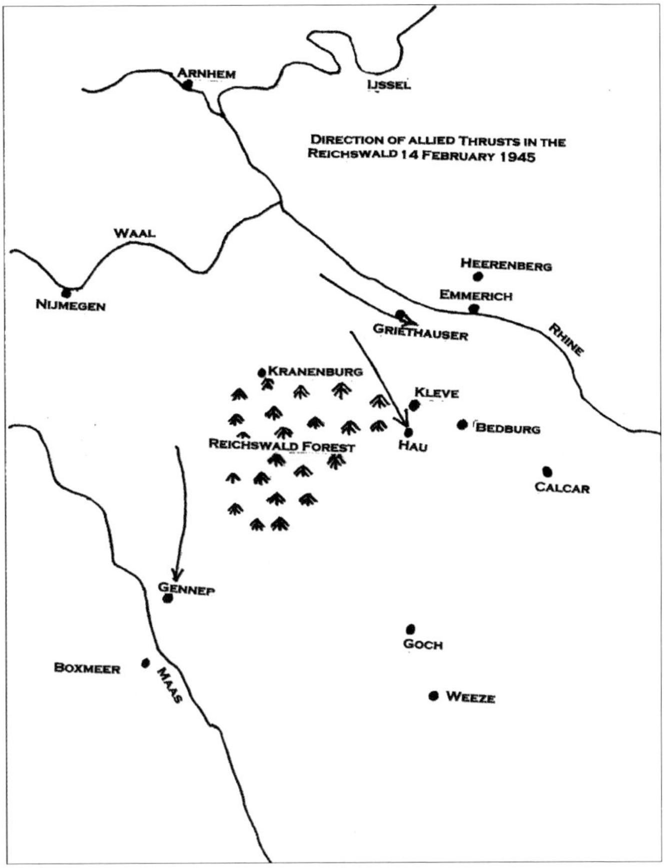

Right: Allied thrusts in and around the Reichswald on 14 February 1945.

Below: British Sherman tanks negotiating floods in Kleve, 11 February 1945. (Courtesy of the National Army Museum, London)

British Churchill tanks in a central Kleve street, February 1945. (No. 5 Army & Photographic Unit)

British armour in central Goch, February 1945. (Courtesy of the British War Museums Collection)

Above: British tanks advance through the rubble of Udem on 28 February 1945. (Courtesy of the National Army Museum, London)

Below: The remains of Castle Blijenbeek, which was the scene of heavy fighting between elements of the 52nd Lowland Division and German paratroopers during Operation Veritable. (Courtesy of Kastelbeer, 2010)

Spitfires on a forward airstrip near Schijndel in the Netherlands, 1945. (Courtesy of the Dutch National Archives)

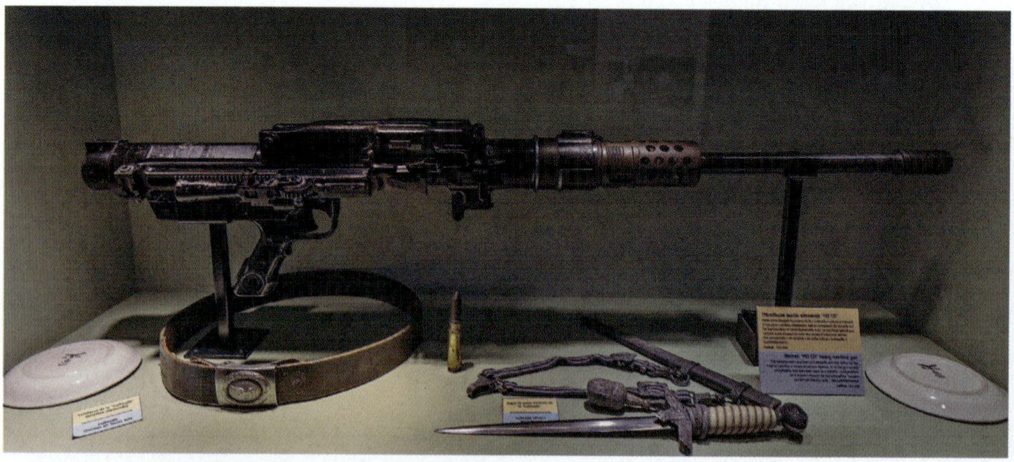

German Second World War MG131 Spandau machine gun. (Courtesy of Falcon [R] Photography)

An M-29C Second World War Water Weasel. (Courtesy of Bz6568)

A 21cm German Nebelwerfer (left) and a British-devised Land Mattrass multiple-rocket launcher (right). The loud screaming noise of incoming Nebelwerfer rockets led to Allied soldiers nicknaming the missiles 'Moaning Minnies'. The Land Mattrass was used in action by British and Canadian troops from summer 1944 onwards. (Courtesy of Mzajac – Canadian War Museum, Ottawa)

Above: German soldiers, captured by the 53rd Welsh Division during Operation Veritable, make their way to POW camps. (Courtesy of the Canadian War Museum, Ottawa)

Left: Major Ronald Balfour, King's Royal Rifle Corps and Monuments Man, attached to the First Canadian Army. (Courtesy of King's College Cambridge Archives Centre)

Right: The pre-war Goch Steintor, saved from complete destruction by the efforts of Major Balfour (as photographed by Erwin Quedenfeldt, 1869–1948).

Below: The Kleve Stiftskirche (St Maria Himmelfahrt). The original Stiftskirche was constructed between 1341 and 1426, but it was destroyed in a matter of hours by the RAF during February 1945. Major Balfour was killed as he tried to rescue medieval wooden carvings from inside the ruined church, hit by a random long-range shell fired by Germans on the last full day of Operation Veritable – 10 March 1945. Subsequently, the church was restored, with historically accurate towers, during the course of a twenty-four-year project, between 1945 and 1969. (Courtesy of Salander 177)

Top: The devastated town of Wesel in March 1945. A few walls were still standing, along with the gutted shell of a church, but virtually everything else was obliterated by Allied bombing. (Courtesy of the National Museum of the U. S. Air Force)

Above: Ruins of the Wesel railway bridge, blown up on 10 March 1945 by the Germans. The bridge was never rebuilt. (Courtesy of Daniel Ullrich, 2005)

Left: Situated in the middle of the forest, the Reichswald military cemetery is the largest Commonwealth War Graves Commission military cemetery of the Second World War in Germany, containing the graves of many of those killed during Operation Veritable.

right flank fully secure. On the left flank, however, German resistance in the town of Sonsbeck, just south of the Hochwald, remained a problem. The 11th Armoured Division had been trying to break through the Hochwald Layback and capture high ground north of Sonsbeck since 27 February. Formations of the 11th Armoured Division's 159th Infantry Brigade, including the 3rd Battalion of the Monmouthshire Regiment, finally broke through these defences on 2 March, after heavy fighting, and were able to occupy this northern high ground overlooking Sonsbeck. The losses incurred in gaining this strategic spot were so severe that individual companies of the 3rd Monmouths had to be merged before the battalion was moved out of the Hochwald Layback on 5 March and ordered to advance on Sonsbeck itself. By the end of 5 March, German resistance in parts of Sonsbeck was still very determined. Shell craters and well-defended pill-boxes made the western approaches to the town very difficult to penetrate. However, on the morning of 6 March, the 7th Canadian Brigade attacked Sonsbeck from the north and the Regina Rifles Regiment pushed through and captured the town with surprising ease.

Sonsbeck had been a thorn in the side of the Allied advance for some time, but by the end of 6 March the town was entirely in the hands of the First Canadian Army. In any event, the problem of Sonsbeck on the left flank wasn't allowed to impede the advance of XXX Corps to the south. In effect, the town was bypassed by British formations as they flooded south to effect a junction with the U.S. 9th Army. The nature and scale of the fighting experienced by British divisions during this final push to the south and east differed enormously. In some parts of this once prosperous part of the Rhineland, there was no resistance at all. After the savage fighting at Weeze, the 8th Armoured Brigade set off towards the town of Kevelaer in hot pursuit of the retreating Germans. Tanks entered Kevelaer unopposed early on the morning of 3 March, and 8th Armoured Brigade soldiers observed that 'Kevelaer was the first town to be entered in Germany which was not a complete ruin'.[5] From the west, the 52nd Division also advanced, initially at least, without encountering much in the way of German resistance. The 6th Cameronians, for example, seized Wemb, south-west of Weeze, on 3 March without encountering any German opposition. However, the village wasn't captured without incident or casualties. The 6th Cameronians' commanding officer, and all its company commanders, set off to reconnoitre the route to Wemb in a jeep and hit a recently planted German roadside mine. Two of the jeep's occupants were killed instantly and the CO was badly wounded before the battalion's second-in-command led an unopposed entry into the small town.

As the 53rd Welsh Division moved progressively nearer to Geldern, on the banks of the Niers, and the 1st Commando Brigade pushed eastwards on the extreme right flank of the British advance, German resistance quickly evaporated. This was unsurprising; with the Americans advancing northwards with considerable momentum, German forces positioned to the west of Geldern were likely to be trapped in a British-American pincer movement unless they pulled out rapidly towards the Rhine. The first contact between advancing British forces and the U.S. 9th Army occurred on the afternoon of 3 March at Berendonk, a small hamlet 3 miles north-west of Geldern. Here, tanks of the 4/7th Royal Dragoon Guards, supported by B Company of the 12th King's Royal Rifle Corps, exchanged fire with unknown tanks located just to the south of Berendonk. It was soon ascertained that these 'unknown tanks' were actually from the U.S. 16th Corps, and firing was halted immediately. Thankfully, no casualties were caused by this 'friendly' fire incident, and both sides went on to exchange warmer greetings to celebrate the point at which Operations Veritable, Blockbuster and Grenade finally became one. Subsequently, British infantry and armoured units linked with American forces at various times and locations, dependent on their particular axes of advance. On the right flank of the

XXX Corps advance, patrols of the 1st Commando Brigade entered Langstraat on 2 March and Well on 3 March. On the 4th, meanwhile, the commandos met up with soldiers of the U.S. 17th Cavalry Reconnaissance Squadron at Walbeck. Other British and U.S. military formations met up for the first time right at the end of the Veritable/Grenade campaigns, on 10/11 March. The 6th Cameronians, for instance, took over from American forces garrisoning Fort Blucher, on the banks of the Rhine, on 11 March.

Although XXX Corps forces sped through towns like Wemb and Kevelaer without opposition, in other instances the Germans offered stubborn and determined resistance. In particular, the small towns of Kervenheim and Winnekendonk, both to the north-west of Geldern, were defended with great tenacity by German forces. Both small towns lay in the path of the 3rd Division's advance towards the Rhine, and during the early hours of 28 February, three of the division's infantry battalions were given the task of assaulting Kervenheim. The 1st Battalion of the Royal Norfolk Regiment, the 2nd Battalion of the King's Shropshire Light Infantry (KSLI) and the 2nd Battalion of the Lincolnshire Regiment were all part of the division's 185th Brigade, and together they attempted to storm the small town, aided by three squadrons of tanks from the 6th Guards Tank Brigade. Accurate German machine gun fire made it almost impossible for the infantry to break into the town, and at dusk both tanks and infantry were withdrawn, ready for a fresh attack early on 1 March. At first light on 1 March, all three battalions moved forward with the aim of breaking into the town from the north. Churchill flame-throwing Crocodile tanks of the 4th Coldstream Guards were used to support the 1st Norfolks, and 2nd Lincolnshire infantry advanced in open order behind the 2nd KSLI, crossing fields towards Kervenheim. At first, all seemed to go well with the attack, but fighting increased in intensity as the day wore on and torrential rain certainly hampered the assault. As the

2nd Lincolns war diary recorded on 1 March, 'These operations were carried out in very bad weather, rain turning the ground into a quagmire, making movement on foot and by vehicle, both wheeled and tracked, very difficult.'[6] Nevertheless, British tanks and infantry continued to attack, despite mounting casualties, in order to gain a foothold in the town.

The advance of the KSLI towards Kervenheim was held up by intense rifle and machine gun fire from a fortified farm building, and it was at this point that Private James Stokes, a tough thirty-year-old Glaswegian ex-labourer, took matters into his own hands and attacked the German position on his own. Dodging a hail of bullets, Stokes stormed into the building and killed or captured everyone inside. He later emerged with twelve prisoners and, despite a severe neck wound, rejoined his platoon and indulged in more heroics shortly afterwards, when he single-handedly stormed another German position and captured yet more prisoners. Stokes was shot again during this second attack but still refused all aid, and moved well ahead of his KSLI comrades as they advanced towards the battalion's final objective, which was a German strongpoint formed from a series of deserted farm buildings. Again, without orders, James Stokes ran for 40 yards through a storm of machine gun fire towards the final German strongpoint, before being brought down by gunfire some 20 yards short of his objective. The rest of the battalion then moved ahead of Stokes and captured the strongpoint. The courageous Glaswegian died at the scene of his stupendous martial exploits, and he was later found to have been wounded at least eight times in the upper part of his body. The actions of James Stokes certainly saved the lives of several comrades in the KSLI, and he became the posthumous recipient of one of the very last Victoria Crosses awarded to a British soldier 'for valour' during the course of the Second World War in Europe.[7]

While the KSLI were assailing German strongpoints in one part of the Kervenheim battlefield, the Norfolks and Lincolns were still attempting to break into the northern parts of the strongly fortified small town. Finally, the Norfolks, supported by one company from the 2nd Lincolns, managed to secure ground in a factory area at the north end of the village, and the same infantry also dug in astride the main road leading from Kervenheim to Udem. These gains proved to be the key turning point in the battle for Kervenheim, because on the following morning two companies of the Lincolns used their new positions on the main road, and in the factory area, as a springboard to capture the rest of the town. At 0300 hours on 2 March, the surviving men of the 2nd Lincolns received their reward for slipping, sliding and fighting through the mud and rain of the previous day. As the battalion's war diary records with some delight, 'Most welcome hot meal and rum ration issued to companies, which warmed many a chilled body.'[8] By 1400 on 2 March, Kervenheim was very firmly in the hands of infantry and armour from Britain's 3rd Division.

The hot meal was particularly helpful to the drenched and frozen soldiers of the 2nd Lincolnshires, because later on the same day they were fighting another tough battle against German forces in Winnekendonk, which was just a couple of miles to the south of Kervenheim. Winnekendonk's defences were organised with some precision by soldiers of the 7th German Parachute Regiment, aided by a mixed bag of support troops including Luftwaffe armourers who had at their disposal a range of anti-tank artillery pieces. The 2nd Lincolnshires launched an assault on these defences at 1745 on 2 March. The attack itself was planned with some haste, and was one of a number of rather impromptu military advances launched during the overall Reichswald campaign – by both British and Canadian commanders – where momentum and 'pressing on' were seen to be key requirements. At least one or two of the battalion's senior officers, including the vastly experienced Major P. H. W. Clarke MC, probably had some reservations about the speed of the Lincolnshires' advance, but they nevertheless went on to lead their men with pluck and determination.

The 2nd Lincolnshires approached Winnekendonk from the north-east, along the Hestert road. Approximately 400 men from the battalion were involved in this advance, along both sides of the Hestert road, supported by fifteen Churchill tanks. The advancing soldiers soon came under heavy fire from well-entrenched German paratroopers, and in the ensuing battle both sides suffered heavy casualties. Eduard Winkler was a twenty-four-year-old specialist Luftwaffe armourer who fought with a unit of anti-tank gunners positioned in a root cellar at the junction of the Hestert road outside Winnekendonk. Once battle commenced, Winkler surrendered with some alacrity and was shipped to Britain as a POW. He returned briefly to Germany for a visit but managed to forge a successful career for himself in the British aviation industry, and became a British citizen in 1954. While Winkler surrendered on one side of the Hestert road, during the battle for Winnekendonk, Major Peter Clarke advanced with his men from the 2nd Lincolnshires on the other side of the road. The fickle fortunes of war were far less kind to Clarke, who was killed instantly by a mortar explosion at roughly the same time as Winkler surrendered. Peter Clarke was one of the most experienced officers in the entire regiment. He'd been an officer in the Lincolnshire Regiment since late 1939, and had already been seriously wounded on two occasions: He'd been hit by German shrapnel on D-Day, and was wounded in the face by a booby trap while crossing the Escaut Canal in September 1944. Clarke was later awarded the Military Cross for his actions at the Escaut Canal, and he was allowed home to England to recuperate from his various wounds. During his convalescence, he apparently wrote in the flyleaf of his personal books the comment 'PHW Clarke, KIA (Killed in Action) 1945'. The vastly experienced major possibly thought his luck was bound to run out sooner or later, and so it proved to be. He was just twenty-three years old when he was killed on the Hestert road, Winnekendonk, on 2 March 1945.[9]

The small town of Winnekendonk was occupied successfully that evening, but at a heavy cost. Eighty men were wounded and twenty-two were killed, and the survivors went on to endure an uncomfortable night under constant enemy artillery bombardment. Tanks from the 6th Guards Armoured Brigade supported the infantry during the assault on Winnekendonk, and they too experienced considerable problems. The leading wave of tanks, from the 3rd Tank Battalion, Scots Guards, were all destroyed as they trundled into the town. A second troop of tanks led by Lieutenant Robert Runcie, who later became Bishop of St Albans and Archbishop of Canterbury, then attacked. Under Runcie's command, two 75mm guns and one 88mm gun were destroyed and the enemy's entire stock of 50mm guns was captured. Runcie then went on to personally direct British artillery fire on to areas holding up the 3rd Division's infantry and armoured assault, and he did all this under heavy shell and mortar fire. Young Lieutenant Runcie's actions earned him an immediate Military Cross, and certainly helped ensure the ultimate success of the attack on Winnekendonk.[10] On 3 March, A Company of the 2nd Lincolns went through the area clearing up isolated pockets of resistance, and by midday some semblance of peace had returned to the quiet backwaters of Winnekendonk.

South of Winnekendonk, three battalions of infantry from the Welsh Division's 158th Infantry Brigade were also installed in the moated town of Gelden by the end of 3 March. Although over 80 per cent of the town had been destroyed by shelling, enough housing survived for Gelden to later become a divisional HQ for the Welsh Division.[11] By 4 March, the German military presence west of Gelden had been removed entirely, and Horrocks' XXX Corps could now concentrate on swinging eastwards and reaching the banks of the Rhine. Unsurprisingly, German military resistance to this British push to the Rhine stiffened considerably. Under the able direction of General Alfred Schlemm, German forces established a range of defences around the bridges on the western side of the Rhine, which lay directly opposite the port town of Wesel, situated on the eastern bank of the river. This so-called 'Wesel Pocket' was established to allow German troops and equipment enough time and space to pull back to the eastern side of the Rhine, and the Pocket presented a serious problem to U.S. and British forces seeking to trap German armies on the western side of the Rhine. However, there was far more to this German defensive strategy than just the Wesel Pocket. German strategy proved to be extremely flexible, and involved the ceding of territory in some areas, combined with stubborn resistance and counter-attacks in others. Blown bridges, mines and cratered roads also delayed the advance of the Allies.

On the 53rd Division's sector of the XXX Corps front, a squadron of Sherwood Rangers Yeomanry tanks, along with a battalion of the Oxfordshire & Buckinghamshire Light Infantry, advanced from Gelden to Issum during the course of 4 March. By midday, troops had entered Issum with no German opposition at all, and on 5 March the 1st Oxfords were ordered to advance further east. Here, east of Issum, the 1st Oxfords began to encounter German resistance. Battalions from the 71st Brigade's Highland Light Infantry (HLI) and Royal Welsh Fusiliers (RWF) were then rushed ahead of the 1st Oxfords, and a larger battle ensued. The Highlanders and Fusiliers had to cope with heavy German shelling and mortar fire, along with extremely accurate bursts of fire from well-placed Spandau machine guns. The Germans counter-attacked during the evening, and the Highlanders were pushed back towards Issum. The situation on this sector of the front was only stabilised with some difficulty and, eventually, some 200 German prisoners were taken. As the 53rd Division war diarist recorded on the evening of 5 March, 'It was now obvious that the enemy was determined to hold on to the Wesel bridgehead at all costs.' Defence of the Wesel Pocket was clearly elastic enough to involve fighting for territory just east of Issum. Fighting continued the following day, when the

4th Battalion of the Welch Regiment advanced eastwards into the Die Lieucht forest. The battalion was met by extremely heavy shelling and mortar fire, and had to repulse one German counter-attack through the forest. By this stage, the 53rd Welsh Division had been fighting battle after battle for over a month, through the centre of the Reichswald Forest and the bloody environs of Weeze, and had suffered thousands of casualties. However, its active campaigning came to an end after the fighting in the Die Lieucht forest, and over a staggered period of two days, the 53rd's sector of the Allied front line was taken over by the 52nd Lowland Division.

To the north of the 53rd Division, the Guards Armoured Division was playing a belated but significant role in XXX Corps' final push eastwards towards the Rhine. The division had been held in reserve for much of the Reichswald campaign, largely because of the rain, mud and flooding, which made rapid armoured movements unrealistic. They were, however, let loose during the final stages of the campaign, in order to clear German positions between Kapellen and the village of Bonninghardt, which lay some 9 miles south-west of the Wesel Pocket. The town of Kapellen was occupied by forces from the 3rd Division without any opposition. Nevertheless, Guards tanks had some difficulty in moving from the south-west to Kapellen because of the German demolition of a bridge over the River Fleuth. Tanks from the 2nd Battalion of the Irish Guards had to take an alternative north-western route to Kapellen, via Winnekendonk, and they arrived without incident on 5 March. By this time, troops from the 3rd Division's Royal Norfolk Regiment were already pushing forward into the wooded area of the Winhelscher Busch, to the north of Kapellen, so the Irish Guards could advance to the village of Hamb with their northern flank secure. Irish Guards tanks and infantry arrived in the centre of Hamb without any problems. However, once the leading squadron had stopped and disembarked, German mortar rounds began to land in and around the village. Heavier German artillery shells then landed in the village, and an enemy self-propelled gun opened up, at point-blank range, on Irish Guards tanks. One tank exploded immediately when hit, blocking access into Hamb. After this a 'Moaning Minnie' salvo from a German Nebelwerfer missile launcher landed right in the middle of No. 1 Squadron of the Irish Guards, who were located in the very centre of Hamb. One tank was obliterated with its crew inside, and nearby infantry also became casualties. Despite these localised military reversals, the Irish Guards were soon in control of Hamb, though some German resistance lingered in the woods to the north.

While the Irish Guards were fighting to gain control of Hamb, the 5th Battalion of the Coldstream Guards were ordered to attack Metzekath, which lay a short distance to the north-east of Hamb. The Coldstream attack was launched during the early evening of 5 March, and received support from five field batteries and three medium batteries of artillery. Unfortunately, some of the shells fired by these batteries landed on Guards infantry and tanks as they assembled on their start lines for the attack, but despite these initial setbacks, the overall operation was a notable success. German paratroopers from the 22nd Parachute Regiment put up a tenacious resistance in many of the farm buildings dotted around Metzekath, using bazookas, 88mm guns, and at least one French-made anti-tank gun, but the 5th Coldstreams still crushed all opposition within two hours, and captured well over 100 prisoners.

On 6 March, the 1st Welsh Guards, 2nd Scots Guards and 2nd Irish Guards were all employed in an assault on the village of Bonninghardt. Irish Guards tanks launched what was described in the battalion war diary as a 'limited advance' towards the village in which, ultimately, nine tanks were lost.[12] Elsewhere, the Welsh and Scots Guards had an easier time clearing the wooded areas around Bonninghardt, though the village itself was only captured by the Guards Division after some heavy fighting which lasted until the evening of 7 March. Even then, some German shelling continued, directed by artillery spotters based somewhat precariously on chimney tops in the nearby village of Menzelen. Once the fighting at Bonninghardt had died down, many in the Guards Armoured Division would have expected to take part in an advance along the Bonninghardt plateau towards the Wesel Pocket and the Rhine. Such a Guards advance failed to take place, however, because on 9 March the whole division was withdrawn to rest and refit, in preparation for the imminent operation to cross the Rhine. The Guards Armoured Division's role in Operations Veritable and Blockbuster was at an end, and the very last battles in the campaign were destined to be fought by the men of the 52nd Lowland Division.

16

XANTEN AND THE WESEL POCKET

> Ninety-eight per cent of the historic city [Xanten] was destroyed as the Germans fought savagely to maintain their last foothold on the west bank [of the Rhine]. The German paratroopers fought with such tenacity that when the battle finally wound down, Brigadier Joe Vandeleur, commander of the 129th Brigade, saluted the German survivors as they were marched away to POW cages.
>
> Whitaker, D. & Whitaker, S., *Rhineland: The Battle to End the War*

By the end of the first week in March 1945, there were approximately 6,000 German troops in the so-called Wesel Pocket, acting as a rearguard which allowed Germany's battered forces to cross to the eastern banks of the Rhine. General Alfred Schlemm, commander of the German First Parachute Army, had ultimate control over nine bridges that crossed the Rhine, but the key crossings were at or near the large town of Wesel, and included a road bridge and the massive 1,950-metre Wesel railway bridge, built during the 1870s as part of the Haltern–Venlo railway line. The port town of Wesel, situated at the confluence of the Rhine and the Lippe, was of huge strategic significance in Schlemm's defensive bridgehead: supplies and troops could be funnelled back across the road and rail bridge, and ferries could also be utilised. By the onset of the Second World War, Wesel was already a significant port town of over 24,000 inhabitants, situated predominantly on the eastern bank of the Rhine, though its economic influence, along with a few outlying suburbs, had already extended to the Rhine's west bank. On the western side of the Rhine, numerous foreshore bridge extensions were attached to the main rail bridge, which could all be used as defensive strongpoints by German troops. The nearby Fort Blucher, built in Napoleonic times and named after the Prussian general who did much to bring about Napoleon's defeat at Waterloo, was another defensive strongpoint, manned by 200 German soldiers at the beginning of March 1945. Additional military fortifications were also built on the west bank of the Rhine, opposite Wesel, such as the rather unimaginatively named Fort 1, which had to be neutralised by advancing First Canadian or American armies before the German bridgehead could be closed.

The town of Xanten, situated just a few miles to the north-west of Wesel, had been of economic and political significance since Roman times, and was the other great bastion of Schlemm's defensive bridgehead, designed to fend off the British and Canadians long enough to allow as many German troops as possible to escape across the Rhine. Of course, there was much more to the German bridgehead than just Xanten and the Wesel Pocket. The Germans created a flexible defensive perimeter line which extended north of Xanten to include the small towns of Wardt, Vynan and Luttingen, and southwards to the monastery of Winninthal, and settlements at Veen and Alpen. Allied armies had to surmount all these strongpoints before they could finally reach the western banks of the Rhine and eradicate the bridgehead established by Schlemm's retreating forces.

During the first week of March 1945, Montgomery and others in the Allied High Command structure still thought it might be possible to use Simpson's 9th U.S. Army, and the 52nd Lowland Division, as part of a northbound pincer movement which could cut off German armies from their exit routes across the Rhine. For this purpose, the U.S. 16th Corps was placed under Crerar's command, and the Americans certainly made rapid progress in their advance northwards. On 2 March, elements of the U.S. 9th Army entered Venlo without opposition, and by the evening of 7 March the Americans had entered Millingen and Ossenberg. Even so, this was a much smaller pincer movement than the grand envelopment planned at the start of Operation Veritable, and it still required converging attacks from the British and Canadians in the north and east. As the converging British, Canadian and American armies moved closer to the bridges at Wesel, the ferocity of the German resistance increased dramatically, making the prospect of closing the pincers and trapping the remaining German forces west of the Rhine increasingly unlikely.

To the north of the Hochwald, and east of Kalkar, the 43rd Wessex Division – under Canadian command – had been, for some time, driving the Germans back across an extensive area of land stretching all the way to the banks of the Rhine. By 4 March, the 1st Worcesters had captured Vynan, north of Xanten, and sent patrols onwards to the town of Wardt, in order to assess German strength in the area. Their patrols were met by machine gun fire in which one Worcester soldier was killed, but Wardt was still occupied successfully by the 1st Worcesters during the morning of 5 March. Once ensconced in Wardt, the battalion established static patrols along the banks of the Rhine. It escorted Royal Engineers on river-borne patrols, and the men of the battalion claimed for themselves the distinction of being the first British troops in the Liberation Army to conduct a 'Watch on the Rhine'.[1] The battalion stayed in Wardt until it ended its participation in the 43rd Division campaign on 11 March, when it was pulled back to Afferden for rest and recuperation. During their time in Wardt, the 1st Worcesters were far from inactive.

Shelling from German positions on the east bank of the Rhine was a constant problem. On 7 March, for example, Wardt church was hit by a German shell, and on 9 March two Worcesters were killed and three injured by a direct hit from a German artillery position. By this time, the Worcesters were also assisting British artillery in observing and firing upon German observation posts situated on the eastern banks of the Rhine.

Despite random shelling from German positions, Wardt still became an assembly point for soldiers from the 5th Wiltshires, in addition to those already present in the area from the Worcestershire Regiment. The 5th Wiltshires concentrated in Wardt prior to launching an assault on German positions at Luttingen, just a few miles to the north of Xanten. The Wiltshires' attack began during the very early hours of 8 March and involved two main phases. To begin with, two companies of infantry tried to secure the largely rural approaches to Luttingen, which proved to be a complex and time-consuming endeavour. A and C Companies of the 5th Wiltshires were halted in their tracks by heavy German machine gun and mortar fire. At least two platoons were cut off and surrounded by Germans, while the rest of A and C Companies were withdrawn under cover of smoke and artillery fire. By the time of their withdrawal, both companies had been reduced to platoon strength. At 1330 hours on 8 March, the two remaining, largely intact, companies of the 5th Wiltshires – B and D – launched their delayed assault on Luttingen itself. The attack went well, even though it involved some hand-to-hand fighting and trench clearing, and by 1845 hours the battalion was lodged securely in northern Luttingen, while the 4th Wiltshires cleared the rest of the large village. By early morning on 9 March, elements of the 4th and 5th Wiltshires had met in the centre of Luttingen without encountering any opposition. The Germans had gone, and in the afternoon soldiers from the 7th Somerset Light Infantry took over the positions in Luttingen recently won by the two battalions of the Wiltshire Regiment. After Luttingen was cleared, elements of the

43rd Division then moved on to seize the Xanten ferry crossing, where the Germans had recently constructed a barge bridge to evacuate both men and equipment across the Rhine.

While the Wiltshires were assaulting the approaches to Luttingen, the 4th Battalion of the Somerset Light Infantry (4th SLI) were participating in a major Anglo-Canadian offensive against the German bastion of Xanten. This combined operation, sometimes referred to as Blockbuster II, was designed to capture one of the very last escape routes used by the Germans to funnel both men and equipment across the Rhine. The 4th SLI advanced into the town from the north-west across a long stretch of open ground, shielded by a 3-mile-long patch of dense smoke oil put up by British artillery. The advance was difficult, requiring them to traverse a major anti-tank ditch and minefields, but by the end of the day the battalion had achieved all its objectives. On the following morning, the 4th SLI went on to clear remaining German positions in the north-eastern parts of Xanten.

To the right of the 4th SLI in the initial assault on Xanten were the Canadian Essex Scottish Regiment and the Royal Hamilton Light Infantry (RHLI). The objective of these two formations was to seize the western areas of Xanten. The artillery bombardment which supported both British and Canadian troops as they advanced at 0530 on 8 March was certainly effective, and in the words of one Canadian veteran of the battle, it 'came down perfectly – like all hell breaking loose'.[2] As was the case with the 4th SLI, the Essex Scottish experienced some difficulties as they advanced towards the north-western parts of Xanten. The initial attacks took place in fine rain, across flat, wet and soft ground where it was difficult to provide effective tank support. Infantrymen had to move through barbed wire defences and cross open fields and waterlogged ditches on their own, and they did so under heavy German mortar, machine gun and sniper fire. Not surprisingly, casualties were heavy. The Essex Scottish war diary, for instance, records the fact that the regiment sustained 119 casualties during the fighting for Xanten.[3] Once British and

Canadian troops had broken into Xanten, German fortified houses and pill-boxes still had to be overcome, in generally short but gruelling street battles. In many cases, German resistance was only ended with the aid of British and Canadian Crocodile flame-throwing tanks, which could be deployed on some of the streets of Xanten, though not in the waterlogged areas outside the town. During the night of 8/9 March, the 5th Canadian Infantry Brigade moved through the areas captured at some cost by the Essex Scottish and the RHLI, and seized the high ground and ridge south of Xanten. During this last phase of the operation to capture Xanten, patrols were sent out towards Ginderich and the Rhine bridges, and the focus of Allied military efforts shifted towards other areas of the rapidly shrinking German bridgehead on the western side of the Rhine.

Just 4 miles to the south of Xanten, tanks and infantry of the 4th Canadian Armoured Division attacked German positions in the village of Veen, which lay directly on the route eastwards to Wesel. The advance was slowed considerably by cratered roads and mines, and once in the village the men of the Canadian 10th Infantry Brigade became embroiled in a savage fight for almost every cellar and house. The village was full of improvised concrete pill-boxes which spouted machine gun fire, and German infantry used their Panzerfausts to great effect. The fighting for Veen was so intense that neighbouring British units referred to it in their individual war diary entries. The 2nd Irish Guards, for instance, mentioned on 7 March that the Germans were 'still holding Veen to the north of us, a village from which the Canadians did not finally dislodge them until some days later, and only with considerable difficulty'.[4] In fact, Veen only fell to the Canadians two days later, on 9 March, and the 4th Canadian Armoured Division was only able to move on a short distance to the east before it was again involved in an epic fight with German paratroopers defending a monastery at Winnenthal. The defenders fought on in the monastery ruins, in small groups, until almost all were either killed or wounded, and fighting only ceased on

10 March. Pushing back the German defensive line to the west of the Wesel Pocket was proving to be a gruelling and bloody affair.

To the south, the advance of the 52nd Lowland Division towards the Wesel Pocket also proved to be challenging. During the night of 8 March, the 6th Cameronians advanced on to a ridge overlooking the small town of Alpen, which lay close to the left bank of the Rhine. The town lay astride a key road which descended from the Bonninghardt plateau, and during the very early hours of 9 March it became the scene of one of the very last battles of the Anglo-Canadian military campaign which began in the Reichswald Forest on 8 February. The 6th Cameronians spent an uncomfortable night on the Alpen ridge, and suffered eight casualties as a result of constant German shelling and mortar fire. During the dark hours early on 9 March they moved down the ridge and attacked Alpen, supported by the 7th Cameronians, the 4/5th Royal Scots Fusiliers, one Sherman tank squadron and a divisional artillery bombardment. The ensuing battle against well-organised and well-led German paratroopers would be brutal.

The 6th Cameronians approached the town from the north, seizing a railway embankment roughly 1,000 yards from the centre of Alpen, and then blocking the main road which ran into the town from the north-east. The northern outskirts of Alpen contained factories and farm buildings, and B Company of the 6th Cameronians was ordered to move into a dairy plant situated in this area, near to Alpen's railway station. Here, the company was pinned down by intense German small-arms fire, which originated from inside the factory building itself. B Company was cut off and surrounded at the factory until late in the afternoon, when the 7th Cameronians arrived to relieve the hard-pressed men of its sister battalion. On the other side of the dairy plant, even heavier fighting erupted in positions occupied by C Company of the 6th Cameronians. This particular company had moved to the blocking position covering the main road to the north-east of Alpen. At approximately 0700 on 9 March, German infantry, artillery and tanks attacked C Company positions in overwhelming numbers, and poured shells into Cameronian slit-trenches from a distance of just a few hundred yards. Serious battles then developed in various parts of Alpen, which sucked in the rest of the 6th Cameronians, the 7th Cameronians and other British units.

All contact was lost with some of the leading Cameronian platoons, and in order to find out more about what was happening at the dairy plant, Lance Corporal William Robertson of the 6th Cameronians led a reconnaissance patrol right into the centre of the fighting, through open ground swept by machine gun fire. His patrol captured two prisoners, ascertained the precarious position of the Cameronians in the plant, and then returned to battalion headquarters with valuable information. For this action, Robertson was given a Bar to his Military Medal, originally awarded during the Walcheren campaign of November 1944, making him the only Cameronian to win this extra accolade during the entire course of the Second World War. Using Robertson's information, the Cameronians moved back into the dairy plant and found that the Germans had gone. Groups of paratroopers had fought on to the last man, while others had pulled back to join the exodus to the fast-disappearing Wesel bridgehead. The scene they left behind them in Alpen was one of general devastation, and the dairy plant was full dead and dying British and German soldiers. Men of the 7/9th Royal Scots advanced into Cameronian C Company positions and found everyone dead apart from the company's lieutenant, Clancey, who had a terrible injury to the throat. Lieutenant Clancey was taken away for treatment, but died shortly afterwards. The 6th battalion's history summed it all up quite accurately when it declared that 'the Company fought a magnificent but hopeless battle'. During the fighting, four officers and 169 other ranks from the 6th Cameronians had been either killed or wounded, and the battalion's official history had little option but to describe the outcome as a 'Pyrrhic victory' for the regiment.[5]

The battle for Alpen was the last great military challenge faced by the 52nd Division during the campaign. Elements of the division attacked Haus Loo Fort during the early morning of 9 March, and fighting was intense, but by the early afternoon, the Germans had withdrawn. On 10 March, Ginderich was occupied with little difficulty, and a set-piece attack on Menzelen had been planned to take place at 0900, involving battalions from the Glasgow Highlanders and the Highland Light Infantry (HLI). No assault was needed, however, as patrols soon discovered that the Germans had pulled out of the small town, and Menzelen was occupied without a fight during the early afternoon. The HLI and the Glasgows suffered only one casualty (a result of shelling), and the biggest problem faced by the troops in Menzelen was how to deal with the large numbers of Russian and Polish POWS they found hiding in the town's cellars, used as expendable forced labour by the local Nazi authorities.

By the time of the Pyrrhic Cameronian victory at Alpen, and the planned assault on Menzelen, the 52nd Lowland Division was very near to closing the remaining German bridgeheads at Wesel. The so-called Wesel Pocket had proved to be an immensely difficult defensive line to break. This in itself wasn't too surprising as, during the first few days of March, when the Pocket was at its height and stretched westwards on to the Bonninghardt plateau, north to Xanten and Luttingen, and south to Alpen, Ossenberg and beyond, the German defensive line – at least according to some American estimates – comprised more than 50,000 men.[6] Alfred Schlemm's bridgehead contained four parachute divisions, the remnants of the Panzer Lehr and 116th Panzer Divisions, and a panzer grenadier division. On some occasions these troops fought tenaciously, and British battalion war diaries often made references to the 'fanatical' resistance encountered in the 'pocket'. Undoubtedly, some fought on 'fanatically' as a result of National Socialist indoctrination and zeal; others were probably just defending the fatherland, and many had no option but to fight on as deserters were shot, and the remaining Wesel bridgeheads were full of security troops preventing able-bodied men from crossing to the east bank of the Rhine.

Given the enormity of the task involved in smashing the Wesel Pocket, Allied commanders hoped that the Americans would be able to sweep in from the south and take the Wesel bridges from the flank. Such a plan fitted in with the original concept of Operation Veritable as part of a pincer movement trapping German forces between Anglo-Canadians on one side and Americans on the other. Once Simpson's U.S. 9th Army had crossed the Roer, its rapid progress made it seem quite possible that they could advance to capture the remaining bridges at Wesel and so trap Schlemm's forces on the west bank of the Rhine. On 27 February, the U.S. 84th Division advanced 9 miles. On the last day of February, and on 1 March, the 9th Army advanced between 7 and 10 miles along its entire front, and on 1 March a single regiment of the 29th Division captured the key industrial area of Monchengladbach with little opposition. So spectacular was the progress made by the Americans that Simpson and his planning staff began to plot an impromptu crossing of the Rhine between Dusseldorf and Uerdingen. Once across the Rhine, Simpson's army would then push northwards and clear the east bank of the river for further Allied crossings.

These new plans certainly went against the original premise of Operation Veritable. Montgomery, not surprisingly perhaps, given the fact that Operation Grenade had already been delayed by flooding, turned down the proposal.[7] General Anderson's U.S. XVI Corps was given the task of continuing a push north-eastwards, towards the Wesel bridges. Between 28 February and 3 March, Anderson's corps encountered little serious opposition. However, as XVI Corps moved closer to the bloody battlefields north of the Niers, contested by the First Canadian Army since early February, so German resistance began to intensify. The U.S. 35th Division's Task Force Byrne only seized the town of Sevelen, 5 miles south-east of Geldern, after heavy fighting on 3 March. Further to the east, other formations of General Baade's

35th Division advanced to capture Rheinberg on 4 March. The U.S. advance to the town proved to be a slow and bloody one. American armour and infantry were halted on the way to Rheinberg by heavy small arms, mortar and artillery fire. On the following day, thirty-nine out of fifty-four tanks deployed to capture the town were destroyed in heavy fighting, and 343 infantrymen were either killed, wounded or posted as missing.

These salutary reminders of German military potency, between 5 and 8 March, certainly slowed down the pace of the American advance. Ossenberg, for instance, was only captured by U.S. forces after two days of gruelling street battles in which the Germans seemed prepared to fight to the death for every ruined house and building. After this, however, resistance seemed to collapse almost overnight, and the U.S. 134th Infantry Division swept all the way to the west bank of the Rhine, opposite Wesel, with practically no opposition.

On 6 March, the German High Command in Berlin had finally given Schlemm permission to evacuate the forces in his sector of the Front by no later than 10 March, despite Hitler's 'heavy heart' in acquiescing to such a decision. Schlemm lost no time in acting upon the permissions received, and by midnight on 6 March several German divisions had already pulled back across the Rhine. The Germans fought rearguard actions at Xanten, Winnenthal, Alpen and elsewhere with the remnants of three parachute divisions, the 116th Panzer Division, a battlegroup of the 346th Infantry Division, and a varied assortment of flak and anti-tank units. The British, Canadians and Americans all came very close to trapping this German rearguard at Wesel, and 'bouncing' a bridge across the Rhine at the same time, but none quite succeeded. Capturing an intact bridge across the Rhine was certainly a difficult task. The U.S. 9th Army tried on a number of occasions, without success, as it advanced towards Wesel. Of course, to the south of the First Canadian Army sector, on 7 March, the U.S. 9th Armoured Division of Courtney Hodges' 1st Army managed to capture, intact, the Ludendorff Bridge at

Remagen, when a portion of the German explosives wired to the structure failed to explode as required. This German military and strategic disaster, rather ironically, made the task of capturing another bridge in a different sector of the front even more difficult, with German engineers and their commanders even more careful to ensure that their detonation charges actually worked. When, under Schlemm's orders, the Wesel road and rail bridges were blown up on the morning of 10 March, large portions of both structures were destroyed beyond repair.

Well before the retreating Germans blew up the Wesel road and rail bridges on 10 March, RAF Bomber Command had plenty of opportunities to destroy Wesel's bridges. Between 16 February and 7 March, Bomber Command launched seven separate raids on the town, which involved a total of 913 aircraft.[8] During this time, 97 per cent of the buildings in the main town area were destroyed. Poor visibility certainly reduced bombing accuracy on occasion, but at other times large numbers of Lancasters, Halifaxes and Mosquito fighter-bombers flattened the town in good, clear flying conditions. On 16 February, for example, 100 Lancasters attacked Wesel in clear skies, and 'the town and the railway were seen to be smothered in bomb bursts'. No specific references were made in Bomber Command records to attacks on Wesel's key bridges. Precision targets were often difficult to hit, but on 18 February 160 Lancasters attacked Wesel, in cloudy conditions, using the G-H radio navigation system, which had entered service in October 1943 and was used to assist Bomber Command in improving its target location and bombing accuracy. Furthermore, on 6 March, forty-eight Mosquitoes attacked the town, with one Mosquito using the Oboe bomb-aiming system, which allowed aircraft to bomb targets in any type of weather, day or night. The Oboe was in operational use by March 1943 and was probably the most accurate bombing system used during the course of the war. The Oboe-equipped Wesel-bound Mosquito dropped flares on the intended targets, which were then used as bombing markers for all the following aircraft. 6 March was a key date in Wesel, when considerable daytime German military traffic crossed from west to east along the two remaining bridges. Even so, and despite the use of Oboe technology, only limited damage was done to the vital river-crossing points. It seems probable that RAF Bomber Command could have destroyed the Wesel bridgeheads completely had it been ordered to do so. However, Allied commanders still hoped, right up to the last moment, that they could seize the Wesel bridgeheads intact. As MacDonald and his team of American military historians pointed out succinctly in their account of the last days of the Wesel Pocket, functioning road and rail bridges were a key Allied objective 'because they held out promise for crossing the Rhine with dry feet'.[9] Unfortunately for the First Canadian Army, and for the Americans, surviving German forces used the still-functioning Wesel bridges to escape across the Rhine in reasonably good order before destroying the structures themselves.

After more than a month of continuous fighting, Operation Veritable and the later variant of Operation Blockbuster had come to an end, as had the delayed American Operation Grenade. There was to be no spectacular capturing of a bridge over the Rhine at Wesel to end the Allied campaign, and there was no mass encirclement and surrender of entire German armies. Instead, General Schlemm had been able to orchestrate a highly effective fighting retreat to the Wesel bridgehead and a subsequent evacuation across the Rhine. It was to be another two weeks before British troops entered devastated Wesel, on 24 March, as part of Mongomery's massive Operation Plunder offensive across the Rhine.

17

COUNTING THE COST: TREATMENT OF THE WOUNDED

A skilful leech is better far than half a hundred men of war.[1]

The guns didn't fall silent after the last of Alfred Schlemm's German forces had retreated across the Rhine. The killing continued, though at a reduced rate, as British, Canadian and American troops confronted the Germans in an uneasy stand-off, which continued until the launching of Montgomery's last great set-piece battle of the Second World War – the assault across the Rhine on 24 March. American troops in Ginderich and Fort Blucher were soon replaced by garrisons from the 52nd British Lowland Division, patrols along the Rhine were organised, and both sides shelled each other. Moreover, RAF Bomber Command re-arranged the rubble in Wesel with further mass attacks involving 218 aircraft on the night of 23/24 March.[2] Some rest and recuperation was certainly needed for the regiments and divisions involved in the campaign which had brought the British and Canadians, aided by the Americans, to the banks of the Rhine, in this northern sector of the Western Front. British and

Canadian medical units, which had coped with the demands of a campaign which began in and around the Reichswald Forest and then spilled out into the Rhineland plains, and ended on the western banks of the Rhine, also needed time to rest, recuperate and resupply. Leave was granted to some, while others trained for upcoming battles across the Rhine, and new replacement doctors and orderlies were received.

British and Canadian medical services had certainly been put to the test during the period of the Reichswald campaign. Feasby, in his substantial *Official History of the Canadian Medical Services 1939-1945*, concludes that between 10 February and 10 March 1945 some 20,640 casualties, of all types, were evacuated from the battle area by First Canadian Army medical personnel. In addition to this, American medical units processed approximately 7,300 casualties sustained by the U.S. 9th Army during its seventeen-day Operation Grenade campaign.[3] As the 9th U.S. Army pushed northwards and linked up with elements of the 52nd British Lowland Division, it processed its casualties in similar ways to the British and Canadians. The chain of care for wounded American servicemen began with combat medics, rather than stretcher-bearers, who provided initial care on the battlefield and assessed whether injured soldiers needed evacuating to battalion aid stations. Urgent surgical operations could be carried out at divisional clearing stations, though in most cases the crucial 'definitive' care took place at the U.S. Army's massive range of military hospitals based in the U.K. or continental Europe. Long-term care and rehabilitation could also take place in military hospitals located back in the USA – referred to as the Zone of the Interior in much of the medical documentation of the time.

The task of caring for tens of thousands of injured soldiers, right in the middle of a series of often bloody military engagements, was certainly an immense one. The field ambulance units of the Royal Army Medical Corps (RAMC) were at the absolute centre of British efforts to care for the wounded during the Reichswald campaign. To begin with, the

RAMC trained army stretcher-bearers. Stretcher-bearer training of the sort undertaken by the RAMC was of crucial importance on the battlefields of the Second World War. During the Reichswald campaign, in particular, the activities of stretcher-bearers on all sides helped save many lives. In the Reichswald Forest itself, the closely packed trees, incessant rain and lakes of mud meant that moving the injured by motor ambulance was impossible. Instead, the wounded initially had to be treated close to where they fell, and then carried on foot, using stretchers, by teams of stretcher-bearers. Privates George Atkin and Henry Lambeth were stretcher-bearers attached to the 2nd Seaforths as the battalion fought its way through the southern part of the Reichswald Forest. Atkin and Lambeth carried their wounded comrades on stretchers through the forest for over 800 yards on at least forty occasions. They often did so under fire, and frequently dressed wounds in forest clearings right on the front line. During the period that the battalion fought in the forest, the two dedicated stretcher-bearers carried their wounded comrades through mud and rain to aid stations for a total of more than 18 miles, and received well-deserved Military Medals for their actions. Their award citations say much about the high regard in which both men were held by their Seaforth colleagues. As regards Atkin, the citation stated that he was 'the embodiment of all that is finest in the British soldier. His constant cheerfulness, courage and devotion to duty could not have been excelled.' The citation regarding Lambeth was equally fulsome in its praise, stating, 'He has been a constant inspiration, and a devoted, cheerful comrade on the front line. No praise is too high for his consistency and bravery.'[4]

Perhaps as a consequence of the fine example set by Atkin, Lambeth and others, courses in stretcher-bearing could be very popular when volunteers were called for from the rank-and-file of the British army. On 28 February 1945, for example, the 153rd Field Ambulance Unit, resting at Tilburg in the Netherlands after a posting to the Reichswald, accepted fifty-six volunteers for stretcher-bearer training from just three Scottish battalions also recently returned from the Reichswald fighting. Such training obviously allowed these putative stretcher-bearers to escape from the normal routines of army life away from the front line, but it also involved five full days of courses and attendance at first aid lectures.[5] With an eye to the imminent crossing of the Rhine, this training was geared to equipping candidates for waterborne casualty treatment and evacuation.

Once Reichswald battlefield casualties were secured on stretchers, their first port of call was often the regimental aid post, situated at some location near to the fighting, where at least a modicum of rudimentary medical assistance could be provided. Either from this regimental aid post, or direct from the battlefield itself, the wounded would progress to an Advanced Dressing Station (ADS) where RAMC personnel would carry out initial medical checks and treatment. These were located more or less on the front line, close to regimental aid posts, in ruined buildings, dugouts and other locations, and from here the injured could be moved on rapidly to RAMC run Casualty Collection Points (CCPs) and/or Casualty Clearing Stations (CCSs). A CCP was, in reality, the location where further ad hoc first aid treatment would take place alongside assessment of wound severity. Those with the most severe injuries could expect to be evacuated to base hospitals and other significant medical facilities. A field ambulance unit in Britain, or one not on active campaigning duties, could be housed entirely at one location. During the Reichswald fighting, however, as with other campaigns, individual ambulance units were dispersed. One field ambulance unit was allocated to each brigade within an army division, and the CCPs, CCSs and ADSs within an individual ambulance unit were set up separately and followed their 'parent' brigade around the battlefield, opening and closing according to the strategic needs of the moment.

The war establishment of a typical field ambulance unit was specified in Army Council Instructions issued in June 1940. A unit was to establish a headquarters and possess two companies – A and B. Unit staff allocated to the headquarters facility had to create, equip and run a main dressing station, while personnel assigned to companies A and B had to function as stretcher-bearers and equip and run forward ADSs, CCPs and CCSs. The 1940 Army Council Instructions also recommended that a typical field ambulance unit should have a full complement of 222 other ranks personnel and eleven medical officers, all commanded by a lieutenant-colonel. On occasions, there might also be a twelfth officer who acted as the unit chaplain. Companies A and B would each be commanded by a major or a captain. In addition to RAMC personnel, field ambulance units also included Royal Army Service Corps soldiers, who drove and maintained the formation's ambulances and other vehicles.[6]

RAMC field ambulance units certainly had a heavy workload during the period of the Reichswald campaign, and it was a workload made heavier by the ever-present rain, flooding, mud and low temperatures which characterised the Rhineland area during February–March 1945. Even before the Reichswald Forest campaign began on 8 February, field ambulance units were dealing with those injured in road accidents caused by the quagmire-like conditions in and around the area targeted for the offensive. For example, the 194th Field Ambulance Unit, which supported the 44th Lowland Infantry Brigade, commented in its war diary entry for 6 February that 'rain and road [conditions were] dreadful. We have never had so many casualties from road movement.' The same ambulance unit went on to report, on 12 February, that they were cut off from the brigade they were supporting by the sheer scale of the localised flooding.[7] In these circumstances, casualties could only be evacuated directly to clearing stations via DUKW amphibious vehicles. The RAMC's 193rd Field Ambulance Unit, which supported the 46th Highland Infantry Brigade, took on the crucial role of managing the First Canadian Army's only DUKW Casualty Evacuation Point, which was situated just to the west of Kleve. Here, between 14 and 25 February, 193rd Field Ambulance

Unit superintended the amphibious evacuation of 4,000 casualties from the entire Allied army.[8] After this date, the Canadians took over responsibility for the same amphibious casualty-clearing services, which remained crucial throughout the entire Reichswald campaign because of the parlous state of the main Kleve–Nijmegen road. In addition to its crucial general evacuation responsibilities, 193rd Field Ambulance Unit began to accept cases from the 43rd Wessex Division, and all Canadian divisions, from 21 February onwards. The unit also continued to accept casualties from its parent brigade, the 46th, during this period, and like all other field ambulance units it treated German POWs. Between 9 and 20 February, 193rd Field Ambulance Unit treated sixty-three POWs at its various stations, while the 153rd Field Ambulance Unit, which was attached to 227 Highland Infantry brigade, treated sixty-two POWs between 9 and 24 February.[9]

The information that individual field ambulance units chose to record in their war diary entries differed from one unit to another. The 193rd Field Ambulance Unit, for example, chose to list separately the Canadian officers and other ranks it treated at its various stations – 129 in total. By contrast, 153 Field Ambulance Unit chose to give figures for the sick, non-battlefield patients it admitted between 9 and 24 February, which amounted to 161 service personnel. Despite these differences in emphasis, the number of surgical interventions and treatments carried out by doctors and medical orderlies on the various Reichswald battlefields was undoubtedly massive. The 153rd Field Ambulance Unit alone treated 636 patients between 9 and 24 February, while the 193rd Field Ambulance treated 1,066 patients between 9 and 20 February. Given the fact that there were usually three field ambulance units in each division, and that there were many divisions utilised during the Reichswald campaign, the massive scale of Allied casualties can be easily deduced. Between 10 February and 10 March 1945, Feasby records that 5,689 casualties were evacuated from the battle area by road, 4,275 by air and 10,676 by ambulance train.[10]

Evacuating such large numbers of casualties, along with POWs, was certainly a major achievement. There were obviously delays and problems, caused mainly by the terrain. Some medical officers commented on the deterioration in the condition of wounded soldiers as they made their way between ADSs, CCPs and more advanced centres of treatment. Only DUKWs could be used in some areas of the battlefield, and two-stretcher ambulance jeeps proved to be one of the few vehicles appropriate for sliding over mud heaps and traversing slippery slopes to rescue the wounded. In some areas of the Reichswald Forest, injured soldiers had to be carried by their comrades for considerable distances before significant medical treatments could be administered. Yet despite such problems and delays, the RAMC field ambulance units still managed to save countless lives. Part of the reason for the success of the service undoubtedly lay in its considerable mobility and flexibility. Units were constantly on the move, setting up and dismantling HQs, CCPs and ADSs, in order to stay as close as possible to the fighting. The war diary entries for the 193rd Field Ambulance Unit provide a clear example of this extreme mobility. On 6 February, two days before the launch of the Reichswald Forest campaign, the Unit's A Company established a CCP at Groesbeek, while B Company remained at a base in Nijmegen. On 8 February, the unit's headquarters staff, together with B Company, established an ADS at Nebo monastery at Heilig Landstichting, to the east of Nijmegen. A Company then moved its doctors, orderlies and RASC personnel to Nutterden on 11 February, and to a small house on the Kleve–Donsbruggen road on the following day. On 13 February, the unit's headquarters moved to a shoe factory on the outskirts of Kleve, where the crucial amphibious Casualty Evacuation Point for the entire First Canadian Army was established.

The 193rd Field Ambulance Unit continued to move from one battlefield site to another until its part in the Reichswald campaign was over. Its constant movements and changes in location were replicated in other ambulance units across the entire First Canadian Army front line. Of course, being on the move for much of the time did mean that, on occasions, individual units were not able to receive patients. However, keeping as close as possible to the fighting also meant that once a large battle had been fought, ambulance units were able to deal quickly with an influx of casualties. On the opening day of the Reichswald offensive, for instance, the 193rd was receiving patients from 0830, and by the end of the day 277 casualties had passed through the hands of A company's CCP at Groesbeek. A further 508 British, Canadian and German casualties were treated by the unit on 9 February. Doctors from the 153rd Field Ambulance Unit were also close at hand on the opening day of the campaign, and therefore able to deal with approximately fifty Allied soldiers suffering from sometimes hideous injuries sustained during the crossing of undetected minefields scattered along the German front line. As the location of the fighting moved on to Nutterden, Kranenberg, Kleve, Goch, Gennep and elsewhere, the field ambulance units were never far behind. During the heavy fighting in the Schloss Kalbeck area, for instance, ambulances of the 193rd were destroyed by German mortar fire.

Front lines were often very fluid during the Reichswald campaign, and field ambulance unit members could sometimes, through accident rather than design, find themselves ahead of their own troops, and clashing directly with the enemy. Private William Imrie was a member of the 176rd Field Ambulance Unit, and on the night of 13/14 February he crossed the Niers at night, along with an assault formation from the Black Watch Regiment. Imrie was given stretcher-bearer duties and assisted in the organisation of a Regimental Aid Post (RAP). The river crossing was a contested one, and somehow Imrie and his RAP party ended up ahead of the rest of the Black Watch assault group. Once the RAP group had crossed the Niers, they attempted to set up an aid post in a nearby building which they presumed to be deserted. As the unarmed medics and orderlies approached the building, they heard the unmistakable sound of German Spandau machine gun fire, and the group sensibly took cover in a nearby ditch. However, they'd been spotted by at least one German soldier, who advanced towards them with a Spandau. Private Imrie, even though he was unarmed, leapt out of the ditch and fought with the German. In the ensuing struggle, Imrie seized both a Spandau and a luger pistol from the German and left the unfortunate enemy soldier alive but unconscious on a muddy trackway. Imrie's speedy actions prevented members of the RAP party from being either killed or captured, and an aid post was soon established for injured Black Watch soldiers. William Imrie, ambulance unit stretcher-bearer, was later awarded a Military Medal for his lone struggle against the Spandau-toting German soldier on the trackway beside the Niers.[11]

Canadian stretcher-bearers, like their British and German counterparts, often had to tend to the wounded in the heat of battle, under the most trying of circumstances. Private Lloyd Head, for example, was a stretcher-bearer with A Company of the Canadian Essex Scottish Regiment. On 19 February 1945, the regiment was involved in heavy fighting near Louisendorf, situated roughly halfway between Kalkar and the Kleve forest. Private Head was wounded early on in the operation but still continued to treat the wounded of the regiment. At the end of a particularly ferocious engagement, the Essex Scottish decided to withdraw to a safer position, but they left behind them six soldiers who were too badly injured to be moved. These severe stretcher cases were abandoned in a no man's land between Canadian and German positions. Lloyd Head volunteered to stay behind with these severely wounded soldiers until further help and assistance could be given. In fact, he looked after his six wounded charges for nearly two days, under constant shelling, until this further medical support was received. The stretcher-bearer was awarded an immediate Military Medal for his obvious commitment to the injured men stranded with him in the narrow stretch of no man's land just west of Louisendorf.[12]

The field ambulance units of the Royal Canadian Army Medical Corps (RCAMC) operated in much the same way as British field ambulances. Indeed, there was a good deal of cooperation between British and Canadian field ambulance units. Injured Canadian soldiers were treated in British field units, and British casualties were looked after in Canadian medical facilities. The 11th Canadian Field Ambulance Unit's takeover of the 15th Scottish Division's amphibious vehicle casualty loading points at Kleve also went very smoothly indeed – over 500 casualties were evacuated from this key facility during the course of a single day by the 11th Canadian Unit. Canadian field ambulance units had to deal with three main Allied offensives during the Reichswald campaign. During the first three days of the campaign, Canadian forces were mostly situated to the north of the Reichswald Forest, along the banks of the Rhine, protecting the flanks of Horrocks' XXX Corps. Casualties during this initial phase weren't severe, with the combined field ambulance units of the 2nd Canadian Infantry Division evacuating just 145 casualties. Canadian casualties were much heavier during the period from 19 February onwards, when the 2nd and 3rd Canadian divisions, along with the 43rd Wessex Division, began their attacks south-east, towards Xanten. In preparation for an influx of casualties, the 11th Canadian Field Ambulance Unit opened a CCP at Bedburg, and No. 18 Canadian Field Ambulance Unit established an ADS at the same location, which dealt with 131 casualties, including eleven POWs, on 20 February alone.

Canadian medical services were, however, tested to their utmost during the bitter fighting in the Hochwald and Balberger Wald between 1 and 4 March, when field ambulance units were very close to the front line, and moved up even further as the fighting progressed. The field ambulance units established CCPs, and then evacuated the injured from these collection points to the nearest ADSs. On 1 March, the 18th RCAMC Field Ambulance Unit opened an ADS at Udem for casualties of the 2nd Canadian Division, and on 4 March the 10th Canadian Field Ambulance

Unit moved to the western edge of the Hochwald to treat cases. During this particularly savage period of fighting, the Canadians added some effective refinements to the service offered by the British in the Reichswald campaign. On 22 February, No. 5 Canadian Field Dressing Station established an advanced surgical centre at Bedburg and three days later, No. 3 Canadian CCS set up its facilities in buildings adjoining the new Bedburg surgical centre. The advanced surgery centre dealt with severe chest and abdominal injuries, while other cases were sent to the CCS next door. The 11th Canadian Field Ambulance Unit set up a similar recovery centre at Kleve, which was earmarked for the use of injured members of the 2nd Canadian Infantry Division. Other Canadian recovery centres were set up at Bedburg for the use of the 3rd Infantry Division, and the 4th Armoured Division. On 1 March, the 18th Canadian Field Ambulance Unit opened an ADS at Udem, and on 4 March No. 12 Field Dressing Station launched a new advanced surgery centre, intended only for very serious cases, in buildings which adjoined the ADS in Udem. As a result of all these RCAMC medical initiatives, it became possible for at least some Canadian service personnel to be wounded, treated, and then recover, without ever leaving the region of the Rhineland.

German medical practices on the battlefields of the Reichswald were, like British and Canadian practices, efficient, detailed and quite advanced in a number of ways. While British and Canadian army doctors were engaged in pioneering work with penicillin, German military doctors were using steel plates to repair fractures in a way that was far in advance of procedures followed in Allied military hospitals. On paper, at least, the German methods for dealing with battlefield casualties seemed logical and sound. The template for dealing with German military casualties was really established by the short Polish campaign of August–September 1939. In May 1940, Hans Hartleban, a senior German military doctor, wrote a paper for the German army which described the system adopted for the Polish campaign, and it was a system which continued to influence German battlefield medical procedures for the rest of the war.[13] To begin with, Hartleban explained that every German soldier on campaign should have one large and one small first aid packet, and should receive a modicum of training on how to apply dressings. By February 1945, however, it's probable that at least some of Germany's new recruits were slipping through the net without such basic advice and training.

The German stretcher-bearer system at the Reichswald was certainly more detailed and complex than that practised by either the Canadians or the British. To begin with, there were the Hilfskrankentragers, who were the auxiliary stretcher-bearers, called upon in the heat of battle to drop their weapons and assist wounded comrades to the nearest battalion first aid station. There were perhaps eight such Hilfskrankentragers in a full-strength company. There were also four permanent stretcher-bearers to be found in a company, who were called krankentragers, and received a more rounded, complete education in first aid. A fully equipped krankentrager carried a considerable medical supply kit with him, but by the time of the Reichswald campaign much of this equipment was in short supply, and at least one resourceful krankentrager was reduced to using a British medical kit bag captured at Arnhem in order to care for his battlefield patients.[14] Every German battalion was also allocated one medical officer and a medical assistant, who were given the job of establishing a battalion aid station as near to the front line as possible during periods of fighting. At these stations, which were very similar to British and Canadian regimental aid posts, all kinds of treatment were attempted apart from surgery. Casualties were picked up from these battalion aid posts by divisional medical services and taken to divisional aid stations and hospitals where surgery could take place.

Theoretically, German divisions at the Reichswald could call upon a motorised field hospital able to accommodate up to 200 patients, together with two motor ambulance trains, made up of fifteen ambulances in each train. By the time of the Reichswald, however, fuel to run such a large number of ambulances was in short supply. Even if ambulances could be put on the road, there was really nowhere for them to go. Flooding had made many roads impassable, and Allied bombing had destroyed much of the road and rail network connecting the Rhineland with the rest of Germany. As a result, German casualties were crammed into a narrow bottleneck of land just behind the front line, where evacuation to the interior of Germany was difficult to organise on a large scale. St Nikolaus's Convent Hospital at Kalkar was one of the main hospitals used to accommodate German casualties from the Reichswald campaign. The convent hospital had been modernised during the 1920s and was run by a group of nuns from the Order of the Sisters of Charity. On 7 February 1945, the town was attacked by RAF Bomber Command, and twenty local civilians were killed and a further twenty were seriously injured. Six bombs actually landed on the hospital, severely damaging the roof, isolation house and chapel. Even so, St Nikolaus's was still selected by German army medical teams as one of the main hospitals to be used for Reichswald casualties. During the halcyon days of 1940, when the German army reigned supreme in much of Europe, Hartleban had said in his report on German military medical organisation that military hospitals should never exceed 500 beds. At St Nikolaus's in Kalkar, however, over 1,000 injured German soldiers were accommodated within the largely ruined buildings. By 15 February, most of these injured service personnel had been moved on, but the nuns remained. The German army had left behind a huge ammunition dump at the front of the hospital, and on 22 February, a large fire started which soon caused this dump to ignite in a huge series of explosions. Most of the hospital buildings were destroyed, and the nuns finally had to admit defeat and leave the area. In April, however, the Sisters of Charity returned, in order to begin the long process of rebuilding both the convent and its adjoining hospital facilities.[15] The most seriously injured of those removed from St Nikolaus' Hospital faced a precarious future in war-ravaged Germany, where long-term care would be increasingly difficult to secure. Indeed, those German POWs treated in British, Canadian or American military hospitals had a much better chance of survival and recovery.

Of course, for thousands of critically injured British, Canadian and American soldiers, treatment at field ambulance units, or by combat medics represented only the first stage in medical interventions which could last, in some cases, for an entire lifetime. Those with life-changing injuries could be passed through a series of military hospitals in Europe and the UK, and Canadian and American soldiers might then be shipped across the Atlantic for further treatment in North America. Major Peter Albery, a former paratrooper who'd transferred to the 2nd Battalion of the Royal Warwickshire Regiment, was shot through the spine while leading his men into action during the 3rd Division's grim battles south of Udem and Goch. By May 1945, he was being treated at the Queen Elizabeth Hospital in Edgbaston, Birmingham. He was married in Edgbaston on 12 May, and taken by wheelchair and ambulance from the hospital to attend the wedding. His bride was the actress and playwright Sylvia Read, and the marriage ceremony was performed by the Free Church chaplain of the Queen Elizabeth Hospital. At this stage, Albery was paralysed in both legs, but the prognosis for his medical recovery seemed good, at least according to the *Birmingham Mail*, which commented that Peter was responding well to treatment 'and hopes to get back the full use of his legs', so grievously injured in the battle of the Reichswald.[16]

Such hopes proved to be overly optimistic, and Peter Albery spent the rest of his life in a wheelchair. These life-changing injuries, sustained in battle, meant – according to theatrical newspaper *The Stage* – that in 1945 Peter 'was confined to a wheelchair and pronounced totally unemployable, but with untiring courage he built a new life in the theatre'.[17] The former Royal Warwickshire Regiment major was a member of the Albery theatrical dynasty, and he used these connections, together with an abundance of natural talent, to forge a new career as a prolific playwright, and as the founder of a new Christian theatrical group called Theatre Roundabout. Late in 1978, Peter endured his last illness, which was directly related to the injuries he sustained thirty-three years earlier during the Reichswald campaign. He had a heavy fall and broke his leg, but the break remained undetected because of the paralysis sustained during the war. Infection set in, and Peter Albery spent months in the Royal Free Hospital before he finally passed away in June 1979 at the age of sixty-six. Albery's obituary in *The Stage* commented on the frequent bouts of pain that the playwright experienced as a result of his crippling wartime injuries, but these injuries certainly hadn't stopped the former paratrooper and infantry major from leading a full and productive life.

Terrible injuries were sustained by Allied troops who strayed on to undetected minefields in the Reichswald Forest and its adjacent areas. Mortar explosions caused similar hideous wounds, and one such mortar round shattered Frederick Tilston VC's legs as he led the Essex Scottish attacks on the Germans in the Hochwald. Tilston had both legs amputated and lost the sight in his left eye. He was treated in various hospitals for a year before he was 'back on the payroll again', as Tilston himself put it, in an administrative position in the Canadian forces. Tilston certainly endured moments of deep depression as a result of his terrible injuries, but during his recuperation he encountered other soldiers with horrific burns, and a British soldier who had been paralysed from the neck down. The suffering of these other soldiers made Tilston think better of his own position, and he went on to enjoy a long and fruitful life in post-war Canada. He became honorary colonel of the Essex Scottish Regiment, and CEO of the Sterling Drug Company. Tilston explained that at least some of the reason for his contentment lay with 'good surgery', and he continued to walk on prosthetic legs, perhaps somewhat stiffly, until his death in 1992.[18]

18

COUNTING THE COST: THE DESTRUCTION OF MONUMENTS AND CULTURAL CENTRES

> Shortly we will be fighting our way across Europe in battles designed to preserve our civilisation. Inevitably, in the path of our advance will be found historical monuments and cultural centres which symbolise to the world all that we are fighting to preserve. It is the responsibility of every commander to protect and respect these symbols wherever possible.
>
> Memorandum from General Dwight D. Eisenhower, 26 May 1944[1]

The devastation wrought by the Anglo-Canadian Veritable offensive, and the subsequent Blockbuster breakout, was certainly extensive. RAF bombers pulverised Kleve on the night of 7 February 1945, dropping 1,384 tons of high explosives on the town.[2] Kleve was further reduced to rubble by British and Canadian infantry and armour who fought on to clear the town of German defenders, often located in heavily defended cellars and other strategic locations. The towns of Emmerich, Udem,

Weeze, Goch and Wesel were also bombed heavily by Allied forces. Horrocks' reluctance to sanction the aerial destruction of the medieval town of Kleve, once home to Henry VIII's fourth wife, Anne of Kleves, is well documented. Nevertheless, he did acquiesce to its destruction, for military reasons. While much of the history of Kleve and other nearby Rhineland towns was literally going up in smoke, one man – Ronald Edmond Balfour, aided by some supporters in the attacking Anglo-Canadian forces, and by a few local German civilians – was doing as much as he could to preserve the area's cultural heritage from the depredations of war.

Ronald Balfour was an unlikely-looking soldier, slightly built and rather short-sighted, but he proved to be a supremely appropriate individual for rescuing timeless artistic and historical treasures and artefacts from destruction during wartime. Balfour was born into an affluent military family in 1904, and educated at Eton before winning a scholarship to study history and theology at King's College, Cambridge. He proved to be a scholar of considerable brilliance, securing a double-first in his studies and then moving on to become a history lecturer and a Fellow of King's itself. When war broke out in 1939, Balfour joined the French desk at the Ministry of Information. The Cambridge academic was, however, keen to play a more active role in the war, and within a year he'd left his desk job at the Ministry of Information in order to join the British Army. In 1940, he was commissioned as a 2nd Lieutenant in the King's Royal Rifle Corps (KRRC) and was promoted to the rank of captain during the following year. The newly promoted captain was then seconded to a post at the Recruiting Branch of the War Office, where he might have seen out the war had he not been attracted by the proposition of utilising his medieval history expertise as a member of the Supreme Headquarters Allied Expeditionary Force (SHAEF) Monuments, Fine Arts & Archives (MFAA) organisation.

The MFAA was created by the Allies in 1943 and integrated within the overall SHAEF military structure as part of its

G-5 Division, tasked with safeguarding as much as possible of Europe's architectural and artistic heritage from the ravages of war. The MFAA certainly had the backing of Supreme Commander Dwight Eisenhower, who issued a memorandum to his leading ground, air and naval commanders on 26 May 1944, reminding them of their responsibility to try and ensure the protection of historical monuments and cultural centres, wherever possible.[3] The creation of the MFAA, and its positioning within the overall structure of SHAEF, supported by both political and military leaders, was certainly a significant moment. As Ross points out, 'It was the first time in history that such an organisation was set up at the highest headquarters at the beginning of an operation and continued through all its phases until the end.'[4] With Eisenhower's support, the MFAA began planning operations in continental Europe (all based on the presumption that D-Day was successful). There were never more than 350–400 individuals – the so-called Monuments Men and Women – involved in working for the MFAA, and the body was influenced heavily by the American museums establishment. Despite this American influence, however, the MFAA leader in the UK was the British art historian Geoffrey Webb, Cambridge University's Slade Professor of Fine Art. By 1 April 1944, Ronald Balfour was a key member of Webb's planning staff, and the two obviously got on well together, because Webb later selected Balfour to become one of the first wave of Monuments Men to accompany the invading Allies across the English Channel into continental Europe after D-Day.

By 30 August 1944, Ronald Balfour had been appointed as the Monuments Officer to the First Canadian Army, which was engaged in a long series of bloody battles with German forces, taking it across much of northern France, Belgium and the Netherlands. Balfour's difficulties in actually getting to the First Canadian Army were considerable. He seems to have made his journey through the various battle zones quite independently, relying on lifts and commandeered trucks that were perpetually on the point of breaking down. Nevertheless, the Cambridge Monuments Man made it to the front line successfully, and he was soon using his negotiating skills to persuade the Allies not to bomb the Church of St Katharina in Hoogstraten (a municipality in the Belgian province of Antwerp). On 29 November 1944, Balfour sustained a serious ankle fracture in a traffic accident, and the injury kept him out of action for the following two months. He eventually returned to his MFAA duties with the First Canadian Army in February 1945, just on the eve of that army's great offensive against German positions in the Reichswald Forest, and its adjacent flood plains.

By the time the Allied guns opened up on the Reichswald during the early morning of 8 February 1945, Ronald Balfour was a major in the British Army. Despite his senior rank, though, Balfour had no permanent dedicated staff allocated to him – there was no specific platoon of men who would do the major's bidding and carry artefacts or secure locations of historical interest. Ronald Balfour did his work in the Reichswald area largely on his own, using whatever human and material resources he could lay his hands upon.[5] Mobility and transportation was extraordinarily difficult given the conditions prevailing in the Reichswald campaign, but despite all this Balfour managed to move about the region, and either visited or communicated with towns of historical interest such as Goch, Kleve, Spyck, Kranenburg and Xanten.

Front lines were extremely fluid during the Reichswald campaign, with individual buildings, streets and defensive positions sometimes changing hands between British, Canadian and German forces on repeated occasions. As a consequence, Balfour sometimes attempted his Monument recovery work just behind enemy lines. On other occasions, he was a mile or so behind the British front line. It was certainly dangerous work, carried out in the middle of one of the most savage battles of the entire war in Europe. Balfour rose to the occasion, however, and accomplished some great work. Indeed, he seems to have enjoyed the added frisson of danger. On 3 March 1945, he wrote to Geoffrey Webb with some excitement about an occasion when the building he was in was shelled by German artillery. He also recorded with some pleasure an encounter with a battalion of his own regiment, the KRRC, a mile behind the British front line. He ate lunch with his regimental colleagues before resuming his work for the MFAA.[6]

During February 1945, Balfour joined First Canadian Army forces assaulting the town of Goch. He persuaded commanders not to destroy Goch's fourteenth-century entrance gate as they moved into the town, and later on, in the town itself, he discovered the abandoned archives of Kleve's Stifts-Kirche (Collegiate College) which he had transferred to a monastery in Spyck for safekeeping. Balfour's work in rescuing the area's ancient archival material was much appreciated by the local inhabitants. Ten years after the end of the Second World War, in 1955, the *Rheinische Post* recorded with some gratitude that 'with his own hands, Balfour salvaged the archives of several towns, including those of Goch, Kleve, Kranenburg and Xanten'.[7]

Major Balfour's focus on the once beautiful medieval environs of Kleve was intense. Whatever Horrocks and the other Allied military supremos thought, Balfour believed that at least some of the destruction wrought in the town had been unnecessary. He told Webb on 3 March that looting in Kleve was endemic, and that virtually every house, every cupboard, and every safe in the town had been searched and ransacked.[8] There was, according to Balfour, only one building in Kleve with its roof, walls and doors still intact, and with considerable foresight the MFAA man had ensured that he could store rescued works of art and archives in the attic room of these premises. Balfour used a local monk (the only person allowed to move freely about the town) to ensure the security and preservation of this secret treasure store. By 3 March he'd rescued two sixteenth-century carved and painted wooden retable fragments from Kleve Stifts-Kirche and taken them to safety. On 10 March he was back at the same fourteenth-century church, this time rescuing two sculptured altarpieces from destruction. A small group of German civilians were helping him load them on to a handcart[9] when one solitary German shell landed in the street nearby. The cart and its precious cargo were left totally untouched by the resultant explosion, and the Germans helping Balfour also escaped injury, but Ronald Balfour was killed instantly. He was the first of only two Monuments Men to be killed on active service.

Senior officers who knew of Balfour's work in the MFAA were quick to express their sadness at news of his untimely death in Kleve. Lieutenant-Colonel Leonard Woolley, Adviser to the War Office on Monuments, Fine Arts and Archives, wrote shortly after Balfour's death:

> It is a great and unexpected blow. He was so cheerfully delighted at being at the front and was killed when actually engaged in saving some of those works of art which he loved so much. The whole field of art history has suffered a tragic loss.[10]

Ronald Balfour's vast knowledge of art history and medieval history would certainly have been of great use to the Allies in the last weeks of the war, and in the post-war period, when extensive efforts were made to track down artworks and treasures stolen by the Nazis. Despite his early death in Kleve, however, Balfour left a considerable legacy behind him. King's College, and the wider University of Cambridge, gained his private library of over 8,000 books (one of the most substantial personal libraries in the entire country) and King's College subsequently renamed an archives room in his honour. The Monuments Man's all-consuming passion for history and heritage was also much appreciated on the continent of Europe. On the fiftieth anniversary of the reconstruction of the huge 105-metre tower of the church of St Katharina in Hoogstraten, Belgium, it was obvious that local people hadn't forgotten Balfour's pivotal role in preventing the church's total wartime destruction. When the municipality organised an exhibition to celebrate the tower's reconstruction, the event was held in 'grateful commemoration of Major Ronald Balfour'.

It was in the Reichswald area, though, that Balfour's wartime legacy was most profound. During a brutal, sometimes merciless campaign between the British, Canadian and German forces, Balfour lost his life trying to preserve the heritage of newly occupied German territories. His efforts and sacrifice were clearly recognised and venerated in the towns destroyed during the 1945 Reichswald battles. During the 1960s, he was posthumously awarded the Johanna Sebus medal for bravery by the town of Kleve. Earlier, in the summer of 1955, the municipal authorities in Goch constructed an archives room in the town's famous 600-year-old Steintor building. This room was dedicated to Ronald Balfour's memory, and it contained a photograph of the Monuments Man inscribed with the motto '*Alle ehre sei seinem andenken*' ('All honour to his memory'). Ronald's mother, May, and his younger brother, Kenneth, were guests of honour at the ceremony unveiling the room, which went on to house Goch's city archives for the next twenty years.

19

AFTERMATH

> I am getting ready for the next battle. The Rhine is some river, but we shall get over it.
>
> Montgomery to his son, David, early March 1945[1]

Between 8 February and 11 March 1945, the First Canadian Army advanced roughly 40 miles eastwards from the Nijmegen area to Xanten and Wesel on the banks of the Rhine. During this time, a collective total of nearly 40,000 British, Canadian and German troops were either killed or wounded in the forests of the Reichswald and Hochwald, the gutted towns of Kleve, Goch, Weeze, Udem and elsewhere, or on the flooded polders along the banks of the Rhine. According to the First Canadian Army Intelligence Summary issued on 17 March 1945, approximately 22,000 German military personnel were either killed or seriously wounded in the struggle to resist the British and Canadian advance.[2] British forces suffered the most casualties of the three Allied armies involved in Operations Veritable, Blockbuster and Grenade. From the time the offensive was launched, just to the west of the Reichswald Forest, until Menzelen and Xanten were captured on the banks of the Rhine, 10,330 British soldiers were either killed or wounded.[3] The Canadians lost a total of 5,304 men killed or wounded during the same period, though the bulk of their casualties occurred after the launch of Operation Blockbuster on 26 February.[4] In this period after Blockbuster, between 26 February and 11 March, 243 Canadian officers and 3,395 Canadian other ranks were either killed or wounded.[5]

To the south of the British and Canadians, Simpson's U.S. 9th Army sustained roughly 7,300 casualties as it pushed across the Roer and advanced north-east towards Sevelen, Rheinberg and Wesel. The 9th Army also inflicted some 16,000 casualties on German forces, mostly from the 15th Infantry Division, as they tried to resist the progress of Simpson's southern pincer movement aiming for the Wesel bridgeheads. Thus, as a result of its battles against British, Canadian and U.S. forces in this northern sector of the Western Front, German armies had lost some 38,000 men killed and wounded. The U.S. 9th Army also took 29,739 German POWs during its two-week campaign advance from the Roer to Wesel, and the First Canadian Army took a further 22,239 POWs during its drive from the Reichswald Forest to Xanten and Wesel. In bald statistical terms, therefore, the converging operations of the British, Canadian and U.S. armies had cost the Germans roughly 90,000 men killed, wounded or captured, and the western Allies had themselves suffered just short of 23,000 casualties.[6] The 90,000 men lost by the Germans were, of course, irreplaceable, as were the Panther and Tiger tanks, artillery pieces, transports and other military equipment seized or destroyed during the intense fighting between 8 February and 11 March. Moreover, the soldiers who fought the British and Canadians were increasingly drawn from the crack units of Schlemm's First Parachute Army, who often fought to the last man in a vain attempt to stem the onward march of the First Canadian Army. These tough professional soldiers were sometimes frittered away in desperate small-scale skirmishes, and their ranks were much reduced by the time the Allies crossed the Rhine in late March.

The offensive which began to the west of the Reichswald Forest was also significant because it proved to be the first in a series of rolling offensives to the south, which brought Eisenhower's entire Allied army up to the banks of the Rhine. On 1 March, the U.S. First Army launched Operation Lumberjack, which was intended to bring substantial numbers of American forces right up to the banks of the Rhine. The key strategic significance of Lumberjack lay in the somewhat fortuitous capture of the Ludendorff bridge at Remagen, sometimes referred to by historians as the 'Remagen windfall'. The bridge was seized, intact, on 7 March, and before the structure collapsed on 17 March some 25,000 U.S. troops had crossed to the eastern side of the Rhine and established a significant bridgehead. In the overall military scheme of things, a 25,000-strong bridgehead remained quite small, but it still offered the western Allies the opportunity of enveloping the vital Ruhr industrial region via the Remagen bridge, as well as via Montgomery's First Canadian Army in the north. Operation Undertone was the second major offensive, launched on 15 March by the U.S. Third and Seventh Armies and by the French First Army. This southern offensive cleared the Saar–Palatinate area, and advanced American and French forces up to the banks of the Rhine between the towns of Mainz and Mannheim. On 22 March, Patton's Third Army crossed the Rhine at Nierstein, in the Mainz–Bingen area of the Rhineland Palatinate, to form yet another bridgehead. Even so, it was to the north, in Montgomery's sector of the front, between Wesel and Rees, that the main planned Allied assault across the Rhine took place, just one day after Patton's successes at Nierstein. Clearly, by mid-March 1945, Eisenhower's favoured 'broad front' had been established firmly across a vast stretch of territory running along the western banks of the Rhine.

On the Western Front as a whole, between 8 February and 14 March, SHAEF estimated that the Germans had lost 210,000 men. Of this number, at least 42 per cent had been captured, wounded or killed in the German army's bitter battles with the

British, Canadian and Americans during Operations Veritable, Blockbuster and Grenade. In modern military parlance, this represented a considerable 'degrading' of German military capacity, and it was a degrading largely made possible by the efforts of the British and Canadian divisions of the First Canadian Army. As had happened in Sicily during the Italian campaign, and at Caen during the Normandy campaign, Montgomery's armies had drawn in the cream of Germany's reserves to oppose them. It was left to the Americans, in the form of the U.S. 9th Army, to exploit the gaps left by the Germans as they focused on the advances made by the First Canadian Army. As MacDonald points out, there was no army more suitable than the American army, with its vast transportation resources, to take advantage of such a strategic situation.[7]

The whole question of whether the Germans should have fought Allied forces at all on the Rhineland plains west of the Rhine has exercised military strategists for some time. Montgomery, for one, certainly believed that the Germans had committed a huge strategic mistake in fighting for every strip of territory to the west of the great river. Had the Germans simply retired to the east bank of the river and dug in, without resisting the forces of Montgomery, Simpson, Patton and others, they would have presented a formidable barrier to the continued advance of the western Allies. However, as a result of Hitler's increasingly hysterical and irrational reluctance to sanction retreats, huge numbers of German soldiers were killed, wounded or captured on the western side of the Rhine. Even if the German armies had been able to pull back across the Rhine in much greater numbers, it's doubtful whether Germany could have survived for much longer, with Rhine river traffic brought to a standstill. The Rhine was a vital economic artery of the Third Reich, and unimpeded access along its waterways was essential for a whole host of reasons: the German navy, for example, relied on coal shipped along the river to fuel much of its Baltic fleet. In the event, Germany's willingness to fight 'tooth and nail' to the west of the Rhine, in the Rhineland, the Saar and the Palatinate irrevocably altered the course of the war in the west. Eisenhower, just after the end of the war, identified three critical elements which led to ultimate victory in Western Europe. The first element, not surprisingly, was the success of the Normandy landings in June 1944. Second was the closure of the Falaise Pocket, and thirdly, and very significantly, Eisenhower believed that Allied battles to the west of the Rhine in February and March 1945 were a crucial tipping point which brought about Germany's final defeat in the west. Of course, the first and longest of these Rhineland battles began in the Reichswald Forest on 8 February and ended on 11 March at Wesel, and was led by the British and Canadians of the First Canadian Army, along with the U.S. 9th Army. This brutal campaign, forgotten by most in Britain, was clearly of major military and historical significance.

After the Veritable/Blockbuster campaign ended at Wesel, the composition of the First Canadian Army began to change almost immediately. Operation Veritable had involved a series of British and Canadian battles, fought under a Canadian general who followed orders from a British field marshal, who in turn was subordinate to an American supreme commander. The British 3rd Division, 15th Scottish Division, 43rd Wessex Division, 51st Highland Division, 52nd Lowland Division and 53rd Welsh Division, along with XXX Corps as a whole, had all fought as part of the First Canadian Army. General Horrocks always seemed to appreciate that he and his men were fighting a 'Canadian battle', and this fact seems to have caused few if any problems. Generals and their men seemed to be content with the situation. For the purposes of Operation Plunder and the crossing of the Rhine, however, this arrangement was turned on its head. During the planning of Operation Plunder, on 20 March, the 2nd Canadian Corps passed completely under the operational command of Miles Dempsey's British 2nd Army. At the same time, the Canadian 3rd Division was placed under the control of Horrocks' XXX Corps, and even Canada's 9th Infantry

Brigade was destined to operate under the command of Rennie's 51st Highland Division. To make up for the gaps in the post-Veritable First Canadian Army, Harry Crerar's command was bolstered by news that the 1st Canadian Corps was to join his forces with immediate effect. The 1st Corps had been fighting in Italy for some time and made the long journey to western Germany in multiple stages between late February and 3 April 1945. The 1st Canadian Infantry Division, the 1st Canadian Armoured Brigade and the 5th Canadian Armoured Division all joined the First Canadian Army during this period, making Crerar's command more truly Canadian than ever before.

Of course, even the 'new' post-Veritable First Canadian Army still existed as part of Montgomery's 21st Army Group. But there were even changes to this higher-level organisational structure when Simpson's 9th U.S. Army was withdrawn from Montgomery's command at midnight on 3/4 April and passed to Omar Bradley's American 12th Army Group. This move, completed much to Montgomery's chagrin, led to a scaling back of 21st Army Group campaigning plans in Germany. Nevertheless, the First Canadian Army remained an integral part of the 21st Army Group, and as part of the planning for Operation Plunder, Crerar's forces were allocated the difficult task of crossing the Rhine and seizing the large industrial town of Emmerich, which lay some 25 miles to the north-west of Wesel, on the eastern banks of the Rhine. The usual population of Emmerich was about 16,000, though many inhabitants had undoubtedly left the area to escape heavy Allied bombing. The town had featured during the planning stages of Phase 2 of Operation Veritable, when Crerar had advocated capturing the localities of Weeze, Udem, Kalkar and Emmerich. Though the first three had fallen, the latter's position on the eastern side of the Rhine had made it unassailable, at least during the early stages of Veritable, and the First Canadian Army had contented itself with observation of the town, and its ferries, from the opposite bank of the Rhine.

In reality, the battles to reach the banks of the Rhine during February and March 1945 proved to be far harder and more costly than the actual battle to cross the river. Montgomery's set-piece battle to get across – Operation Plunder – began late on 23 March, and bore similarities to the earlier Veritable, Blockbuster and Grenade campaigns. To begin with, many of the British, American and Canadian brigades and divisions used in the Rhine assault were the same as those used in the earlier offensives through and around the Reichswald Forest and – in the case of the Americans – across the Roer river. The German resistance to the crossings in this sector was also provided, largely, by the men of Alfred Schlemm's First Parachute Army, which had provided such a stern test to the Allies during the prosecution of Operations Veritable, Blockbuster and Grenade. Above Schlemm, however, there had been significant changes in the German military command structure. On 11 March, after the successful conclusion of Operation Veritable and the loss of the Remagen bridge, Field Marshal von Rundstedt was dismissed by Hitler as commander-in-chief of German forces in the west. Rundstedt's replacement was the very capable Albert Kesselring, who was transferred from Italy, where he had conducted a highly effective defensive campaign against the British, American, Canadian, Polish and other Allied forces. In the context of the general military situation in western Germany, however, Kesselring had an unenviable task ahead of him. As 21st Army Group Intelligence stated, rather theatrically, on 20 March, he had in fact 'inherited a bankrupt estate'.[8] As with Veritable, Operation Plunder began with a huge artillery bombardment, and after this three Allied formations led the initial assault across the Rhine. Horrocks' ubiquitous XXX Corps led the way, along with the British XII Corps and the American XVI Corps, which had advanced towards the Wesel bridgeheads at the tail end of Operation Grenade. The survivors of the 51st Highland Division's Reichswald campaign, bolstered by replacements, were the first to attack across the Rhine, near Rees, at 2100 on

23 March. In the early hours of 24 March, the 15th Scottish Division also began landing between Wesel and Rees, and the 1st Commando Brigade entered the bomb-cratered wasteland of Wesel with little trouble. Elsewhere, formations from the U.S. XVI Corps landed south of Wesel.

Huge British and U.S. airborne landings took place to the rear of German positions on the Rhine during the morning of 24 March, and it was the primary task of the 15th Scottish Division to push eastwards as quickly as possible to link up with these Anglo-American airborne troops. In general, German opposition to the crossings was very light. There was fierce resistance in some areas, however, to the airborne landings, and the Scottish 15th and 51st Divisions were involved in some heavy fighting against well-positioned German machine gun emplacements. Thomas Rennie, the 51st Division's renowned 'bash on' general, was killed by mortar fire, and the entire 9th Canadian Infantry Brigade had to come to the aid of the 7th Black Watch, which had encountered particularly fierce German resistance at Bienen, north of Rees. In many sectors of the battlefield, though, there was little if any German response to the Allied crossings, and a firm bridgehead was soon established on the eastern banks of the Rhine. To the north, the First Canadian Army attacked Emmerich on the night of 27/28 March, but the town was only secured on 31 March after three days of fighting in which the Canadian Scottish regiment alone sustained 172 casualties. By the end of 27 March, the overall Rhine bridgehead was roughly 35 miles wide and 20 miles deep. Moreover, Schlemm's First Parachute Army, which was really the most effective German formation in the sector, was unable to withstand the pressure of the Allied assault and began to retreat in a north-easterly direction towards Hamburg and Bremen. Schlemm himself was wounded on 27 March and took no further part in directing the fighting. General Gunther Blumentritt replaced Schlemm as commander of the First Parachute Army, and together with General Blaskowitz, who was the overall commander of Germany's Army Group H covering the Netherlands and northern Germany, he began organising a careful withdrawal from 1 April. The German First Parachute Army had been severely depleted by its actions in resisting the Allies during Operations Veritable, Blockbuster and Grenade, and this led directly to its inability to cope with the assaults across the Rhine on 23/24 March. To this extent, the battle to cross the Rhine was really won earlier on, during the fighting in the forests of the Reichswald and the Hochwald, and in the lower Rhine towns of Kleve, Goch, Weeze and Wesel. The Battle of the Reichswald, and Operations Veritable and Grenade as a whole, had sapped the strength of the remaining German armies in the lower Rhineland. For this reason, Allied casualties during Operation Plunder were much lighter than those suffered during the preceding campaigns. British forces suffered 3,968 casualties during the Rhine crossings compared to over 10,000 during Operations Veritable and Blockbuster. The Americans sustained 2,813 casualties during Plunder compared to over 7,000 during Operation Grenade.[9]

Schlemm's paratroopers retreating to the north-east also opened up a dangerous gap between the 1st Parachute Army and the German 15th Army on the Ruhr. The British, Canadians and Americans were then able to pour substantial armour and infantry into this gap, and the end of the war in the west was clearly in sight. On 4 May 1945, less than six weeks after the bridgeheads had been established over the lower Rhine near Wesel and Rees, all German armies in north-west Germany, the Netherlands and Denmark surrendered to Montgomery on Luneburg Heath, a few miles south of Hamburg. By the time that peace came to the shattered continent of Europe, the surviving British and Canadian veterans of Operation Veritable were spread throughout western Europe, from the Netherlands to central Germany, where the 15th Scottish Division led the assault across the Elbe – Operation Enterprise – on 29 April 1945. The significance of these soldiers' earlier achievements during Operation Veritable, when they'd surmounted every obstacle both the weather and the enemy could throw at them, was clearly recognised and appreciated at the time. On 26 March 1945, Eisenhower wrote a letter to General Crerar:

> The purpose of this note is to express to you personally my admiration for the way you conducted the attack by your army, beginning 8 February and ending when the enemy had evacuated his last bridgehead at Wesel. Probably no assault in this war has been conducted under more appalling conditions of terrain than was that one.

Four days later, on 30 March, Crerar responded to Eisenhower with a letter which was just as laudatory about the achievements of both British and Canadian soldiers who had battled through the Reichswald Forest, the Hochwald, fortified towns such as Kleve, Goch, Weeze and Xanten, and onwards to the western banks of the Rhine:

> I believe that no troops could have put up a finer exhibition of enduring gallantry and determination than was demonstrated during those weeks of bitter, bloody and muddy fighting. With such soldiers, British and Canadian, no Commander could ever fail in the tasks he had been set to accomplish.[10]

The letters of both Eisenhower and Crerar act as a fitting tribute to the sacrifices and achievements of the British soldiers who fought in a campaign which has largely slipped from the collective consciousness of the British public today. The letters also offer a stirring reminder of the glittering role played by Canadian armies in the final and complete defeat of German military power in western Europe.

20

REFLECTIONS ON THE CAMPAIGN

> The fighting in the Reichswald was part of a broader battle that took place along the entire length of the river [Rhine]. Both sides suffered heavy losses in this battle for the Rhineland. It took the Allied forces just as long to negotiate the last 30 kilometres to the Rhine as it took them to cross the next 300 kilometres into the heart of Germany...
>
> Liberation Route Europe Foundation, 2019

Charles Perry Stacey, who possessed history degrees from Toronto University and Corpus Christi College, Oxford, along with a Doctorate of Philosophy from Princeton, became the official historian of the Canadian Army during the Second World War. He was given unprecedented access to documents and key personnel of the time, and he adjudged that in the executions of Operation Veritable and Grenade 'the teamwork of the two Allied armies [First Canadian and 9th U.S.] had produced an excellent result and a great contribution to the final victory, now not very far away'.[1] Stacey, who collated his research in the ten years or so after the end of the Second World

War, was surely right to emphasise the unity and cohesion that existed between British and Canadian forces during the Veritable campaign, and the positive results that this brought about. However, successful teamwork with the Americans was, by February 1945, somewhat harder for Montgomery to achieve, because by this time the British field marshal had developed a strained relationship with some of the higher echelons in the American military.

During the height of the Battle of the Bulge crisis, Eisenhower gave Montgomery temporary control of a number of U.S. armies and formations, as part of an effort to beat back the German offensive. This action antagonised several leading American generals, including Omar Bradley, head of the U.S. 12th Army Group, who found it hard to forgive Montgomery for his public comments claiming much of the credit for developing the Allied strategy which defeated the German offensive. Bradley then went on to make a private (but recorded) telephone call to General Patton on 10 February in which he expressed some personal glee at the fact that Montgomery's northern offensive in and around the Reichswald was being slowed by fierce German resistance.[2] Given these somewhat less than propitious circumstances, the U.S. 9th Army went on to cooperate very effectively with the First Canadian Army during the period of the Veritable and Grenade operations. Bradley, perhaps unsurprisingly, gave much of the credit for this cooperation to the 'uncommonly normal' civility of U.S. 9th Army staff, who were apparently less temperamental than their colleagues in the U.S. First Army. Montgomery himself, though, must be given much of the credit for this collaboration during the Veritable/Grenade offensives. He handled William Hood Simpson and his 9th U.S. Army with some finesse. There were no traces of frustration or impatience in Montgomery's dealings with Simpson. The decision about postponing Grenade, which had severe consequences for British and Canadian soldiers fighting in the north, was left up to Simpson, as was the decision about when to recommence the offensive. Indeed, Simpson and Montgomery seem to have had cordial personal relations – a fact trumpeted in the British press, which claimed that the two worked well together because they both took care to avoid unnecessary casualties on the battlefield. Again, Montgomery went on record to thank Simpson and the U.S. 9th Army for its role in Operation Grenade. During a letter written on 10 March, just a few weeks before the 9th reverted back to the command of Omar Bradley, Montgomery told Simpson:

> I would like to tell you how very pleased I have been with everything the Ninth Army has done. The operations were planned and carried through with great skill and energy .... I can truthfully say that the operations of the Ninth Army since 23 February last have been up to the best standards.[3]

Though the letter certainly didn't contain the fulsome tributes paid to Crerar, it was nonetheless a courteous expression of thanks for the assistance provided by Simpson and his 9th Army during the preceding months.

Far fewer problems stood in the way of British–Canadian military unity and teamwork during the delivery of Operations Veritable and Blockbuster. Canada's links to the UK were particularly strong during this period, and these links were never more closely illustrated than in the shared Scottish ancestry and military traditions of many who lived in the two nations. Canada had its Camerons and its Argyll and Sutherland Highlanders, as did the British Army, and both fought together well during the Reichswald campaign. These shared Scottish cultural affinities proved to be advantageous during various parts of the fighting, and never more so than during a Gordon Highlanders night assault on a German strongpoint near Gennep, south of the Reichswald. The British Gordons commander was afraid of his soldiers being hit by 'friendly' fire in the darkness, and so ordered his bagpipers to play the regimental march. Out of the darkness, and above the sound of gunfire and bursting shells, the response of the pipers of the Queen's Own Cameron Highlanders of Canada could be discerned quite clearly, and a 'friendly' fire incident was averted. German forces in the area were apparently much disconcerted, and somewhat baffled, by the plaintive wail of the pipes. The impact of these Canadian Scottish bonds was enduring, even among the many English-born soldiers who served in Scottish regiments. Rifleman Adrian Bridge, for example, of the 9th Cameronians, was born and brought up in Liverpool, and came into close contact with Canadian soldiers north of the Reichswald, and at Kleve, Goch and elsewhere. Later on, inspired by these battlefield friendships and connections, he was one of many British veterans who applied for, and was granted, the right of permanent settlement in Canada.[4]

The links between the British and Canadian generals who directed the progress of Operation Veritable were also very close. Guy Simonds, Canadian II Corps commander, was born in Bury St Edmunds, Suffolk, and Christopher Vokes, commander of the Canadian 4th Armoured Division, was born in Armagh. Other Canadian commanders had either been based in the UK, or with UK forces, since the outbreak of the war in 1939. The process wasn't all one-way, however. The 51st Highland Division's commander, Thomas Rennie, had very close connections to Canada. In 1936, his wife and family travelled to Canada on board the passenger liner RMS *Empress of Japan*, and two years later they finally emigrated, travelling on board the same ship. At the apex of the Anglo-Canadian military structure, Horrocks, Crerar and Montgomery all seem to have got on well together during the campaign. Montgomery often receives a bad press because of his alleged egocentrism, and because of a supposedly entrenched belief in his own personal infallibility in matters of military strategy. Nevertheless, he comes across quite well during the isolated glimpses we have of him during Operation Veritable. When his staff car was caught up in one of the interminable traffic jams so characteristic of the early days of the Reichswald campaign, Montgomery personally stepped out to try and get the traffic moving again.[5] The newly promoted field marshal may well have had some previous reservations about Crerar's rapid rise to generalship. He may also have been somewhat antagonised by the Canadian's failure to appear at an Operation Market Garden briefing session in autumn 1944 because of a prior engagement at a Dieppe raid commemoration. If so, he didn't allow this to influence their relationship during Operation Veritable. Montgomery gave Crerar all the backing and support he needed, and when the European war ended in May 1945 he wrote an extremely effusive 'Dear Harry' letter which was exceptional for the warmth and gratitude it exhibited. The letter, quoted below, says much about the close bonds forged between the armies of the two nations:

> My dear Harry,
> I feel that on this day, I must write you a note of personal thanks for all that you have done for me since we first served together in this war. No commander can ever have had a more loyal subordinate than I have had in you. And under your command the Canadian Army has covered itself with glory in the campaign in western Europe. I want you to know that I am deeply grateful for what you have done. If ever there is anything I can do for you, or for your magnificent Canadian soldiers, you know that you have only to ask.
>
> Yours always,
> Monty.[6]

Unlike Montgomery, XXX Corps commander General Horrocks had few problems dealing with the Americans. In fact, everyone seemed to like Horrocks – nicknamed 'Jorrocks' by those who knew him – be they American, British or Canadian. This was perhaps no real surprise, as 'Jorrocks' was that most unusual of creatures, a modest, self-deprecating general. The

American brigadier general James Gavin, commander of the U.S. 82nd Airborne Division, who got to know Horrocks well during Operation Market Garden, said of the XXX Corps leader that he was 'truly a unique general officer and his qualities of leadership were greater than any I have ever seen. General Horrocks was the finest general officer I met during the war and the finest corps commander.'[7] These sentiments were supported by Eisenhower, who went on record to state that Horrocks was 'the outstanding British general under Montgomery'. In addition to considerable personal charm, and an undoubted capacity for leadership, Horrocks was also a general who'd experienced life at the sharp end during the Second World War: he was shot in the chest and stomach by a stray German fighter plane during June 1943, and only returned to front-line action after five operations and fourteen months of recovery time.[8]

The bonds of loyalty and affection between Brian Horrocks and Montgomery were particularly strong. Both had joined the 8th Army in North Africa during August 1942, Horrocks as a corps commander and Montgomery as the general-in-charge. Churchill visited both within a week of their arrival and was apparently unimpressed by Horrocks' focus on defence rather than attack. 'He's no good, get rid of him,' he urged Montgomery. 'Look sir, you stick to your sphere, and I'll stick to mine' was Montgomery's response, and Horrocks never forgot this level of support and backing from his new superior officer. For Montgomery, and for many others – British, American and Canadian – Horrocks and XXX Corps were the natural choices to lead the charge through the Reichswald on 8 February, despite the earlier delays and challenges of the Market Garden campaign in September 1944. If, on the basis of a brief interview in 1942, Churchill believed that Horrocks lacked a suitable appreciation of the virtues of attack rather than defence, then the offensive through the Reichswald and on into the Rhineland plains was to prove him very wrong indeed.

Crerar and Horrocks, together with the team of British and Canadian divisional commanders involved, all subscribed to the policy of speed, momentum and constant forward movement. The guiding principle behind the offensive was neatly and accurately summed up by Crerar in his message to troops of 7 February 1945, when he stated, 'Whatever the difficulties of ground and weather, the forward thrust through the enemy and his defences will be pressed without respite.' This is indeed what happened. There were very few 'respites', and British and Canadian troops continued to attack, day and night, through driving rain, hail, snow, oceans of mud, and often knee deep in flood waters, for over a month.

The policy of constant, relentless attacking, whatever the weather, led to heavy casualties at Goch, Weeze, Udem, the Hochwald and elsewhere, but the soldiers kept on moving forward, even if the pace was somewhat slow on occasions. The British 3rd Division, for example, managed to advance eastwards at the rate of about 3 miles a day despite encountering heavy German resistance at Kervenheim, Winnekendonk and elsewhere. Disputes and disagreements occur in every military campaign, however, and the offensive through the Reichswald was no different in this respect. At the time, and ever afterwards, the Canadian major-general, Christopher Vokes, was criticised for continuing to push his infantry and armour through the slaughterhouse of the Hochwald Gap. The Canadian II Corps commander, Guy Simonds, together with Vokes and a few others, also clearly believed that Daniel Spry, major-general in charge of Canada's 3rd Division, didn't possess the aggressive 'pressing-on' mentality needed to push the Veritable/Blockbuster offensive onwards to a successful conclusion. For his part, Spry thought – probably correctly – that Vokes and Simonds didn't appreciate properly how difficult it was for front-line soldiers to fight in the mud, rain and confined spaces of the Hochwald Gap. At the end of the campaign, Crerar transferred

Major-General Spry to England, where he was appointed head of the Canadian Reinforcements Unit. Simonds and Vokes continued in post and played key roles in the Canadian Army's push into the Netherlands and Germany. Vokes continued, in a forthright manner, to divide opinion and court controversy. Between 11 and 12 April 1945, he ordered the German town of Friesoythe, in Lower Saxony, to be razed to the ground after one of his closest friends and proteges, Lieutenant-Colonel Frederick Wigle – who'd been a significant supporter of Vokes' Hochwald strategy – was shot dead by a German sniper.

On the British side, there was also an undercurrent of resentment in some quarters about the precipitate nature of some of the localised attacks launched during the offensive. Planning for the attack on Winnekendonk by the 2nd Lincolnshires was very brief, and the same was true for several other attacks carried out by various British battalions and regiments during the campaign. Rapid, improvised planning of this sort, based on sometimes inadequate intelligence about the nature and scale of German opposition in a particular village, wood or field, undoubtedly led to heavy casualties on some occasions. Such occurrences were inevitable given the nature of the fighting which took place during the Reichswald campaign. Horrocks himself conceded that once his divisions were launched forward on 8 February, the exercise of generalship became very difficult indeed. Command and control became almost impossible to exert in a lunar landscape of shell craters, rubble and flood waters. Instead, individual battles were often decided by the actions of soldiers, NCOs and officers on the spot.

The terrain over which these battles was fought was not ideal for the proper conduct of armoured warfare. In the rubble of towns like Kleve, Goch, Weeze and Xanten, tank mobility was much reduced, and flooding in the forests and rural areas meant that large numbers of Shermans, Churchills and Valentines became bogged down irretrievably in mud and water. Many infantry assaults had to take place without tank support, which led to higher casualties. Veterans' recollections often mention the lack of armoured support. While this was undoubtedly true, armoured formations still played a key role in some of the major battles of the campaign at Winnekendonk, at Hochwald and in and around the Reichswald itself. The impact of the spring thaw, freezing temperatures and flooding upon the Reichswald campaign was obviously immense, and has led some post-war strategists to criticise Allied military planners, principally those in the 21st Army Group, for not anticipating such problems in advance. Obviously, February and March in the German Imperial Forest was never likely to be warm, but as it turned out, First Canadian Army Buffalos, Weasels and other 'funnies' were sufficiently numerous to sustain the offensive despite flooding and the spring thaw. The failure to seize the Schwammenauel dam before its walls were blown by German engineers was a definite Allied strategic oversight, however, which – because of the consequent flooding – delayed Operation Grenade and changed the nature of Operation Veritable irrevocably.

Flooding caused by dam and dyke blowing, and by the spring thaw, certainly slowed down the Reichswald offensive, meaning that the timetable for the attacks was wildly awry from the very beginning. Even before elements of the 15th Scottish Division had seized the Materborn heights above Kleve, during the first day of the offensive, the drive eastwards along the northern flank of the Reichswald was already eleven hours behind schedule. Further to the west, at Wyler, Den Heuvel and Hochstrasse, the Canadians fell some five hours behind schedule during the first day of the offensive. In essence, Operation Veritable was intended to be a rapid, carefully timetabled offensive with the Reichswald Forest at its centre. British divisions incorporated within XXX Corps, and supported by the Canadians, would smash eastwards through and around the Reichswald, debouch into the Rhineland plains and then hopefully seize a bridge across the Rhine. The reality was very different, and involved a blood-soaked slog through the mud which lasted for more than a month and involved many complex, interlinked stages.

In the end, though, the British and Canadians achieved a significant victory, which did indeed help shorten the duration of the war in the west. British and Canadian military achievements during Operation Veritable were, in essence, due to the partnership between infantry, armour and, where weather allowed, air power. At the heart of the UK's military partnership was the brigade, a military structure in which men from all parts of Britain fought together and, in some cases, died together. By the time of Operation Veritable, the British brigade was a more polyglot structure than ever before. Montgomery and his team of senior officers took a keen interest in trying to ensure that no more than one battalion from a particular regiment was included within a brigade. The reasoning behind this policy was sensible: if a brigade was involved in what Montgomery referred to as a 'sticky situation', then the consequent casualties would be spread across the UK rather than coming from just one particular location. By following such a policy, the British Army could avoid repeating the disasters of the First World War, when the annihilation of local Pals battalions on the Somme meant that whole streets and neighbourhoods in parts of Bradford, Leeds and elsewhere were denuded of their menfolk. On a few occasions, battalions did slip through the net and end up fighting in the same battle. The 6th and 7th Cameronians, for instance, fought at Alpen during the last days of Veritable, though it was the 6th battalion that suffered the bulk of the casualties. Thus, in the brigades of the British Army that fought from the Reichswald through to the Rhine, men from the Derbyshire Yeomanry fought as part of the 51st Highland Division, and Englishmen in the Oxfordshire and Buckinghamshire Light Infantry fought as part of the 53rd Welsh Division. In addition, there were countless Scots in English regiments, and many, many Englishmen fought in Scottish regiments involved in Operation Veritable.

In many ways, the Reichswald Forest campaign, in all its complexity, showed the UK at its very best: a picture of cohesion and unity in adverse conditions. Similarly, Canadian regiments, evolving from both the English and French historical and linguistic traditions of that country, fought together and died together during Operations Veritable and Blockbuster. Of course, both armies fought under the banner of the First Canadian Army, which says much about the ties of Commonwealth and Empire at this particular time in history. The fact that nearly 40,000 British soldiers stood up and advanced into battle on 8 February 1945 as part of a Canadian army was in itself a remarkable event, and one which deserves to be remembered with considerable awe and respect.

APPENDIX A

Reichswald Forest Campaign: Code Names & Passwords from the Original War Diary of 9th Battalion The Cameronians (Scottish Rifles), February 1945

Towns & Villages

Code Name	Town/Village
Aberford	Grafenthal
Alford	Rindern
Ashdown	Forest of Kleve
Bangor	Goch
Brideford	Middelaar
Brighouse	Heumen
Bromyard	Zelderheide
Carwood	Qualberg
Conway	Grave BR
Crawford	Kamp
Croxton	Riethorst
Dalby	Hau
Darton	Horst

Code Name	Town/Village
Daventry	Zyfflich
Digby	De Hoise
Driffield	Schottheide
Farlow	Kessel
Fastville	Grafwegen
Fonham	Breedweg
Grasby	Frasselt
Hatfield	Emmerich
Hinton	Kellan
Hipfield	Heikant
Holyhead	Kranenburg
Howden	Bruuk
Kirkham	Smorenhook
Lublow	Wyler
Markfield	Mehr
Mirfield	Heikant
Plumtree	Materborn
Ratby	Nutterden
Ravensfield	Groeningen
Repton	Reichswald Forest
Ripley	Zelder
Rotherham	Marienbaum
Rugby	Xanten
Stainforth	Groesbeek
Stamford	Hanselaar
Tadcaster	Aaldon
Tuxford	Mook
Welby	Donsbruggen
Wellington	Grave
Wembley	Malden
Wigan	Kleve

Rivers & Canals

Code Name	River/Canal
Trent	Maas
Humber	Niars
Clyde	Kalflach
Windermere	Dasmeer
Shannon	Rhine
Welland	Spoy Kanaal

Crossroads & Road Junctions

Code Name	Road Feature & Grid Ref
Holborn	Crossroads (852580)
Aldgate	Road Junction (817553)
Hampstead	Road Junction (869573)

Passwords

From	To	Challenge	Reply
1200 - D-1	1200 - D-Day	Father	Thames
1200 - D-Day	1200 - D+1	Virgin	Snow
1200 - D+1	1200 - D+2	Silver	Ring
1200 - D+2	1200 - D+3	Jolly	Farmer
1200 - D+3	1200 - D+4	Mother	Superior
1200 - D+4	1200 - D+5	Sour	Grapes
1200 - D+5	1200 - D+6	Simple	Simon
First	Spare	Plum	Duff
Second	Spare	Short	Odds

Movement Orders & Objectives

Code Name	Movement Order/Objective
Argus	4th bt. Royal Welsh Fusiliers (RWF) move forward
Barham	160 Infantry Bde move at 30 mins notice
Dido	158 Infantry Bde move within 1 hour
Hollyhock	4th bt. RWF objective
Honeysuckle	2nd bt. Monmouthshire regiment objective
Ivanhoe	1st bt. Highland Light Infantry (HLI) pass 1st bt. Oxford/Bucks regiment
Kimberley	160 Bde to move
Lion	Intermediary Objective Phase 2
Marigold	Final Objective Phase 3
Ramillies	Objective Phase 1
Sydney	158 Infantry Bde to move
Snapdragon	160 Infantry Bde objective
Verbena	6 bt. RWF objective

APPENDIX B

Divisional Order of Battle (Operation Veritable)/Allied Commanding Officers

General Officer in Command of 21st Army Group: Field Marshal B. L. Montgomery

First Canadian Army: Lieutenant-General Harry Crerar

British XXX Corps: Lieutenant-General Brian Horrocks

Division	Commanding Officer
3rd Canadian Division	Daniel Spry
2nd Canadian Division	Albert Bruce Matthews
4th Canadian Armoured Division	Christopher Vokes
15th (Scottish) Division	Colin Muir Barber
51st Highland Division	Thomas Rennie
53rd (Welsh) Division	Robert Knox Ross
79th Armoured Division	Percy Hobart

Added as Campaign Progressed

Division	Commanding Officer
3rd British Division	Lashmer 'Bolo' Whistler
11th Armoured Division	George Roberts
43rd Wessex Division	Ivor Thomas
52nd Lowland Division	Edmund Hakewill-Smith
Guards Armoured Division	Allan Adair

German Commanding Officers

General der Fallschirmtruppe (First Parachute Army): Alfred Schlemm

Division	Commanding Officer
84th Infantry Division	Heinz Fiebig
6th Parachute Division	Hermann Lukas Plocher
7th Parachute Division	Wolfgang Erdmann
47th Panzer Corps, comprising:	Heinrich Freiherr von Luttwitz
15th Panzer Grenadier Division & 116th Panzer Division	Wolfgang Maucke
346th Division	Walter Ludwig
Panzer Lehr Division	Friedrich Steinmuller
15th Infantry Division	Horst Niemack (Jan–April 1945). Intended as a reserve formation, but ultimately used against the U.S. 9th Army.

Allied Air Force Supporting the First Canadian Army during Operation Veritable

British	Commanding Officer
RAF Bomber Command	Sir Arthur 'Bomber' Harris
RAF No. 2 Group, 2nd Tactical Air Force	Basil Embry
RAF No. 83 Group, 2nd Tactical Air Force	Harry Broadhurst
No. 84 Group, 2nd Tactical Air Force	E. C. Hudleston

U.S.	Commanding Officer
U.S. 8th Air Force	Ira Eaker
U.S. 9th Air Force	Otto P. Weyland

APPENDIX C

153rd Field Ambulance Unit (1). Patients treated 9–24 February 1945 during the Reichswald Campaign.

Date (2)	Battle casualties	Sick (3)	POWs	Evacuated (4)
9	25	2	4	30
10	73	12	20	110
11	46	20	13	102
12	29	14	3	40
13	31	30	1	73
14	20	17	3	40
15	2	6	0	8
16	1	2	0	3
23	84	23	17	96
24	102	35	1	0

(1) Attached to 227 Highland Infantry Brigade, 15th Scottish Division.
(2) On 8 February, approx. 50 casualties were treated at the unit, mostly suffering from injuries sustained in minefields, but no further specific details were given.
(3) Non- battlefield injuries inc. road accidents, pneumonia etc.
(4) Those needing more intensive treatment were evacuated to base hospitals and other institutions. On 23 February, 28 badly injured service personnel were also given priority evacuation.

Between 17 and 22 February, the Unit was relocated and received no patients. During the night of 24/25 February, 227 Brigade was pulled out of the front line, and 153rd Field Ambulance Unit returned to Tilburg in the Netherlands for further training, rest and recuperation.

Source: 153rd Field Ambulance Unit War Diary, February 1945

193rd Field Ambulance Unit (attached to the 46th Highland Infantry Brigade) 15th Scottish Division. Patients treated 9–20 February 1945 during the Reichswald Campaign.

Date	British officers & other ranks	Canadian officers & other ranks	POWs
9	496	1	11
10	9	-	-
11	2	-	-
12 (1)	-	-	-
13	4	4	-
14	57	2	-
15	120	20	17
16	57	27	20
17	37	4	8
18	39	20	3
19	33	19	2
20	20	2	2
TOTAL (2)	874	129	63

(1) On 11–12 February, A Company of the Unit moved its medical staff and facilities to Nutterden.

(2) The patient totals treated represent only a fraction of the unit's activities during this period. Between 14 and 25 February the Unit played a major role in evacuating 4,000 casualties, via amphibious vehicles, to a range of other medical facilities.

Source: 193rd Field Ambulance Unit War Diary, February 1945.

War Diary: 399th Company Royal Army Service Corps (RASC), 1–8 February 1945 (Unpublished)

Date	Hour	Activity
1	0600 onwards	Twelve 3-ton vehicles collected petrol & then distributed 10,932 gallons.
2		Fifteen 3-ton vehicles collected petrol, oil & lubricant (POL) from Depot. Thirty 3-ton vehicles collected tank tracks for 6th Guards Tank Brigade. Twelve 3-ton vehicles collected & transported tank tracks for other formations. Four 3-ton vehicles collected DERV.
3	0600	Two 3-ton vehicles collected DERV. Nineteen 3-ton vehicles collected POL. One 3-ton vehicle carried blankets to battalions.
4		Twenty-one 3-ton vehicles collected POL.
5		Six 3-ton vehicles collected POL 8,000 gallons of fuel issued.
6		24,747 gallons of fuel issued. Twenty-seven 3-ton vehicles collected POL.
7	0200	6007 gallons of fuel issued. Nineteen 3-ton vehicles collected 25 pounder artillery shells. Twenty 3-ton vehicles collected 2,400 rounds of 17-pounder high explosive artillery shells. Two 3-ton vehicles distributed loud hailers & jerry cans to the 15th Division.
8		13,201 gallons of fuel issued. Three 3-ton vehicles loaded oil & proceeded to Goirle, south-west of Nijmegen. Thirty-two 3-ton vehicles collected POL. Eight 3-ton vehicles collected coal and delivered the load to Goirle. Four 3-ton vehicles proceeded to Nijmegen.

War Diary: 62nd Company, Royal Army Service Corps (RASC) February 1945 (unpublished)

Date	Hour	Activity
9	0830	Convoy of seventeen vehicles moved from Groesbeek to Kranenburg.
10		Twenty 3-ton vehicles 'humping' ammunition from Nijmegen to Gemert.
11		Maintenance of small arms ammunition supply for 15th Division.
12		Forward base at Kranenburg cut off owing to floods.
17	1000	Vehicles 'humping' ammunition from Zeeland to Nijmegen.
18		Forward ammunition dump established at Kranenburg. DUKWs employed in ferrying ammunition to forward ammunition dump.
19	1500	Sixteen vehicles proceeded to Veghel and joined a convoy of sixty lorries delivering 25-pounder ammunition to Kranenburg forward dump.
20	1500	Twenty-six vehicles proceeded to Veghel, collected 25-pounder ammunition, and joined a convoy of sixty-six lorries travelling to Kranenburg forward dump.
21		Six DUKWs loaded with small arms ammunition and taken to Kranenburg forward dump.
22		Every vehicle engaged in 'humping' 25-pounder ammunition from Veghel to 25-pounder forward gun sites.
23		Every available vehicle engaged on dumping programme of 25-pounder ammunition to forward gun sites.
25		Orders received for Company to move to Tilburg (Netherlands). Some leave allocations then issued.

APPENDIX D

105 Military Awards & Decorations Granted to British & Canadian Service Personnel During Operation Veritable (Reichswald Forest Campaign), 8 February–11 March 1945

VC Victoria Cross
DSO Distinguished Service Order
MM Military Medal
MC Military Cross
DCM Distinguished Conduct Medal
Bar When the same award is won on multiple occasions (e. g. MC Bar indicates that the recipient was awarded the Military Cross, and then judged to be worthy of the same award on a later occasion).

Lewis Aitken, 3rd Tank Battalion Scots Guards, Kranenburg (MM)
Private George Atkin (Stretcher-bearer), 2nd Seaforth Highlanders, Reichswald Forest (MM)
Lieutenant Harry Haultain Badger, Royal Winnipeg Rifles, Louisendorf (MM)

Private Henry Bailey, 5th Seaforth Highlanders, Hekkens crossroads (MM)

Lance Corporal Joseph Baron, 1st Black Watch, Reichswald Forest (MM)

Sergeant Maurice Bausse, Le Regiment de Maissonueve, Kalkar/Xanten road, Distinguished Conduct Medal (DCM)

Captain Beaton, 5th Cameron Highlanders, Kleve/Hekkens road (MC)

Major Walter Beckhhurst, Somerset Light Infantry, Goch (MC)

Lance Corporal Alexander P Blades, 1st Black Watch, Niers Bridge, Kessel (MM)

Lieutenant Cuthbert P. S. Bowlby, No. 3 Troop – Fife & Forfar Yeomanry, Gennep (MC)

Lieutenant Colonel Berenger 'Bill' C Bradford, 5th Black Watch, Goch (DSO)

Major Alexander C. C. Brodie, 5th Black Watch, Goch (DSO)

Sergeant C. H. Byce, Lake Superior Regiment, Hochwald Gap (DCM)

Sergeant John Joseph Cain, 3rd Irish Guards, Vrij (MM)

Major Donald Fraser Callender, 5th Cameron Highlanders, Reichswald Forest (DSO)

Lieutenant Colonel Henry R. Carr, 274 Field Company, Royal Engineers, Niers bridgehead (Bar to DSO)

Major Charles Thompson Cathro (C. O.) 1st Black Watch, Reichswald Forest (MC)

Sergeant Wilfred Corker, 107 Regiment, Royal Armoured Corps, Reichswald Forest (MM)

Sergeant Aubrey Cosens, Queens Own Rifles of Canada, Kalkar/Udem road (posthumous VC)

Lieutenant Douglas Crockett, 5th Black Watch, Gennep (MC)

Captain Paul A. Cropp, Essex Scottish Regiment, Goch/Kalkar road (MC)

Sergeant Sidney Curtis, A Company, 4th Wiltshire Regiment, Eselsberg (MM)

Lieutenant James R. Cuthbertson, 5/7 Gordon Highlanders, Weeze (MC)

Harry A. Davies (Driver), 147 Company, Royal Army Service Corps, Niers Bridge (MM)

Major L. H. Denison, Royal Winnipeg Rifles, Moyland Wood (DSO)

Colour Sergeant Major F. L. Dixon, Canadian Essex Scottish, Kalkar/Xanten (Bar to MM)

John W. Drennan (Driver), 147 Company, Royal Army Service Corps, Niers Bridge (MM)

Major Drewry, Royal Hamilton Light Infantry, Goch/Kalkar road (DSO)

Lieutenant Douglas J. Dudley, 1st Fife & Forfar Yeomanry, Kleve/Hekkens road (MM)

Lieutenant Colonel Claude Dunbar, 3rd Battalion Scots Guards, Louisendorf (DSO)

Major Ian A. Duncan-Millar, 276 Field Company, Royal Engineers, Niers bridgehead (MC)

Lance Corporal Angus D. Elliot, Fort Garry Horse, Goch/Kalkar road (DCM)

Major Basil O. P. Eugster, 3rd Irish Guards, Hommersum (DSO)

Major William D. D. Evans, 1st Welsh Guards, Hassum (MC)

Major Charles Farrell, 3rd Tank Battalion, Scots Guards, Groesbeek (MC)

Sergeant Major William John Foster, Essex Scottish, Louisendorf (MM)

Captain John Fyffe, 79th Medium Regiment (Scottish Horse) Black Watch, Villers (MC)

Major James Ian Gammie, 5/7 Gordon Highlanders, Reichswald Forest (MC)

Major Ronald Grantham, Royal Tank Regiment, Reichswald Forest (Bar to MC)

Lieutenant Patrick Hugh Grant, 5th Seaforth Highlanders, Frasselt/Hekkens road (MC)

Colour Sergeant Major Green, 2nd Argyll & Sutherland Highlanders, Reichswald Forest (DCM)

Lance Corporal Francis E. Griffee, 1st Black Watch (Signals Division), River Niers crossing (MM)

Private Lloyd P. Head (Stretcher-bearer), Essex Scottish, Louisendorf (MM)

Lieutenant David Heaps, 18th Canadian Anti-Tank Battery, C Troop, Goch/Kalkar road (MC)

Lieutenant David Heaps, Royal Hamilton Light Infantry, Louisendorf, Military Cross (MC)

Captain James C. Hogg, 126 Field Regiment, 1st Black Watch, Niers crossing (MC)

Private William Imrie (Stretcher-bearer), 176 Field Ambulance, Royal Army Medical Corps, Niers crossing (MM)

Acting Corporal P. P. Katchanoski (Junior NCO), 1st Canadian Scottish, Moyland Wood (DCM)

Lieutenant W. L. Keating, Regina Rifles Regiment, Moyland Wood (MC)

Corporal Arthur J. Kelly, Royal Hamilton Light Infantry, Kalkar (MM)

Captain Duncan F. Kennedy, Royal Hamilton Light Infantry, Schrannenhof (MC)

Captain Ian Lesley Kidd, 1st Gordon Highlanders, Heyen (MC)

Colour Sergeant Major Ernest C. Knott, Royal Hamilton Light Infantry, Kalkar (Bar to MM)

Private George Henry Lambeth (Stretcher-bearer), 2nd Seaforth Highlanders, Reichswald Forest (MM)

Sergeant Eric A. Maclean, Mechanic, 107 Regiment, Royal Armoured Corps, Bruuk (MM)

Private Allan MacDonald, Royal Hamilton Light Infantry, Goch/Kalkar road (MM)

Major B. F. MacDonald Essex, Scottish Canadian, Kalkar/Xanten (DSO)

Major Bruce F. MacDonald, Fort Garry Horse, Goch/Kalkar road (DSO)

Sergeant Frederick H. J. Maxey, 5th Black Watch, Robenhof (DCM)

Sergeant David McClew, 5th Cameron Highlanders, Kleve/Hekkens road (DCM)

Major Kenneth W. McIntyre, Essex Scottish, Goch/Kalkar road (DSO)
Sergeant James McIvor, Royal Winnipeg Rifles, Louisendorf (DCM)
Corporal Hugh McKeown, 7th Black Watch, Hekkens village (DCM)
Sergeant Robert J. McLelland, Royal Hamilton Light Infantry, Goch/Kalkar road (MM)
Lieutenant John S. McMartin, 107 Royal Armoured Corps, Reichswald Forest (MC)
Private Robert Middleton, 7th Black Watch, Breedweg (MM)
Lieutenant William Moore, 3rd Irish Guards, Hommersum (MC)
Lance Sergeant William H. Moriarty, Essex Scottish, Goch/Kalkar road (MM)
Major Morrison, Gordon Highlanders, Thomashof (DSO)
Major John H. F. Morton, 7 Argyll & Sutherland Highlanders, Goch (Bar to MM)
Major Mumford, D Company, The Hampshire Regiment, Berkhofel (MC)
Major Leonard Naylor, C Company, The Hampshire Regiment, Berkhofel (MC)
Sergeant Richard Newell, 2nd Seaforth Highlanders, Kleve/Kessel road (MM)
Lieutenant Anthony Francis McLeod Paget, Oxford & Buckinghamshire Light Infantry, Asperberg (DSO)
Lieutenant Colonel J. E. C. Pangman, Canadian Essex Scottish, Kalkar/Xanten (DSO)
Major Anthony Parsons, A Company, 4 Wiltshire Regiment, Eselsberg (MC)
Lieutenant Daniel Pullen, 1st Worcestershire Regiment, Kellen Reigel (MC)
Captain Frank Quilter, 2nd Seaforth Highlanders, Reichswald Forest (MC)
Captain William Booth Rae-Smith, Black Watch, Bruuk (MC)
Lieutenant Frederick R. Rig, 2nd Canadian Anti-Tank Regiment, Goch/Kalkar (MC)

Lance Sergeant, Thomas Roberts, 32nd Guards Armoured Brigade, Welsh Guards, Hommersum (MM)

Major D. M. Rogers, Black Watch (Royal Highland Regiment), Kalkar/Udem road (DSO)

Lieutenant Robert Runcie, 3rd Scots Guards, Winnekendonk (MM)

Lieutenant David Scott-Barrett, 3rd Battalion Tank, Scots Guards, Kranenburg (MC)

Lieutenant Alexander M. Scott, 5/7 Gordon Highlanders, Reichswald Forest (MC)

Lance Corporal Leslie Harry Shorthouse, 1st Black Watch, Hekkens crossroads (MM)

Private Leo Sloat, Royal Hamilton Light Infantry, Kalkar (MM)

Private James Stokes, Kings Shropshire Light Infantry, Kervenheim (posthumous VC)

Corporal Donald Swatman, 5th Black Watch, Gennep (MM)

Major Peter Taylor (Acting Commanding Officer), 1st Black Watch, Reichswald Forest (DSO)

Lance Bombardier Alexander Thomson, 94 Field Regiment, Royal Artillery, Eselsberg (MM)

Sapper Thomson, 274 Field Company, Royal Engineers, Niers Bridgehead (MM)

Lieutenant Ronald Tilling, C Company, 4th Dorsetshire Regiment, Eselsberg (MC)

Major Frederick A. Tilston, Canadian Essex Scottish, Hochwald Layback (VC)

Sergeant Thomas William Todd, Royal Winnipeg Rifles, Louisendorf (MM)

Captain Anthony Townshend, 94 Field Regiment, Royal Artillery, Eselsberg (MC)

Lieutenant Horace R. Tucker, Essex Scottish, Kalkar (MC)

Lieutenant Ian T. P. Ventris, 1st Gordon Highlanders, Thomashof (MC)

Sergeant Arthur E. Vousden, 61st Anti-Tank Regiment, Gennep/Ottersum (MM)

Lieutenant Colonel William D. Whitaker, Royal Hamilton Light Infantry, Louisendorf (Bar to DSO)

Captain Richard O. M. Williams, 154 Brigade, Signals Division, River Niers (MC)

Captain William Michael Wingate-Gray, 154 Brigade HQ, Black Watch, River Niers (Bar to MC)

Gunner John N. Willson, 79th Medium Regiment (Scottish Horse) Villers (MM)

Sergeant William York, 61st Anti-Tank Regiment, Goch fortress (MM)

APPENDIX E

Aubrey Cosens' Citation for the Victoria Cross

Department of National Defence, Ottawa, 22nd May 1945

THE CANADIAN ARMY

The KING has been graciously pleased to approve the posthumous award of the VICTORIA CROSS to:-
No.B46495 Sergeant Aubrey Cosens, The Queen's Own Rifles of Canada.

In Holland, on the night of 25/26th February, 1945, the 1st Battalion, The Queen's Own Rifles of Canada, launched an attack on the hamlet of Mooshof, to capture ground which was considered essential for the successful development of future operations.

Sergeant Cosens platoon, with two tanks in support, attacked enemy strongpoints in three farm buildings, but were twice beaten back by fanatical enemy resistance, and then fiercely counter-attacked, during which time the platoon suffered heavy casualties and the platoon commander was killed.

Sergeant Cosens at once assumed command of the only other four survivors of his platoon, whom he placed in a position to give him covering fire, while he himself ran across open ground under heavy mortar and shell fire to the one remaining tank, where, regardless of danger, he took up an exposed place in front of the turret and directed its fire.

After a further enemy counter-attack had been repulsed, Sergeant Cosens ordered the tank to attack the farm buildings, while the four survivors of his platoon followed in close support. After the tank had rammed the first building he entered it alone, killing several of the defenders and taking the rest prisoner.

Single-handed he then entered the second and third buildings and personally killed or captured all the occupants, although under intense machine gun and small arms fire.

Just after the successful reduction of these important enemy strongpoints, Sergeant Cosens was shot through the head by an enemy sniper and died almost instantly.

The outstanding gallantry, initiative and determined leadership of this brave N. C. O., who himself killed at least twenty of the enemy and took an equal number of prisoners, resulted in the capture of a position which was vital to the success of the future operations of the Brigade.

(Source: Supplement 37086. *The London Gazette*, 18 May 1945, published on 22 May 1945, pp. 2607–8)

Fred Tilston's Citation for the Victoria Cross
Department of National Defence, Ottawa, 22 May 1945
THE CANADIAN ARMY

The KING has been graciously pleased to approve the award of the Victoria Cross to:-
Major (acting) Frederick Albert Tilston, The Essex Scottish Regiment, Canadian Infantry Corps.

The 2nd Canadian Division had been given the task of breaking through the strongly fortified Hochwald Forest defence line which covered Xanten, the last German bastion West of the Rhine, protecting the vital Wesel Bridge escape route. The Essex Scottish Regiment was ordered to breach the defence line North-east of Udem, and to clear the Northern half of the forest, through which the balance of the Brigade would pass. At 0715 hours on 1st March 1945, the attack was launched but due to the softness of the ground it was found impossible to support the attack by tanks as had been planned. Across approximately 500 yards of flat open country, in face of intense enemy fire, Major Tilston personally led his company in the attack, keeping dangerously close to our own bursting shells in order to get the maximum cover from the barrage. Though wounded in the head he continued to lead his men forward through a belt of wire ten feet in depth to the enemy trenches, shouting orders and encouragement and using his enemy machine gun post he dashed forward personally and silenced it with a grenade. He was first to reach the enemy position and took the first prisoner.

Determined to maintain the momentum of the attack he ordered the reserve platoon to mop up these positions, and with outstanding gallantry, pressed on with his main force to the second wave of enemy defences which were on the edge of the woods. As he approached the woods he was severely wounded in the hip and fell to the ground. Shouting to his men to carry on without him, and urging them to get into the wood, he struggled to his feet and rejoined them as they reached the trenches on their objective. Here, an elaborate system of underground dugouts and trenches was manned in considerable strength, and vicious hand-to-hand fighting followed. Despite his wounds, Major Tilston's unyielding will to close with the enemy was a magnificent inspiration to his men as he led them in, systematically clearing the trenches of the fiercely resisting enemy. In this fighting, two German Company Headquarters were overrun, and many casualties were inflicted on the fanatical defenders.

Such had been the grimness of the fighting, and so savage the enemy resistance, that the Company was now reduced to only twenty-six men, one quarter of its original strength. Before consolidation could be completed, the enemy counter-attacked repeatedly, supported by a hail of mortar and machine gun fire from the open flank. Major Tilston moved in the open, from platoon to platoon, quickly organising their defence and directing fire against the advancing enemy. The enemy attacks penetrated so close to the positions that grenades were thrown into the trenches held by his troops, but this officer by personal contact, unshakeable confidence and unquenchable enthusiasm so inspired his men that they held firm against great odds. When the supply of ammunition became a serious problem, he repeatedly crossed the bullet swept ground to the Company on his right flank to carry grenades, rifle and Bren ammunition to his troops and replace a damaged wireless set to re-establish communications with Battalion Headquarters. He made at least six of these hazardous trips, each time crossing a road which was dominated by intense fire from numerous well-sited enemy machine gun posts.

On his last trip he was wounded for the third time, this time in the leg. He was found in a shell crater beside the road. Although very seriously wounded and barely conscious, he would not submit to medical attention until he had given complete instructions as to the defence plan, had emphasised the absolute necessity of holding the position, and had ordered his one remaining officer to take over. By his calm courage, gallant conduct and total disregard for his own safety, he fired his men with grim determination and their firm stand enabled the Regiment to accomplish its object of furnishing the Brigade with a solid base through which to launch further successful attacks to clear the forest, thus enabling the Division to accomplish its task.

(Source: Supplement 37086. *The London Gazette*, 18 May 1945, published on 22 May 1945, p. 2608).

James Stokes' Citation for the Victoria Cross
War Office, 17 April 1945

The KING has been graciously pleased to approve the posthumous award of the VICTORIA
CROSS to:-
No. 1592376 Private James Stokes, The King's Shropshire Light Infantry (Glasgow C.1.)

In Holland, on 1st March 1945, during the attack on Kervenheim, Private Stokes was a member of the leading section of a Platoon. During the advance the Platoon came under intense rifle and medium machine gun fire from a farm building and was pinned down. The Platoon Commander began to reorganise the Platoon when Private Stokes, without waiting for any orders, got up and, firing from the hip, dashed through the enemy fire and was seen to disappear inside the farm building. The enemy fire stopped and Private Stokes reappeared with twelve prisoners. During this operation he was wounded in the neck.

This action enabled the Platoon to continue the advance to the next objective, and Private Stokes was ordered back to the Regimental Aid Post. He refused to go and continued the advance with his Platoon.

On approaching the second objective the Platoon again came under heavy fire from a house on the left. Again, without waiting for orders, Private Stokes rushed the house by himself, firing from the hip. He was seen to drop his rifle and fall to the ground wounded. However, a moment later he got to his feet again, picked up his rifle and continued to advance, despite the most intense fire which covered not only himself but the rest of the Platoon. He entered the house and all firing from it ceased. He subsequently rejoined his Platoon – who, due to his gallantry, had been able to advance – bringing five more prisoners.

At this stage, the Company was forming up for its final assault on the objective, which was a group of buildings, forming an enemy strong point. Again, without waiting for orders, Private

Stokes, although now severely wounded and suffering from loss of blood, dashed on the remaining 60 yards to the objective, firing from the hip as he struggled through intense fire. He finally fell 20 yards from the enemy position, firing his rifle until the last, and as the Company passed him in the final charge he raised his hand and shouted goodbye. Private Stokes was found to have been wounded eight times in the upper part of the body.

Private Stokes' one object throughout this action was to kill the enemy, at whatever personal risk. His magnificent courage, devotion to duty and splendid example, inspired all those round him and ensured the success of the attack at a critical moment; moreover, his self-sacrifice saved his Platoon and Company many serious casualties.

(Source: Supplement 37033 to *The London Gazette*, 13 April 1945, published on 17 April 1945, p. 2011).

APPENDIX F

Armoured Vehicles Used by British and Canadian Forces during Operation Veritable (Reichswald Forest Campaign), 8 February–11 March 1945

Armoured Bulldozers Much in demand during the period of the campaign for removing burned-out vehicles, rubble, etc. from both waterlogged rural tracks and urban streets.

AVREs (Assault Vehicles Royal Engineers) Churchill tanks operated by sappers possessing a number of specialised devices.

Bobbins Churchill tanks which carried huge bobbins used to lay carpets of coir and tubular scaffolding across heavy ground.

CDLs (Canal Defence Lights) Searchlights mounted on tanks.

Congers A rocket-propelled tube that would extend across a minefield and detonate to clear the mines.

Crabs A Sherman tank with a flail of chains attached to a cylinder extending from the front. When revolved at a high speed, the chains 'flailed' the ground and detonated hidden mines. A rotary wire-cutter could also be carried by a Crab tank.

Crocodiles Flame-throwing Churchill tanks. The chemical mixture generating the flame was contained in a trailer which could be jettisoned by the crew. When a button was pressed inside the tank, a flame shot out of a turret-like device at the front of the vehicle, and the burning arc of fire could extend to 20 sq. ft by the time it hit its target at a speed of approximately 120 m.p.h. The fire could be bounced over obstacles into trenches, and through tiny holes and slits into enemy pill-boxes. Crocodiles typically had a range of between 100 and 150 yards.

DUKWs ('Ducks') 'D' indicated the model year of 1942, 'U' stood for 'utility,' 'K' for all-wheel drive, and 'W' for dual rear-axels. The vehicle, originating in the USA, had a maximum road speed of 50 mph and 6.4 mph in water (equivalent to 5.56 knots). It could be operated by just one crew member, weighed 13,600 lbs, and had a total length of 31 ft. The DUKW could transport approximately twenty-four troops, or 5,000 lbs of cargo. A Browning machine gun was fitted to roughly one in four DUKWs. Other DUKWs weren't armed but were instead plated with sheet steel for extra protection.

Fascines Large bundles of chestnut paling carried on top of tanks, which could then be dropped to fill in an anti-tank ditch or 'cushion' the drop into a ditch for assaulting infantry.

Kangaroos A tank stripped of its turret in order to carry infantry, used throughout Veritable. A largely Canadian innovation.

LVTs (Landing Vehicles, Tracked) Significant numbers of LV2-Buffalos, developed in the USA, were operated by British and Canadian forces during Operation Veritable. The Buffalo was a tracked amphibian vehicle, sometimes supplied with a 20mm cannon and two machine guns in order to supply extra fire support. LVTs had originally been envisaged as load carriers but later developed into assault troop and fire support vehicles.

M29 Weasels A tracked vehicle which was used extensively by the First Canadian Army from Autumn 1944 onwards. Weasels were useful for crossing minefields as the ground pressure exerted by the vehicle was often too low to trigger off anti-tank mines.

The Weasel was usually operated by a crew of four, weighed 3.800 lb and had a total length of 10 ft 6 ins. The M29 was powered by a six-cylinder 70hp Studebaker engine, and had a maximum speed of approximately 36 mph.

Petards These AVREs fired substantial high explosive charges – nicknamed 'flying dustbins' – which could breach emplacements and concrete walls, and were particularly effective in destroying snipers' posts.

Ploughs Self-propelled 'Bulshorn' ploughs which swept aside mines.

SBGs Small box girder bridges, carried by tanks to bridge ditches and other obstacles.

Snakes Similar to the conger, a device containing explosives which was used to blast a way through minefields.

Terrapins A British-made load carrier which weighed approximately 7 tons and had a total length of 23 ft. Terrapins were operated by a crew of two, and possessed no armaments (other than those carried by troops aboard). The vehicle was propelled by two Ford V8 engines, and had a top speed in water of 5 mph – equivalent to 4.34 knots.

Sources: Falls, C. *Aftermath of War: A Record of the Seventy-Ninth Armoured Division. Illustrated London News,* 27 April 1946. Graves, Charles. *From Crocodiles to Lifebuoys. The Sphere,* 20 October 1945. *Leicester Evening Mail,* 23 November 1961. War Diary: 2nd Battalion Argyll & Sutherland Highlanders, February 1945 (Unpublished).

ENDNOTES

Introduction

1. The Reichswald Forest is a huge stretch of historic woodland situated in the lower Rhineland region of Germany, bordering the Netherlands. The area was once the German Imperial Forest, and existed under the protection of the Holy Roman Emperor. 'Wald' is, of course, the German word for 'forest', so calling the area the Reichswald Forest is, strictly speaking, unnecessary. Nevertheless, many Allied newspapers in 1945 referred to the 'Reichswald Forest' battles and campaign, as did General Horrocks and other leading generals and combatants. As a result, the authors refer to the 'Reichswald Forest' campaign on many occasions during the course of this book. Referring to the former German Imperial Forest in this way also helps to differentiate the Reichswald Forest from the many other smaller 'walds' in the area, such as the Balberger Wald, Tuschenwald, Siebengewald, Hochwald and others.
2. General Crerar's full name was Henry Duncan Graham Crerar, though he was known as 'Harry'. He was born in Hamilton, Ontario, on 28 April 1888, and rose to become

Canada's senior field commander during the Second World War. On 16 November 1944, Crerar was promoted to the rank of full general, and thereby became the first Canadian to hold that rank in the field. He retired from military service in 1946, and received a variety of awards from around the world. He became an aide-de-camp general to both King George VI and Elizabeth II, and attended Queen Elizabeth's 1953 coronation in that capacity. In the opinion of Canadian historian J. L. Granatstein, Operation Veritable was Crerar's 'finest hour' and 'Crerar was unquestionably the most important Canadian soldier of the war' (Granatstein, J. L. *The Generals: the Canadian Army's Senior Commanders of the Second World War.* University of Calgary Press, 2005 ed.).

3. Quoted from Thacker, T. *The End of the Third Reich*, Tempus Publishing, 2006.
4. Illingworth, J. New Phase in the Battle: Enemy Trebles His Strength. *Yorkshire Post*, 14 February 1945.
5. Maps produced by the 21st Army Group in 1945, anglicised the spelling of key town names such as 'Cleve' and 'Calcar'. The Nazis began to introduce spelling reforms in the 1930's, which replaced 'C's with 'K's. Thus, Cleve became Kleve, and Calcar was referred to as Kalkar. This more Germanic spelling of town names has been re-emphasised in modern times, and the authors therefore refer to Kleve and Kalkar, rather than Cleve and Calcar, during the course of this book.
6. Thacker, T. Op. Cit
7. See Chapter 18 for further details of Balfour's exploits.
8. *War Junk*, History Television (Canada).
9. See for example *Greatest Tank Battles: The Hochwald Gap.* Season 1, Ep. 5, produced by Breakthrough Entertainment, aired on British TV channels, and made available on YouTube in April 2021.
10. Elstob, P. *Battle of the Reichswald*. Ballantine Books (1970). Even Elstob's account is really only a partial one, which says

little about the later exploitation phase of the campaign, when British and Canadian forces moved through and beyond the Reichswald, and advanced towards the banks of the Rhine.

1 *The Road to the Reichswald*

1. Quoted by Elstob, op. cit. p.29
2. Ibid p.27.
3. Ryan, C. *A Bridge Too far: The true story of the Battle of Arnhem*, Simon & Schuster, 1974. Also the subject of a feature film, *A Bridge Too Far*, 1977.
4. Elstob, op. cit. p.41

2 *Strategy and Planning for the Campaign*

1. Horrocks, Sir Brian. *A Full Life*, Collins, 1960. & *Corps Commander*, Sidgwick & Jackson, 1977.
2. Longville Bowen, T. 'Master Race' in Fighting Retreat From the Forest to Goch. *Pontypridd Observer*, 24 March 1945.
3. Ironically perhaps, the stockpiling of fuel counted for little in a situation where tank mobility was reduced severely by soft ground and widespread flooding. Many of Operation Veritable's key battles were fought on foot by British and Canadian soldiers, without tank support, because the armour had become bogged down in mud and flood water.
4. DERV was an acronym standing for diesel engine road vehicle fuel. For a more detailed breakdown of the RASC's 62nd and 399th Company activities, see the war diary extracts in App. C.
5. War Diary, 9th Cameronians (Unpublished) February 1945.

3 *The Air Campaign*

1. Quoted from Spartacus Educational, www.spartacus-educational.com.
2. Ep. 19, Pincers, *World at War*, Thames TV, 1972.

3. Campaign Diary, RAF Bomber Command, February 1945.
4. Figures reported in the *Evening Despatch*, 9 February 1945.

4 *The German Defence*

1. Quoted from Holton, Matthew, war correspondent, *Aberdeen Press & Journal*. 13 February 1945.
2. See, for example, the articles of Christopher Buckley, war correspondent for both the *Daily Telegraph* and *The Scotsman*. On 9 February 1945, he referred to the German 84th Division as being 'a division of poor quality, holding an important sector of the Front' in both newspapers.
3. Intelligence about Battle Group Katzmann, and other matters, was circulated to battalion adjutants and then included within overall war diary information (at least this was the procedure followed in the 9th Cameronian war diary collated by J. Sawbridge, the battalion adjutant).
4. See Appendix B for information related to the overall Order of Battle for Allied and German forces involved in the campaign.
5. War Diary, 9th Cameronians, February 1945.
6. Ibid.
7. The 9th Cameronians were caught in an undetected German minefield on the Galgansteen Ridge during the first day of the offensive. Those maimed in the minefield became some of the very first battlefield casualties treated by nearby field ambulance units.
8. Buckley, C. op. cit. *Daily Telegraph* & *The Scotsman*, 9 February 1945.

5 *Into the Valley of Hell*

1. Taken from H. D. G. Crerar's Personal Message from the Army Commander to men in the First Canadian Army, 7 February 1945. Canadian War Museum, Ottawa.
2. Quoted by Longville Bowen in the *Merthyr Express*, 17 March 1945.

3. Delaforce, P. *Red Crown and Dragon: 53rd Welsh Division in North West Europe 1944 -1945*. Thistle Publishing (2015 ed.).
4. The German tendency to 'plug holes' by rushing men up to the front in little more than company strength was, for example, commented upon by the *Yorkshire Post*, in an article entitled 'Allies cut through the Reichswald' on 14 February 1945.
5. Grantham came from quite an unusual background. His father was killed in a Leeds nightclub brawl during the 1930s. After this, Grantham joined the army and enjoyed a glittering wartime career. He resigned his commission in 1946 and retired into private life. Very little is known about his post-war life and career, though nine years after his death in 1999, Grantham's wartime medals and memoirs were sold at auction for £4,950 (Duke of York's Military School website, © A. W. Cockerill).

6 'Tiny' Barber and the Road to Skye

1. *Statistisches Jahrbusch 2013*, Stadt Kleve.
2. Montgomery's efforts at traffic management were reported by the *Bradford Observer* on 12 February 1945. The field marshal apparently told Reuters special correspondent Doon Campbell that 'the battle is going very nicely, but this mud is not helping it'. He wore a couple of leather jackets over a sweater and a mottled airborne jacket to keep out the cold, and while he was trying to sort out the immense local traffic jam he took the time to talk to two mud-caked Canadian soldiers who happened to be in the vicinity.
3. These delays, on the first day of the offensive, caused undoubted friction between the 79th Armoured Division Funnies and at least some of the officers and men of the 2nd Argylls. On 20 February, after the battle for Bucholt, the battalion war diarist criticised the caution of the armoured specialists of the Funnies by stating that they were: 'frightened of taking [the] risks of war. They did not appear to realise that they were there to help the infantry and to get

them forward. They do not realise that there is no such thing as a battle to suit their own book tactics, and whatever they do the infantry still have to go on with or without them, casualties or no casualties.' Other British and Canadian formations sometimes experienced similar delays in securing armoured support, due to flooding and the spring thaw, but the Argylls' war diary was unique in the vehemence of its criticisms. (Scottishdivisionwardiaries.co.uk)

4. See Ch. 4. Endnote 7.

7 *Water Rats, Weasels and Buffalos*

1. Schumines contained 7.5 ounces of TNT and were just 4.72 inches long, 3.55 inches wide, and weighed 1.1 pounds. The small size of these deadly mines meant that they were often difficult to locate as a result of probing and observation. German forces transported Schumines to the Reichswald area in light crates containing twenty mines. Detonators and charges were carried separately. (*Intelligence Bulletin Vol. III. No. 1. September 1944*. U.S. Military Intelligence Service, War Department, Washington)
2. Major General Percy Hobart, nicknamed 'Hobo', was born in 1885, and his sister, Elizabeth, later went on to marry Bernard Montgomery. Thus, the pioneer of 'Hobart's funnies' was in fact Field Marshal Montgomery's brother-in-law, and uncle to Montgomery's much-cherished son, David. Later on, David Montgomery went on to marry Tessa Browning, daughter of Lieutenant-General Frederick 'Boy' Browning, Deputy Commander of the 1st Allied Airborne Army at Arnhem – providing yet another family link between Britain's top wartime generals.

8 *To Bruuk and beyond with the 51st Highland Division*

1. 152 Brigade Operational Order No. 12 – Operation Veritable, 4 February 1945, as quoted in WW2Talk, Veritable 1945: 51st Highland Division, Reichswald Forest.

2. War Diary, B Squadron, 1st Lothian & Border Yeomanry, as quoted in WW2Talk, Ibid.
3. Quoted in the *Dundee Evening Telegraph*, 5 April 1945.
4. The civilian population of Gennep had been evacuated by the German occupying forces during October 1944.
5. WW2Talk, op. cit.

9 *The Battles for Moyland Wood and the Goch–Kalkar Road*

1. The forested area of Moyland Wood consisted mainly of small conifers and extended for 3 miles from Bedburg to a point south-east of Moyland village, from which the nearby wood derived its name. The 46th Highland Brigade's desperate battles in Moyland Wood were, according to the divisional historian, 'the worst experience they had endured since the campaign began'. (Royal Canadian Legion Branch 005: The Liberation of the Netherlands)
2. War Diary, Unit HQ 46 (H) Infantry Brigade, February 1945.
3. War Diary, Unit HQ 227 (H) Infantry Brigade, February 1945.

10 *Goch: Town without a Face*

1. Part of an *Aberdeen Press & Journal* article by Ronald Clark entitled 'Scots in cellars of Goch'.
2. Friedrich, J. *The Fire: The Bombing of Germany 1940-1945*. Columbia U. P. (2008).
3. WW2Talk: Veritable 1945: 15th Scottish & 43rd Wessex Divisions in the Reichswald battle.
4. Sligman, H. *Operation Veritable and the Fighting in the Battle of the Rhineland*. Royal Canadian Legion Magazine, 2020.
5. War Diary, 4th Wiltshire Regiment, as quoted in WW2Talk op. cit.
6. 43rd Wessex Intel. Summary as quoted in WW2Talk. Ibid.
7. The *Illustrated London News* of 3 March 1945 also reported that 'the swiftness of the first [Black Watch] attack,

combined with the darkness and a fog, took the Germans so much by surprise that the garrison commander and his staff were captured in bed'.

8. War Diary, HQ 44(L) Infantry Brigade, February 1945.
9. War Diary, Unit 6th King's Own Scottish Borderers, February 1945.
10. War Diary, Unit 8th Royal Scots, February 1945.
11. War Diary, Unit 6th Royal Scots Fusiliers, February 1945.

11 *Anthem of Death*

1. The early morning of 23 February was really the earliest possible moment that Simpson could launch the offensive. He had been advised to wait another day or two in order to allow flood levels to drop even further. Simpson, however, chose to go early, and thereby achieve an element of surprise.
2. Twenty bridges in total were constructed across the Roer by the evening of 24 February.
3. Crerar's afternoon conference was held in a convent building near the Materborn gap, just north of the Reichswald Forest.
4. Major General George Bradley Roberts – known as 'Pip' – was one of the very youngest British general officers of the Second World War, and 'the outstanding British armoured commander of the war' according to Richard Mead (*Churchill's Lions: A Biographical Guide to the Key British Generals of World War II*, Stroud, Spellmount, 2007).

12 *Operation Leek and the Departure of the 15th Scottish Division*

1. An ancient medieval castle first mentioned in various records way back in 1326. At the time of the fighting in February 1945, the castle was privately owned by the von Vittinghoff-Schell family.
2. Official history of the 46th Brigade, as quoted in WW2Talk.com: The attack on Schloss Kalbeck. Discussion on NW Europe Forum, April 2021.

3. Radley College Obituary, 17 June 1945, Radley College Archives.
4. War Diary Sherwood Rangers Yeomanry, 1 March 1945, as quoted in WW2Talk.com. Weeze.

13 *Aubrey Cosens, Mooshof, and the Fight for the Udem–Kalkar Ridge*

1. Adams, S. 'Aubrey Cosens and the Victoria Cross'. *Legion*, 22 February 2022.
2. C-in-C West, IcNo. 1314/45, 24 February 1945.
3. In total, twenty-five German targets were hit in the Allied air attacks which preceded the launch of the ground offensive.
4. Adams, S. op. cit.
5. For Cosens' full VC citation, see Supplement 37086 to the *London Gazette*, 22 May 1945, in App. E.
6. *Coventry Evening Telegraph*, 27 February 1945. In the same syndicated article, Campbell went on to state that 'hundreds of tanks are today clanking forward, carrying the battle deeper into Germany with a new violence and speed'.

14 *The Battle for the Hochwald*

1. Copp, T. 'A Question of Command', *Legion*, Army Part 45, March 2003.
2. Named after Michael Wittmann, one of the most highly decorated SS tank aces of the Second World War. As a company commander at the battle of Villers-Bocage in Normandy on 13 June 1944, he used his lone Tiger tank to personally engage the rear elements of the British 22nd Armoured Brigade formation. After destroying a number of tanks on the narrow Route Nationale 175, Wittmann simply moved up the column, creating mayhem wherever he went. The Tiger ace destroyed perhaps fourteen British tanks, fifteen personnel carriers and two anti-tank guns within fifteen minutes, for the loss of his own tank. Wittmann was later killed, on 8 August, during another brief but deadly Normandy tank battle.

3. James Curry Jefferson was a seasoned veteran of the Italian campaign, and had already been awarded the DSO and Bar. He commanded the Canadian 5th Brigade for a brief period, before transferring to the 4th Canadian Armoured Division, where he was given control of the Algonquins and the 10th Infantry Brigade (canadiansoldiers.com).
4. Copp, T. op. cit.
5. Copp, T. ibid.
6. For Tilston's full VC citation, see Supplement 37086 to the *London Gazette*, 22 May 1945, in App. E.
7. the-hochwald-gap.project44.ca

15 Rendezvous with the Americans

1. As quoted in WW2Talk.com: Veritable 1945: 51st Highland Division, Reichswald Forest.
2. War Diary, 3rd Irish Guards, 21 February 1945 (Unpublished). National Archives, Kew. WO171/5148.
3. Manger, Warren. 'The Bravest Sniffer Dog of WW2. Denied a Medal then Put Down'. *The Mirror*, 12 August 2016.
4. Main HQ 51st Highland Division. No. 1055/AQ. 3 March 1945.
5. As quoted in *A Short History of the 8th Armoured Brigade,* Hanover, 1946.
6. War Diary, 2nd Battalion Lincolnshire Regiment, Jan–Sept 1945 (Unpublished). National Archives, Kew WO171/5231.
7. For Stokes's full VC citation, see Supplement 37033 to the *London Gazette*, 17 April 1945, in App. E.
8. War Diary, 2nd Lincolns, op. cit.
9. For more detailed biographies of Winkler and Clarke, readers should consult the copiously researched articles and books of Tony Colvin, particularly *The Noise of Battle: The British Army and the Last Breakthrough Battle West of the Rhine, February–March 1945*. Helion & Co. 2016.
10. Robert Runcie (1921–2000) was Bishop of St Albans between 1970 and 1980, and Archbishop of Canterbury

between 1980 and 1991. His MC was announced in the *London Gazette* on 7 June 1945.

11. War Diary, 53rd Welsh Division, 5 March 1945. Library & Archives Canada.
12. War Diary, 2nd Irish Guards, 6 March 1945, Unpublished. National Archives, Kew WO171/5147.

16 Xanten and the Wesel Pocket

1. War Diary, 1st Battalion Worcestershire Regiment, March 1945. (Worcestershire Regiment – 29/36th of Foot Website)
2. McVicar, H. 'Backdoor to War: A Canadian Infantryman at Hochwald and Xanten, February – March 1945'. *Canadian Military History*, Vol. 4, Iss. 2, Art. 9, 1995.
3. McVicar, Ibid.
4. War Diary, 2nd Irish Guards, 7 March 1945. op. cit.
5. *The History of the 6th (Lanarkshire) Battalion. The Cameronians (S. R.).* John Cossar, Glasgow, 1950 ed.
6. MacDonald, Charles B. *United States Army in World War II. European Theater of Operations, The Last Offensive.* Office of the Chief of Military History, Department of the Army, Washington, 1973.
7. Montgomery's rejection of the proposal seems to have aroused the extreme anger of at least some members of Simpson's planning staff.
8. Bomber Command: Royal Air Force Bomber Command 60th Anniversary Campaign Diary, February & March 1945. 60th Anniversary of RAF Bomber Command Website, 2004.
9. Macdonald, op. cit. p. 180.

17 Counting the Cost: Treatment of the Wounded

1. Feasby, W. R. Lt-Col RCAMC. *Official History of the Canadian Medical Services 1939 – 1945, Vol. 1.* The Queen's Press, Ottawa, 1956.
2. RAF Bomber Command: Campaign Diary, op. cit.
3. Feasby, op. cit.

4. Atkin & Lambeth Army Form Citations W3121, from WW2Talk.com – 51st Highland Division, Reichswald Forest.
5. War Diary, 153rd Field Ambulance Unit (FAU), February 1945. scottishdivisionwardiaries.co.uk.
6. Clark, R. *Field Ambulance Royal Army Medical Corps. Researching the Lives and Records of WW2soldiers* (in researchingww2.co.uk/field-ambulance-royal-army-medical-corps/).
7. War Diary, 194th FAU, February 1945, scottishdivision wardiaries.co.uk.
8. War Diary, 193rd FAU, February 1945, scottishdivision wardiaries.co.uk.
9. War Diary, 153rd FAU, February 1945, scottishdivision wardiaries.co.uk.
10. Feasby, op. cit.
11. Imrie Army Form Citation W3121, WW2Talk.com, op. cit.
12. WW2Talk.com – Veritable 1945. The Canadian finale, Moyland Wood, Goch–Kalkar road.
13. Hartleban, Hans. *'The Organisation of the Medical Service of the German Army and its employment in the Campaign against Poland'*. Military review, September 1940 (as translated by the Feldgrau.net Message Forum of the Feldgrau.com research community).
14. A fully equipped German krankentrager often carried the following items: 1 pair of tweezers, 1 clinical thermometer, 1 wooden spatula, 1 nail cleaner, 1 pair of scissors, 3 band aids, 6 band aid packs, 1 ligature-bind, 20 safety pins in a leather case, 1 piece of waterproof band aid, 2 iodine bottles, 50g of soap, 1 roll of Collemplastrum Zinci, 5 band aid packs in paper, 1 tube of Unguentum saliicyclici, 2 tubes of Unguentum Formaldehydi, 1 tube of alcalic eye ointment, 20 tablets of Acidum acetylosalicylicum, 20 tablets of 0.03g opium, 15 tablets of 0.5g Rhizoma Rei, 20 tablets of Cardiazol, 10 tablets of natrium bicarbonic. (German Medics in WW2: Feldgrau.net Message Forum, 2009)

15. The History of St. Nikolaus Hospital, Kalkar. St. Nikolaus Hospital Supervisory Board/Board of Trustees, 2022.
16. 'Ambulance at Wedding. Wounded Major the Bridegroom', *Birmingham Mail*, 12 May 1945. National Newspaper Archives.
17. *The Stage*, Obituary 23 August 1979. National Newspaper Archives.
18. Thames TV. 'Victoria Cross Recipient Fred Tilston Interview', *For Valour*, 1985. YouTube, 20 August 2018.

18 Counting the Cost: The Destruction of Monuments and Cultural Centres

1. Eisenhower, Dwight D. Memorandum from General Dwight D. Eisenhower Regarding Preservation of Historical Monuments in Europe, 26 May 1944. (Eisenhower's Pre-Presidential Papers, Principal File, Box 13, Bradley, Omar N. (6): NAID 7505528)
2. RAF Bomber Command Campaign Diary, op. cit.
3. Eisenhower Memorandum, op. cit.
4. Ross, Marvin C. 'SHAEF and the Protection of Monuments in Northwest Europe'. *College Art Journal*. Vol. 5. No. 2. College Art Association, January 1946.
5. Balfour was, however, in the process of trying to recruit a team to assist him in his endeavours. He made some notes for a speech he intended to give to those who joined his team, but sadly he was killed before he could deliver it. The talk he intended to give contained the following comments: 'No age lives entirely alone; every civilisation is formed not merely by its own achievements but by what it has inherited from the past. If these things are destroyed we have lost part of our past, and we shall be the poorer for it.' From: *University of Cambridge News: Ronald Balfour, Cambridge's own 'monuments man'* (cam.ac.uk/news/ronald-balfour-cambridges-own-monuments-man, 10 March 2014).

6. Ibid.
7. Ibid.
8. Ibid.
9. There were very few German civilians still living in the remains of Kleve. The *Illustrated London News*, 24 February 1945, reported that there were perhaps just fifty left in the town.
10. Lt-Col Sir Leonard Woolley, King's College Archives Centre, Cambridge. (The Papers of Ronald Edmond Balfour)

19 Aftermath

1. Lippman, D. *Operation Plunder: Crossing the Rhine*. WWII History, Vol. 12, No. 5. August 2013.
2. First Canadian Army Intelligence Summary No. 260, 17 March 1945, as quoted in Stacey, C. P. Col. *Official History of the Canadian Army in the Second World War, Vol. III*. The Queen's Press, Ottawa, 1960.
3. By way of comparison, there were 13,560 Allied casualties at the battle of El Alamein, which began on 23 October 1942 and drew to a close twelve days later, on 4 November. Of this number, 58 per cent (7,864) were British casualties, and the remainder were drawn, predominantly, from the large Australian, New Zealand and South African contingents involved in the battle. Figures quoted in Playfair *et al. The Mediterranean and the Middle East, Vol. 4: The Destruction of the Axis Forces in Africa – Official Campaign History*, N & M Press ed. 2021. During Operation Veritable, between 8 February and 11 March 1945, British casualties of 10,330 represented 66 per cent of the total numbers of killed and wounded in the First Canadian Army.
4. First Canadian Army Casualty and Strength rates, February–March 1945, W. D. A & Q, HQ FCA, February and March 1945, App. 17. Quoted in Stacey, ibid, p. 522.
5. British service personnel killed during the campaign were subsequently interred in the Reichswald Forest military

cemetery, which became the largest Commonwealth War Graves Commission (CWGC) Second World War cemetery in Germany, containing 7,654 graves. Other British servicemen killed during Operation Veritable were interred at a range of nearby CWGC cemeteries, including Jonkerbos, Mook, Rheinberg and Milsbeek. At least some of the Roman Catholic servicemen killed were interred at the Ottersum RC Cemetery. Canadian campaign casualties were interred at Groesbeek Cemetery, just across the Dutch border. Groesbeek Cemetery also contains a memorial to missing British, Canadian and Commonwealth service personnel who have no known grave. German soldiers lie at rest in large military cemeteries at Weeze, and in the Reichswald, on the opposite side of the road to the substantial Commonwealth Reichswald Forest military cemetery.

6. Stacey, ibid, p. 522.
7. MacDonald, op. cit.
8. 21st Army Intelligence Summary, 20 March 1945, as quoted in Stacey, op. cit. p. 564.
9. Ford, Kenneth. *The Rhine Crossings 1945*. Osprey Publishing, 2007.
10. General Crerar's diary, March 1945, App. C & D, as quoted in Stacey, op. cit. p. 524.

20 *Reflections on the Campaign*

1. Stacey, op. cit. p. 524
2. Elstob, op. cit. pp. 116-7.
3. Quoted in Stone, R. 'General William H. Simpson – Unsung Commander of U.S. 9th Army'. *U.S. Army War College* XI (2), 1981.
4. The authors interviewed Adrian B. Bridge – the authors' father/father-in-law and a Cameronian veteran of the Reichswald campaign – informally on several occasions between 2010 and 2015 about his wartime experiences. He recalled that once the Rhine was crossed, the playing of

the bagpipes had a noticeable impact on the local populace. In rural areas, German civilians would appear with white flags, and applaud the pipers and the Cameronians as they marched past. However, cattle herds that had previously endured the drone of thousand bomber raids overhead with some equanimity often went berserk at the sound of the pipes, and ran amok through a number of German towns and villages.

5. See Ch. 6 Endnote 2.
6. W. D. G. O. C.-in-C. First Canadian Army, May 1945, App. H. As quoted in Stacey, op. cit. p. 612. Montgomery was certainly in a position to dispense largesse to the Canadians, and many others, by the time the war in Europe ended in May 1945. He was created Viscount Montgomery of Alamein in 1946, and continued to enjoy a stellar army career. He became C-in-C of the British Army of the Rhine (BAOR) and served as Chief of the Imperial General Staff (CIGS) between 1946 and 1948. For eight years, between 1951 and 1958, he was also Deputy Commander of NATO's Supreme Headquarters Allied Powers Europe (SHAPE) before finally retiring from the army in 1958. Away from the army, Montgomery continued to be hugely popular with the ordinary public, however irascible he might have been in private. He was mobbed by large crowds during tours of the UK and Commonwealth, and he was sometimes accompanied by Brian Horrocks. The two principal British architects of the Reichswald/Veritable campaign once enjoyed a post-war visit to Birkenhead, ostensibly to thank locals for their wartime shipbuilding endeavours. Horrocks provided Montgomery with many details about the town, which the field marshal proceeded to ignore completely. Instead, Montgomery delivered an off-the-cuff speech to a crowd of 1,000 people which was received with considerable enthusiasm. After Montgomery's death in 1976, his son David succeeded him as the 2nd Viscount Alamein.

7. Quoted by Warner, Philip. *Horrocks: The General Who Led from The Front.* Hamish Hamilton, 1984.
8. The wounds Horrocks received in North Africa eventually meant that he had to be invalided out of the British Army, in June 1949. After this, he spent fourteen years as Gentleman Usher of the Black Rod, supervising administration in the House of Lords. With characteristic style, Horrocks spent many hours, during long Lords debates, filling in his football pools coupon selections. After his death in 1985, representatives from over thirty British Army regiments attended a memorial service given in his honour at Westminster Abbey.

BIBLIOGRAPHY

21st Army Group (British Armed Forces) 1945. Report on Operation Veritable 8 February – 10 March 1945. U.S. Army Combined Arms Research Library, 2022.

51st Highland Division. Reichswald – Operation Veritable, February 1945. Highland Division (Ross Bequest) Website, Museum of the Royal Regiment of Scotland, 2023.

8th Armoured Brigade Headquarters. *A Short History of the 8th Armoured Brigade*, Hanover, March 1946.

Adams, S. 'Medical Advances Behind the Line, Part 2'. *Legion: Canada's Military History Magazine*, 17 June 2021.

Bradley, Omar. *A Soldier's Story*. Henry Holt, 1951.

Battle for the Rhineland, Parts 1-3. YouTube, 2019.

Clark, R. 'Scots in Cellars of Goch'. *Aberdeen Press & Journal*, 21 February 1945. National Newspaper Archives.

Colvin, T. 'How Fate Played its Hand for Two Soldiers in WW2'. *Lincolnshire Life*, January 2017.

Copp, T. 'The Battle for Xanten'. *Legion*, Army Part 46, May 2003.

'Close Air Support', *Dundee Courier*, 17 February 1945. National Newspaper Archives.

Holton, Matthew, 'German Order of the Day', *Aberdeen Press & Journal*, 13 February 1945. National Newspaper Archives.

'Goch', *Illustrated London News*, 3 March 1945. National Newspaper Archives.

Kervin, R. 'Told with Fluency and Candour: A Full Life by Sir Brian Horrocks'. *The Montreal Gazette*, 14 January 1961.

The Papers of Ronald Edmond Balfour (REB 10 March 2014). King's College Cambridge Archive Centre.

Lindsay, Martin. *So Few Got Through: With the Gordon Highlanders From Normandy to the Baltic*. Pen & Sword Books, 2011 ed.

'Dead End Kids Fought Like Veterans in 51st: Bitter Battles in a German Forest'. *London Daily News*, 26 February 1945, National Newspaper Archives.

Lynch, C. *Coventry Evening Telegraph*, 9 February 1945. National Newspaper Archives.

Manring, M. M. Hawk, A. Calhoun, J. H. Andersen, R. C. 'Treatment of War Wounds: A Historical Review.' *Clinical Orthopaedics and Related Research*, August 2009.

Feldgrau.com research community Forums. German Medics in WW2, 2009.

Monuments Men and Women Foundation (monuments menandwomenfnd.org/balfour-maj-ronald-edmond).

Moore, William. 'Operation Veritable: A Dirty Slogging Match in the mud of the Rhineland'. *War Monthly*, 1976.

Morley-Priestman, Anne. 'Big small-scale successes'. *The Stage*, 21 September 1978. National Newspaper Archives.

Original War Diary of the 9th Battalion, The Cameronians (Scottish Rifles). Unpublished, February/March 1945. Low Parks Museum, Hamilton, Scotland.

Renouf, T. *Black Watch: Liberating Europe and Catching Himmler – My Extraordinary WW2 with the Highland Division*. Little Brown Books, 2011.

'The War Diaries of Major J. M. G. Hendry (1st Battalion Glasgow Highlanders) 1944-1945, Vol. 11'. *A McCreath Miscellany*, 2023.

The War Diaries of the 15th (Scottish) Infantry Division June 1944–May 1945, scottishdivisionwardiaries.co.uk.

The Wartime Memories Project – The Second World War 1939–1945, www.wartimememories.co.uk.

Vannoy, A. 'Operation Grenade: Race to the Roer'. *WWII Quarterly* Vol. 12. No. 3 (Spring 2021).

War Diaries, 53rd (Welsh) and 15th (Scottish) Divisions, Ref. T2425. Unpublished, 1945. Library & Archives Canada/ Bibliotheque et Archives Canada (Department of National Defence, Directorate of History and Heritage).

War Diary, 2nd Battalion Irish Guards, Jan–Dec 1945 (Unpublished). National Archives, Kew, WO171/5147.

War Diary, 52 (L) Div. Int. Summary No. 80 (9 March 1945). Alpen (Alpon) Germany. Operation Blockbuster and Veritable, February–March 1945, ww2talk.com

War Diary, 5th Battalion Coldstream Guards, Jan–Oct 1945 (Unpublished). National Archives, Kew, WO171/5143.

War Diary, 5th Battalion Wiltshire Regiment, 8 March 1945. The Rifles Wardrobe and Museums Trust, Salisbury, 2022.

INDEX